Reviews

Prosecco is the Answer

"Under the Palermo sun lives today an enviable woman who delivers a beguiling tale—part adventure, part crime story, part inspiring autobiography. Clarissa McNair is never less than interesting and witty; her book is a delicious taste of the eternal Sicily."

—Patrick McGilligan, author of
Alfred Hitchcock, A Life In Darkness And Light

"How did a Mississippi belle transform herself into a private eye and end up in Palermo? Prosecco is the answer. A story told with wit and flair."

—Terrance Gelenter, The Paris Readers Circle

Murder, Actually

"It reads like a magic carpet ride. A fast-paced, enjoyable book with Cici loving every caper. Her exploits in Chinatown with counterfeiters illuminate the underbelly of a huge black market very effectively."

—James C. Esposito, F.B.I. Special Agent in Charge (ret.)

"Cici's memoir, in her charming and self-effacing style, leaves you a little breathless and admiring of her courage and determination."

—Jerry Schmetterer, former Metro Editor of the *NY Daily News* and author of *Crooked Brooklyn* and *The Murder Curtain*

Never Flirt With a Femme Fatale

"A classic from the hands of a pro … what makes this book work so well is that the author is part of the drama. A fine and skilled writer. …"

—John Bowers, associate professor, Columbia University, and author of *Love in Tennessee*

Detectives Don't Wear Seat Belts

"This improper Southern belle's memoir as a private detective combines the immediate impact of a newspaper column with the ironic detachment of a fine novel. McNair's crafted vignettes of low-rent detectives are like chocolate truffles: dark, bittersweet and addictive."

—Bruce Schimmel, founder and columnist, *Philadelphia City Paper*

"A wonderful, wonderful read, an amazing true story told in the voice of a born story-teller . . . she's funny, she's honest and completely fascinating. This is a memoir written by someone who made her own life into an adventure story, and who knows exactly how to grab your hand and pull you along."

—Perri Klass, author of *The Mercy Rule*

Prosecco is the Answer

Books by Clarissa McNair

Garden of Tigers
A Flash of Diamonds
Dancing with Thieves
The Demons of Coral Gables

Books by Cici McNair, P.I.

Detectives Don't Wear Seat Belts
Never Flirt with a Femme Fatale
Kiss the Risk
Murder, Actually

Prosecco is the Answer

a true adventure in Palermo

CLARISSA McNAIR

FEDORA PRESS
Philadelphia

Copyright © 2024 by Clarissa McNair

All rights reserved. Except as permitted under the U.S. Copyright Act of 1976, no part of this publication may be reproduced, distributed or transmitted in any form or by any means, or stored in a database or retrieval system, without the prior written permission of the publisher.

First edition September 2024

ISBN: 978-1-936712-11-3 (Paperback)
ISBN: 978-1-936712-14-4 (eBook)

To learn more about the author visit:
www.mcnairwrites.com | www.sleuthstar.com

Book cover and interior design by Scribe Freelance:
www.scribefreelance.com

Prosecco is the Answer

This book is dedicated to James Hadley and Althea Roberto, confidantes and allies; to Gema Hernandez, my wise and cherished friend; and to Sarah Chapman Monahan, a fellow writer, whose laughter on the phone always made me recognize the absurdity of my present situation.

I am particularly grateful to Pietro Silano, the owner of the Hotel Joli, who helped me again and again when I was confused and felt lost.

I salute Giorgia Lo Monaco, my adorable amica in the alley, who made my life richer.

Thank you to Stephen Altschul, Bettie and Ella Petith, Rosita Castro Domínguez, Ron Edens, Betty Gainsborough, Liz Murray and Victor Ciardello.

The Hotel Joli was such a happy experience. I wish to thank all those who made my time so pleasant there: Maria Giovanna Scordato, Giuseppe Caragliano, Salvatore Parisi, Mauro Bafumo, Danilo Di Girolamo and Maria (Mariella) Di Cristina.

Thank you so much to Dorothea Halliday. It is a better book because of Dorothea.

Grazie to my proofreaders.

This book is pieced together from 985 pages of email sent to friends over the span of that first year in Palermo. I appreciate every single one of them for their enthusiasm and encouragement.

Contents

La Tana 15
Hello, Palermo. 49
Exile 85
Extortion, Fraud, Threat of Bodily Harm 147
The Mafia Works on Saturday 227
Ferragosto in Palermo 273
Oscar Wilde's Birthday 289

Prosecco is the Answer

La Tana

Vicolo della Gardenia, 1, Palermo, Sicilia, Italia. I read the typed address again and again as I stood on the sidewalk in front of my building in Astoria, Queens. The biggest man, the one in charge, leaned over my shoulder and tapped a thick finger at the bottom of the page. "Sign there. Every page." I readjusted the clipboard and did as directed. That Sicilian address. I'd found out that it meant Alley of the Gardenia in English. Two movers were slamming the door of the huge truck closed and a third was dealing with one of the dollies.

"You know I'm waiting for one last thing to be delivered," I said. My watch said ten past three.

He nodded. "Yeah, we were told. We're just about finished and after that it's overtime but we'll wait."

Overtime for movers in New York City was probably like paying a brain surgeon by the hour. It was 2021, and months before I'd ordered what was probably the biggest white leather sofa in North America to be delivered the Tuesday after Labor Day between noon and five. Today. Any minute, I prayed. I'd called and begged for an earlier time but been told it was impossible.

The Friday before as I stepped off a train in Rhode Island for the holiday weekend, my cell phone rang. We New Yorkers were in the final throes of COVID and I was delighted to be getting out of town. It was a call from the international shipping company. Lori, an American in Rome who was handling this, said she had a proposition. An idea. "Clarissa, you know that this is the worst time to move anything. The Chinese have all the containers and, as I've told you, your goods may sit in a warehouse on the dock for weeks or months waiting for one. You'll pay storage day after day." I pulled my suitcase over to a bench and sat down, inhaling sea air. "I have one idea. It's a big chance but you must tell me yes or no right now." I waited. "Italy's minister of defense has goods going to Rome and we can consolidate his and yours in the same container." She seemed to take a deep breath before elaborating. "Everything of yours must go by truck to Alabama and be put on a ship there and then on to Italy." I started to ask why Alabama but she was still talking. "We have your goods from Philadelphia but all from New York has to be picked up no later than Tuesday."

"Tuesday?" I yelped.

"That's the only way this will be possible. You have to tell me now. You can't think about it. I must have your answer now."

A few seconds passed. It was a dare. I wasn't ready, I thought I had weeks to leisurely pack. I didn't have the boxes or the paper or the tape. That's minutiae. My God. I looked up at the sky and said, "Okay. Let's do it. Tuesday, Alabama, Italy. Okay!" I hung up as my friend waved "hello" and then I had to tell her in the car that I'd leave on Sunday afternoon instead of staying over til Monday evening. "The international movers are arriving at seven on Tuesday morning." She gasped as I burbled on. "The Chinese have all the containers and that's why I'm doing this now instead of October." I pictured a chubby little Asian boy in a bathtub surrounded by dozens of colored toy boats. "All my stuff will go with the Italian minister's to Rome and they'll unload his property and then the ship will go on to Napoli where my stuff will be loaded onto a truck for Palermo."

I opened the window all the way and sat back and smelled the salt air as Jan chattered about the plans for the weekend.

I am a queen of compartmentalization and had a wonderful few days. The part of my mind that panicked at the idea of being ready by early Tuesday I simply closed off. On the train from Westerly to New York, I planned. Home on Sunday night and I packed until 2 am Monday and then began again at 7 to pack all day Monday. At half past seven on Tuesday morning, the movers rang my doorbell and now all was in the truck except the giant white leather sofa.

My watch said three-twenty.

The three men had arranged themselves on the curb with soft

drinks and sandwiches. I guessed overtime started now. Even if the sofa I'd dubbed Moby Dick arrived on the nose of five o'clock times three men, how bad could it be? I tried to relax. Gema came out of the laundromat and stood beside me.

My best friend in Astoria. Mexican, a single mother, bright, savvy, kind, perpetually good humored, we had the same world view and discussed everything from El Chapo to abortion rights with the hum of washing machines as our sound track. She ran the Egyptian's laundromat on the first floor of my building. Gema could exorcise a weird stain, spot a counterfeit bill, solve any emotional problem.

"You wait for Moby Dick?"

I nodded.

Just then this enormous truck came roaring down Broadway. I felt it coming more than heard it. It stopped right in front of Muncan, the Bosnian/Macedonian butcher shop across the street. The driver leapt out. "It's here!" I shouted at the men munching sandwiches. One of them waded through the traffic but it took four men to get Moby Dick across Broadway. The butchers came out in their long white aprons and watched, my neighbors materialized, Gema was at my side laughing. Then the movers' truck had to be unpacked to make room for the immense volume of Moby Dick and packed again. But it all fit: Haitian paintings, my French day bed, my bike, my grandfather's mirror, the carved screen from Bangkok, books, photographs, hats, clothes, my shoes, the Venetian chandelier.

No overtime. I tipped everyone and thanked them. Gema had her arm around my shoulders as we watched the truck disappear into the afternoon traffic. "To Sicily," she said. "It's on the way."

"Well," I said. "Just one thing I'm trying not to think about."

"No!" she said. "There is nothing else to think about. You packed in time for the movers. It's done! Tonight when I close we celebrate with tequila. And the next time you see everything will be at vicolo della ... what is it called?"

"Vicolo della Gardenia, number one." I sighed. "But Gema, I haven't bought it yet."

Gema's eyes grew wide and she clapped one hand over her mouth and whispered, "Cici!"

Then we both started laughing.

· · ·

This entire Sicilian operation was a breech birth. Everything I owned was gone, to be delivered in three weeks to an address in an alley in the Arab quarter of Palermo. Okay, I told myself, if the sale does not happen I will have time to make a plan before the ship has crossed the Atlantic. I will find another place to buy or I will find a warehouse for my stuff until I find another place to buy. What arrives in Sicily will stay in Sicily.

Meanwhile, I had my old mattress and the TV I would give to Victor, my pal from Trinidad, and an open suitcase with summer clothes in my otherwise empty apartment. I gave my last chair to Gema and spent time sitting on a towel reading out on the terrace.

THE HUDSON RIVER VALLEY PLAN

Pre-COVID, in the last gasp of 2019, was when I decided to leave the city. I found a house in the Hudson River Valley which looked like an illustration in a children's book and I saw myself there in the big kitchen baking Scottish shortbread and brownies to sell at the river market once a week. I saw myself giving dinner parties in the dining room under my Venetian chandelier. I would have an archery range in back. But at five o'clock on the afternoon before I was to buy the Mini Cooper and actually move, the seller changed her mind. She would not sign the final document.

Devastated, I spent January looking for another house instead of time spent hanging paintings in the Coxsackie house. There was nothing I wanted. In February, I watched the sale prices leap skyward following the outbreak of COVID. My realtor said a house on the market in the morning would have five offers before lunch and all over asking price.

Like everyone else, I survived on Netflix and Zoom, but I also rode my bike and had the terrace. I kept looking online at the Hudson River Valley. One afternoon I took a piece of typing paper and wrote in big green letters: WHAT DO YOU REALLY WANT?

I had not put down the pen and I knew. I wanted to live in Italy again. In the 1980s, after a failed marriage to a Canadian, I'd moved to Rome, thrown my wedding ring into the Tiber, worked for Vatican Radio, had friends and adventures. I left that job I loved to co-author a book on contemporary celibacy in the Catholic Church. This meant a year of interviewing nuns and priests about their sex lives; the book was published in at least half a dozen languages. I returned to Rome and wrote a novel then moved to Geneva and wrote a novel. Both were published. I moved to Beverly Hills and worked in film for a year. Back in New York City, my literary agent told me that the market had changed; her suggestions of what I *should* write were singularly unappealing. I thought, okay, I guess I'm not a novelist anymore. Turning to the Yellow Pages for inspiration, I decided to become a private detective. In NYC, I worked undercover with the F.B.I., the Joint Terrorist Task Force and Organized Crime Intelligence of the NYPD. I moved to Miami for a money laundering case, did death penalty cases in Philadelphia, moved to Paris then returned to New York City.

In 2021, I had over 20 years of experience as a P.I. My cases were everything from missing persons to murder.

THE ITALIAN PLAN

Now, I was sure. I would go back to Italy. So began the search for the city, the town, the village. A one-euro house? Online I found the videos hilarious. Middle-aged Americans standing ankle-deep in broken rocks gazing up at a blue sky and raving about the weather as the Italian realtor told them a roof and walls would be advisable. These were offered in villages with dwindling populations and I did not want to be the only person under ninety and the only divorced woman in 300 kilometers. I wanted art galleries and people to meet for wine.

I began to look at cities. Venice? That water problem. Bologna, Milano, Torino? Too much like the rest of Europe. Florence? I never liked it. Rome? Yes, I felt so at home there but I could imagine my life. I'd lived there for a few years and worked at the Vatican. I'd loved the job but my work was in English and everyone I met wanted to speak English so I'd never learned Italian. I wrote my first novel in Rome standing at a typewriter raised high on Rome phone books, wearing a huge hat and a bikini on my terrace overlooking the Tiber. A thousand pages and a terrific tan later, a British publisher accepted it.

As COVID dragged on, I found a conversation partner online for Italian and we Zoomed every Tuesday. She was in Genoa with her parents during COVID, was planning to sell her apartment in Nice where she really lived but also had a house in Sicily. Silvia and I liked each other. We discussed my work as a detective, her childhood, her zany aunts, her relationship with her mother, everything.

Naples? Yes, maybe Naples because I could have Rome *and* Naples. There were over fifty trains going back and forth every day and the trip was about two hours. Then I read that Naples was the poorest city in Europe and that the train station was not safe at night. I considered crime.

Puglia was a possibility. Angela, my fabulous Italian-Australian dress designer in Rome, had relatives there and went all the time.

A town outside Palermo was interesting. Sambuca. I really liked a large house there and kept going back to it online.

On one Tuesday, Silvia told me her house in Sicily was in Sambuca! I would have a best friend upon arrival.

But Palermo intrigued me. The history, being on the sea. But it was eleven hours 35 minutes from Rome on the train. I'd hoped to be nearer but then I thought, why do I have to be close to Rome?

I looked at Palermo properties online and realized I could afford some of them. The city was a cultural one; Teatro Massimo was the third largest opera house in Europe after Paris and Vienna. It was flat so I could ride my bike. One study said that Palermo, among the twelve largest cities in Italy, had the lowest crime rate. I had been all over Sicily twice and liked its exotic feel. Okay. I would live in Palermo.

Research regarding COVID tests and airline regulations proved contradictory and complex but I had a reservation on June 6th on Air France to Rome via Paris then on to Palermo. I thought I'd done everything correctly and was prepared.

At Kennedy, checking in, the French didn't care about my negative COVID test and told me I'd have to quarantine in Paris for ten days. I insisted I was in transit, was proceeding to Rome and Palermo. Didn't matter. "You are entering the Schengen in Paris." The Schengen is composed of 29 countries that have officially abolished border controls. It is all one zone now. France and Italy are in the Schengen.

The French sent me to Alitalia who said, of course, there was no quarantine as I was in transito; I'd be tested upon arrival at Fiumicino. They sent me back to Air France who disagreed then the French sent me back to set the Italians straight. The Italians said the French had lost their minds. They offered me a direct flight to Rome then realized it had left an hour before. Back to the French and one of the snippy women in navy blue happened to ask if I were going for business. I said yes. "In Palermo?" she asked as if no business were ever conducted there. I nodded. Then she wanted confirmation of my business plans, a letter confirming my appointments, and to look at my emails. I had had enough of these people and drew myself up, presented my Press card and said, "I am a journalist going to Sicily for interviews. The people I deal with don't send emails, do not put anything in writing. I will be contacted upon arrival and taken to the appropriate place." Well, that did it. Madame You Must Quarantine for Ten Days in Paris asked, in quite a subdued manner, "Why didn't you tell us that in the beginning?"

"Why didn't you ask?" I countered. I was given a boarding pass and wished bon voyage. I thought, yes, please do imagine I'm going to be blindfolded, put in a car and driven to a hideout up in the mountains to interview a Mafia capo.

Paris was a breeze, no one stopped me for any kind of test. Actually, a trio of Air France flight attendants complimented me on my belt. I told them I'd bought it in Paris a few years before and they twittered in delight. In Rome, testing was done as we walked past an unseen sensor. I was asked to take off my hat and walk past a second time. That was all.

I sat at the gate and surveyed the passengers on my Palermo flight. They looked like reasonable Italians to me. One very chic older woman. My plan was to find a place in two weeks, buy it, stop in Rome for a few days then go back to New York and pack.

The flight was a bit over an hour. I looked down at this triangle of land dropped onto an expanse of lapis lazuli and thought, I am going to live there.

The driver said my taxi ride was 56 euros. No meter. I felt faint in the back seat and said I only had fifty which I handed over. The driver very helpfully pointed to another section of my wallet I'd overlooked and took the five-euro bill with a smile. As much as my room! I'd later learn the taxi should cost 35 euros.

The hotel was near the Teatro Politeama which was spectacular: stone horses dramatically galloped on top of it. I went to an outdoor caffè for a glass of prosecco served with all kinds of little hors d'oeuvres.

Bob, a friend from Paris, called and we had a long talk as I walked on what I'd later learn was via Maqueda. There was a Zara and an H&M so I would be okay. Gema called but we were cut off. She WhatsApped and wrote she missed me. I missed her, too.

The next day was Monday. June 14, 2021. My wedding anniversary. Mother always wanted me to be married which, to her, was being safe. I am not sure I ever liked the idea of being safe and I had not liked being married.

If I'd stayed this would be my 46th wedding anniversary. I would be in Toronto with a man who slept with men OR I would be married to a lawyer who is now a judge. Winters skiing and summers in Muskoka. I wouldn't speak Italian, I would have missed being a detective, I would have never lived in Rome or Paris or Geneva or had all those affairs with people like handsome Genevois Olivier or crazy Welsh Gordon. Maybe I would never have written a book. It is very ok that I am *here now* in 2021.

THE HUNT

I think I was on the first plane out of New York after COVID. Palermo was devoid of tourists and people often asked me why I was there. When I said I would live there, that I wanted to buy a place, the immediate response was, "I can help you."

I had so little time in Palermo and was happy to meet a realtor I'd communicated with via WhatsApp. He arrived at my hotel as promised at 8:45 that first morning but had no listings, nothing for me to see. He had done no preparation at all. I was polite. He left and I called someone recommended by Silvia but Gianni was unavailable and sent his friend also named Gianni. He was young and tall wearing a mask that kept slipping off his rather large nose. Nice but wanted to show me a flat for Euros 100.000. Double over what I said I could afford. His phone rang in the car on the way and it seems the toilet had exploded and we could not see it after all; he was quite upset. He lived in Sambuca and sang its praises, insisted I could do much better there.

My hotel's concierge may remember me forever because I washed a few things and my bra was missing the next morning. I'd put it on the balcony out of sight but somehow it was gone. The concierge tried not to laugh when I asked if anyone had turned in a black lace bra. Of course, with my limited vocabulary I had to act it out. Later it was found in the bushes beside the front door.

A friend in Rome had given me the name of the only person she knew in Palermo. I would discover that Romans think Palermo is another country. Agata was an architect and because she was from Torino, I freely admit to being prejudiced in her favor. The saying was the farther south you go, the more corruption so I trusted a northern Italian over a Sicilian.

I called her and she suggested lunch. Engaging smile with very crooked teeth, a sort of Bohemian outfit with knee-high brown leather boots for June. Loves Palermo, said nobody here cares what you wear, what you think or do. It's very free. She has lived in Bogota, spent time in NYC but wanted a place that was "a bit Arabic, a place in the south that had the energy of New York." She came in 2008.

Friendly, exuberant, promising to show me all the ropes at one nice lunch after another. She could renovate for me, had just started a business to help foreigners navigate buying property and renovating. She could also recommend a realtor she worked with who was "wonderful, bellissimo." I thought she was an answer to a prayer.

Agata designs furniture to order on demand, has her artisans, has craftsmen here. I liked her. That first lunch, she asked if I wanted wine and I said yes and she said, "Oh, let's have Champagne!" Agata greeted two women who stopped at our table. One was dressed in black with frizzy orange hair and mirrored glasses; a little dog's head was poking out of her bag. Another woman greeted Agata wearing an off-the-shoulder red party dress with frilly ruffles of organza. High noon in Palermo seemed to be anything goes.

The following morning, I woke at five with a pain in my chest. Fear? Is that possible? Just because I was leaving all the people I know to live on an island where I have no job and will spend every cent I have saved for shelter? I wished I had done this in 2012 when I had so much money. Palermo instead of Paris? No. I will always have Paris and Bob, Dennis, Faouzi, Cris, Zachary, Violaine, Ruth and Stephen and two hip replacements and rue Elzevir and Nadine and the Sunday memoir class.

Well, Agata's Alberto was not wonderful, as she so enthusiastically claimed. He was the laziest person I'd ever known. I'd find four or five properties online I wanted to see and beg him to call and get the keys, make the arrangements. My Italian was not good but I told Agata I actually could and would do this on the phone rather than be dependent upon the impossible Alberto. "Oh, no," she cried, "he's the best. He is working so hard for you but you don't know it."

Countless hours were spent in my hotel room waiting for him to call and say meet me on via whatever. He never used WhatsApp which would have made my life so much easier. In two weeks, he showed me one place and another one I saw with him and Agata and Luigi, an architect who worked with her. They stood in the middle of 30 square meters (322 square feet) and raved about the space. One area had a ceiling height of less than three and a half feet, about one meter. "Oh, that's perfect for the kitchen!" they exclaimed. Sure. If you are a dwarf. I mentioned wanting a closet. That was easy . . . blah blah. I stared at them: two architects and a real estate agent selling me a hovel up four flights of winding stairs overlooking a courtyard that appeared the Allies had bombed it two days ago. "Don't worry about that," said Agata. "This is an area that is undergoing huge growth. Prices are way down now so you are getting in at the right time. This is a very popular neighborhood."

No realtor asked me to sign any agreement so I connected with Francesca who showed me a small all-white apartment with no windows priced at Euros 280.000. I told every realtor exactly what I could afford but they paid no attention to me. I was shown a larger apartment above the Ballarò market and greeted by the chubby, unshaven, perspiring owner who immediately raised the price. It was so ridiculous that I smiled. I saw several rooms with mattresses on the floor, unwashed clothes everywhere, and stumbled over a running shoe without its mate. He thrust his phone in my face with photos of rooms that the realtor and I were not allowed to enter. Overturned chairs, more dirty clothes. When he raised the price again, I laughed aloud.

I'd found cheaper places online in an area called Zisa but was told it was too dangerous.

The other apartments I found online were 40 and 50 square meters divided into two even three and four bedrooms I would have called closets. The few I saw were up flight after flight of stone stairs which meant light and a view from a window but none had a terrace which is what I deemed mandatory. And though I didn't mind the stairs now I wondered how I'd feel in a few years. I'd had plenty of stairs in Rome but there were wine bottles to go up and that forgotten umbrella once you were at street level. Nothing was right for me.

It was Friday and I was leaving a week from today on the train for Rome. I found places online every day, sent them in the evening to Alberto, Agata's "wonderful" realtor, then followed up with a pleading phone call in the morning and he would tell me they were no longer on the market or the owner was out of town. I didn't believe him.

Realtors don't work here on weekends and, of course, in the States it's the busiest time. The high point of Saturday night was watching *Law & Order* in Italian.

In the evenings I would walk to the nearby outdoor caffé and have a glass of prosecco which would arrive with an assortment of so many appetizers that it qualified as dinner. The weather was glorious and there was always a cool breeze off the water.

But not many frequented the restaurants. I was sad to see all the little tables outside set with tablecloths and wine glasses surrounded by smiling waiters hoping for customers. There were no crowds, which was nice for me but not for them.

Everyone was masked except when eating. I heard that one must still wear a mask in the street or be heavily fined. If one wanted to enter a restaurant then the vaccination proof known as a Green Pass had to be shown. They accepted my white card listing my Pfizer shots but I usually sat outside and no one asked for it.

On Sunday morning, I went to the cathedral which is a fabulous mix of Norman and Arab architecture; it was overwhelmingly elaborate, very grand. The mosaics were stunning and the incense was heavy. Everyone was masked and everyone I talked to had had the vaccine. Italy really suffered.

On Monday of that second and final week, Alberto finally deigned to get the key to a place I had found online with 75 square meters and no bedrooms. A metal shutter roared up and I walked into darkness. The online description had said there was a terrazzo. I winced. The outdoor space was tiny with no sun and an upward view of one air conditioner after another going up five stories of the next building. I said no, absolutely not.

I wrote an email to a friend:

> *The place I saw this morning was pretty ghastly.*
>
> *Only Euros 39.000 for 75 sq meters but BLACK darkness.*
>
> *Ground floor. Two bathrooms which is odd. If you opened the big double doors you had light and if you went all the way to the back there was a square of concrete audaciously calling itself a terrace but that open door afforded a patch of light.*

After seeing this I had lunch with Alberto and Luigi, the architect who worked with Agata. Both men were very cheerful. I told them how disappointed I was to have been shown just two properties by them my entire trip when I was leaving in four days. I was told, "Oh, but if you had let us know you were coming we would have been prepared." I swallowed my anger with the swordfish. I was finding properties online every day.

They must have told Agata I was not happy for she called that afternoon with a place she said would suit me perfectly. When I asked how large and did it have outdoor space, she was evasive and just said, "It's unusual but I think you will fall in love with it." The address was in Kalsa on via Divisi which I liked as it was lined with bicycle shops. I missed my bike. A realtor named Elena showed us two storage rooms without windows. I was ready to say no thanks but Agata was snapping photos like it meant something as I was thinking, a waste of time, get me out of here.

One space was ten square meters and the other was smaller. This was ground floor and up on the Italian first floor were the two "apartments." They weren't even side by side! Just a piece of rubber for a door over each dark room across the hall from each other. This cover hung from a nail. One "apartment" was a room without a window and about eight square meters; the other "apartment" was a room across the hall with a window overlooking a neighbor six feet away and a trace of light. A second window overlooked the grotty courtyard. All told, it was 35 square meters for the two rooms. Agata was ebullient. "Make a staircase to go down to the storage room and have a blind bathroom down there. Across the hall have a kitchen." I stared at her. "Across the hall?"

Agata was talking quickly. Renovation costs would be 15.000 euros. Ceilings are done but reno would be a kitchen, a bathroom, three layers of plaster for the walls. The realtor said the owner would accept 45.000 euros. Probably two tax bills because I would be buying two properties. "Live in it for two years and sell it. Smooth the floor in the storage area and sell it for people to keep their motorcycles. Make 7.000 euros," said Agata triumphantly as if the deal were closed.

I thought of John Gotti in Colorado. If given the choice, he would have preferred to stay where he was. I diplomatically told Agata that I was amazed at her optimistic ideas but I wanted to be settled and not in the business of renovating and selling. I wanted to shout, you have wasted my time!

• • •

That evening in my hotel I kept thinking about the 75-square-meter place. I did the math; it's very easy. I used the metric system way back working for Herbert in Toronto. The U.S. is only one of three countries in the world that doesn't use it. The others are Myanmar and Liberia.

The space was between 800 and 900 square feet. I could afford

39.000 euros and that would give me some money for renovation. The euro was $1. 20. I called Alberto and said I wanted to see vicolo della Gardenia or Alley of the Gardenia again. He acted as if that were a problem. The reason was incomprehensible. There was always a wrong number, a phone that didn't answer, it was already sold, the owner was out of town or had changed his mind. Alberto just didn't want to bother. I called Agata and said I might want to buy it and could I see it again tomorrow? She said, "Well, just buy it! Why do you want to see it again?"

My enthusiasm about Agata, even after several granitas and lively lunches, was diminishing fast. I said I had to see it again before making a decision. The next evening at 6 p.m. I was at vicolo della Gardenia waiting for her. The area seemed to be populated by Africans and Arabs, there was a motorcycle shop nearby and motorcycles stored across the narrow alley in rooms with metal shutters like number one.

The longer I waited in the alley, the more hesitant I became. Several people stared at me in my black T-shirt dress, my silver sandals with the rhinestones and the straw Panama I wear all summer. Agata arrived with a very handsome Tecnorete realtor who handled the property; he pulled up the metal shutter then unlocked a pair of wooden doors maybe 12 feet tall.

Agata said she thought I could get it for Euros 30.000 which was welcome news as I had seen nothing at that price. She was enthusiastic to the point of gushing about all she could do to make it spectacular. She never took a measurement or examined anything but stood in the middle of the open space and watched me walk around. The tiles which lined the walls up to waist height could be removed in a day. This and this could be done in half a day. That in a few hours. I wanted a wrought iron front door for security and light and a second interior door of glass. Absolutely! Could I have a loft for storage? Of course! All my questions were answered in the effusive affirmative.

One bathroom would be the new kitchen, the second one would be redone as the new bathroom. I wondered aloud why there were two bathrooms. Agata didn't answer. She had the workers and all would be completed in two weeks. "Fantastic!" she exclaimed again and again. I asked about the plumbing and the electricity since it had not been occupied for ten years. She didn't answer me. I said I had to have an inspection before buying, I had to know the condition, liens on the property, what taxes. She told me the notary did all that. It was agreed that Alberto would take me to Tecnorete to make an offer the next day.

That evening sitting at what was now my caffé where my waitress gave me extra appetizers with a conspiratorial smile, I thought about Agata. Her "wonderful" Alberto was a washout. Agata's website did not inspire confidence. Her furniture was hideous. Raw wood as if a 9th grader had hammered raw lumber together in shop class. The kitchens pictured were pretty, to be sure, but impractical with no counter space, no cabinets. I decided to buy vicolo della Gardenia and find someone else to renovate. I wished it were larger but it was quite large, according to Palermo standards. It was open space which was maybe the best thing about it.

I called Bettie in Rome who had given me Agata's name and Rosita, another friend in Rome who knew her. They said I shouldn't trust her. Agata was out for Agata. I said I didn't know if the lunches and granitas were friendship or business and my Roman friends said probably a mix but to watch out. Warnings were a bit late but I had only asked if anyone knew anyone in Palermo and not requested a character reference.

I wrote my thoughts in green ink on a yellow legal pad beside my flute of prosecco.

> *First—remove the pull-down shutter, remove the double doors. Put in a pair of wrought-iron doors (I think a leaf pattern) that can be locked and will let in air and light. A 2nd set of doors inside that will be thick glass they use for banks. This means A.C. and heat will stay inside. It may also cut down on street noise.*
>
> *The front part is GREAT for my desk, books. That is light. Fine. It is a larger space than I remembered.*

Part of the ceiling is false so that will be removed. The realtor said there are rafters /beams up there that can be exposed. Kitchen in the bathroom to the left. There is a window there out to the terrace for ventilation. Ha! terrace?

The other bathroom is big enough for free-standing tub, bidet, etc. Also has two tiny windows.

At the back, over the bathroom and kitchen will be a loft for storage 6 feet wide or deep. It can have 6 foot ceiling height up there. Stairs can go up to it.

I want black and white marble floors.

Floor is even, walls are fine but new bathroom, a kitchen, loft, and removing that tile and fake ceiling, plastering and painting.

Agata said I could fix it up in October and sell it in November as it will be worth much more when renovated and that it could be an artist studio.

I'd asked about it being commercially zoned and she said you can do that for 2500 euros if anyone wants to buy the space to use for a shop or art gallery. It is street level so when I unlock those wrought-iron doors I am home! I can wheel my bike in. I am also five minutes walk from Palazzo Gangi which was in the movie, *The Leopard*. The area is on the edge or just inside the Centro Storico, the historical center. I am a short walk from via Maqueda which is a wide, no cars allowed avenue.

I sipped my prosecco. Agata was doing the math and would send me all the figures tonight. I would look at her estimates but I was firm in my decision to find someone else for the renovation. Both my friends in Rome were with me on this.

Yes, this is good, I decided. I thought of what the other realtors had shown me. The one that I'd seen the week before was Euros 58.000 and looked like a bomb had hit it. There are plenty of buildings here that a bomb *had* hit and no one has cleaned up the rubble yet. American bombs. I decided it was before I was born so I stopped feeling guilty.

All this walking, all the outdoor caffès, the magnificent architecture, the history—I liked Palermo.

THE DECISION

I went to my caffé and wrote Stephen, an English friend, that vicolo della Gardenia is the biggest and the cheapest and means I can actually move to Palermo. He wrote back: '*75 square meters is amazingly large if you could arrange something with glass and mirrors without going for the whole Amsterdam red light look. Soft candlelight can be romantic.*'

I smiled, picturing life as a vampire. I kept reading his email. He addressed my fear of not fitting in and told me my presence "would enhance the area." I laughed and my cute waitress approached me and topped up my glass. I said, grazie, took a sip and thought, I am buying Alley of the Gardenia and will make it beautiful and live there.

THE OFFER

Everything in Palermo is walk walk walk. I stumbled behind Alberto over broken sidewalks for what seemed like a kilometer. It was an area of wholesale souvenir shops, fabric and kitchen utensil stores and we were finally there. As we opened the glass door, two pretty young women at desks pulled on their masks as Alberto and I did. Then I was fist-bumping Sergio, the capo of the office, who was beefy, pink-faced and large behind a black mask. I said, "Ho avuto due Pfizer" and the men nodded and we all took our masks off.

Sergio had this way of half closing his eyes when talking in a low voice looking down and I imagined that he might be planning a hit. He sat with large belly behind his desk as Alberto and I sat before him. I said something about dealing with the Mafia and Sergio was offended and said this is not the Mafia. It was a tasteless attempt at humor and a terrible gaffe and I would not understand how terrible until a few months later. In Sicily, you do not make jokes about the Mafia. Too many people have suffered too much.

I offered 29.000 euros and Sergio shook his head but he thought that the owner would accept 30.000 so that was my offer. The seller would be contacted and I would be emailed his answer. Alberto talked very quickly to Sergio and though I said I didn't understand, no one slowed down or attempted to explain when I asked. Sergio then said the agency fee was 4880 euros and I said okay. I passed over my passport which one of the women took and photocopied and then I was asked to leave a check for 5.000 euros as a deposit. I explained I did not have my euro checkbook with me. Shrugs from the men so I wrote a check for $5,000 and passed it across the desk.

Line by line we went over everything on page after page as Sergio read aloud.

When we were leaving, he, stout and tall, stood up, said his birthday was the 29th of January and that we were both Aquario. I fist-bumped him and said, "Siamo i migliori!" We are the best! Everyone overhearing this in the office laughed.

I walked outside and into the sun and thought, the realtor talked so fast, Alberto talked so fast and I signed all those papers in Italian. Did I just give away a kidney?

* * *

Agata and I met for a granita at Piazza Bellini which is my favorite piazza. Bellissima. Built in the 1100s. She was grinning with her little crooked front teeth and said, "Well, you did it." I didn't mention work estimates which she had promised the night before but not sent. We talked about how great it was going to be. She told me she had been considering a move to Mexico from Torino but Palermo made her feel good so she decided to come here. All her friends said, "Oh, no, Mexico would be better." I told her a few of my friends were aghast at the idea of Palermo. Agata said that Palermo gave her the confidence to do her own designs.

We talked about speaking Italian. I said, "I think it's like music." I remembered Ethiopia. "All these beautiful people were speaking Italian. That was a long time ago."

"But how, why were you there?" she insisted.

"I was traveling all over Africa that year," I began. "Ethiopia! In Asmara I met this adorable Italian with a red Sports Spider. I was going to Massawa on the Red Sea and so was he and he insisted we fly together. I wanted to take the train but gave in and flew. The next morning at breakfast we learned that bandits attacked the train, got everybody off, robbed them and then pushed the train over a cliff." Agata was horrified but I continued. "I was furious! He had made us fly instead of taking that train and we missed all the excitement. Imagine bandits on camels in the middle of the desert and an entire train going over a cliff!"

Agata was wide-eyed and said, "You are crazy but I can see why our friend in Rome loves you and I love you, too!"

A PRIVATE CELEBRATION

That evening in a spirit of celebration, hoping that the owner would accept my bid, I went to the glorious Grand Hotel des Palmes. Stephen, my English friend, the opera critic, had said I would feel at home there. "Have a cocktail where Wagner finished Parsifal." The sweet concierge named Bruno took me on a tour, told me an English family, who made all their money with Marsala wine, built it along with the Anglican church across the street. Then Italians bought the house and turned it into a hotel. I was escorted to the bar and sat in a room with a spectacular ceiling above me. There was no one there but me, the three bartenders plus a man who looked as if he'd taken root and might have to be extracted from the red velvet banquette like a bad tooth. Several empty glasses in front of him were a testament to his thirst.

Yes, there was Wagner but this ritzy hotel was also the setting for meetings with Lucky Luciano, Joe Bonanno, Maggadino who ran

Buffalo and a few other Mafia chieftains less illustrious.

I gazed into space and thought. What have I done? A few people in New York said, "Palermo? But you don't know anybody! You don't have any friends there!" My answer was: The population is over 800,000 so I'm counting on one or two people liking me.

My mind darted around like a rabbit. When I'd first seen the place at midday in darkness, it felt like a bunker. Now I decided to call it La Tana, which means the lair in Italian. My dictionary said a lair was 'the resting or living place of a wild animal.' Perfect. A jumble of thoughts. The dark is actually good for my lithographs as they are ruined by the light.

Palermo is very safe. Women are highly respected here. No violent crime. That afternoon some teenaged boys were talking in a group and one stepped back, barely touching me and every one of the five couldn't say "I'm sorry" enough times. I wondered if that would happen in the U.S. with boys that age.

People appear so kind. The maid, the people at the coffee bar. I've been here two weeks and people recognize me and say buongiorno. It is very different from Rome. The way the fathers always tend to the crying baby or the hurt child in the restaurant or in the street. The mother sits it out. I hadn't seen anyone yank a leash; the dogs sniff and the owners wait. People smile so much. I love television here. Channel 39. All crime shows. *Midsomer Murders, Law & Order, The Mentalist, Poirot*, etc.

There was no English bookstore or radio station. I could not find an English-language newspaper or magazine for sale anywhere. Fine, I decided. I will be immersed in Italian.

My prosecco and a plate of appetizers arrived, ending my reverie. A last thought as I reached for the flute: I am changing my whole life.

A HANDSOME CONDUCTOR and THE ANSWER IS YES

My plan was to go to Rome for a few days and then on to New York.

I'd give Silvia, my online conversation partner, power of attorney so that she could stand in for me at the sale in July. She was in Sambuca at this point and didn't mind the short trip to Palermo for the closing. Meanwhile, I'd be packing and preparing to come back to Palermo to live.

The next morning I took the train to Rome and loved it. Paying an extra 30 euros for first class meant I was alone in the carriage. About four hours in, the train was loaded onto the ferry and I scampered up several flights of iron stairs to the deck. Crossing the Straits of Messina, being in the wind and sun, watching the island of Sicily recede across blue water as we neared Italy delighted me. Then the train was off-loaded to land and raced beside the lush, green fields of Calabria. I found it all exhilarating and thought, this is my new country.

No reason for me to have any affinity at all for this boot-shaped peninsula giving a kick to an island called Sicily. I grew up with boys named Jimmy and Steve and Bill. I bet there was not one Italian in the state of Mississippi. I did have a teenaged fascination with the Mafia. How many girls who are meant to be trying out for cheerleader are busy memorizing every capo of every crime family? I was fourteen or fifteen when a pizzeria named Pasquale's opened in Jackson. The parking lot was jammed. Mother and my sister and I went and had our first pizza. We never told Daddy. The only thing I knew about Italians was that they were on a list of people that he hated. Quite a long list: anyone in New York City, everyone in Washington, D.C., Jews, Polish people, the Irish, anyone in California particularly Los Angeles, chiropractors and Italians.

At about nine hours in I asked the handsome conductor directions for the bar car to buy water. He told me that because of COVID, there was no place for food or drink on the train. All this was in my basic Italian. He later returned and gave me a large bottle of orange drink. I was terribly thirsty and very grateful. Hours later as I prepared to descend the steps at Termini in Rome, he took my suitcase, stared into my eyes and said, in perfect English, "You are a very beautiful woman."

I was quite surprised but smiled and said thank you as I let him help me down the steps. I was reminded again of how much I loved Italy.

In Rome on Sunday, I went to the Anglican church on via Babuino and from behind a mask a woman said, "Clarissa?" in an English accent. It was Philippa whom I hadn't seen for years. After the service we went to a lovely place with wine bottles on shelves right up to the sixteen-foot ceiling and drank prosecco. I talked to her as I never had before because my mentor at Radio Vaticana had died and she knew him. No one else in my life had. I heard details of his last weeks with cancer and wiped away tears. She said, "Palermo? You must meet my friend who is going to be the vicar of the Anglican church there." I was delighted at the possibility of a new friend.

While in Rome, I had news from the realtor that my offer was accepted!

I flew back to New York in a state of euphoria. Silvia knew of my bad experience with Alberto and told me that the first Gianni and not the Gianni who'd wanted to show me the exploding toilet property could help me with the sale. I could dump Alberto. She praised Gianni's father, Luca, who had renovated the kitchen of her Sambuca house and said he'd have workers for me. The drive to Palermo was less than an hour. Silvia adored Luca so much she could not say his name without sighing and declaring, "I want to marry him." To me, he became Luca Iwanttomarryhim. Silvia knew he was married and that his wife was blonde. The two of us, me in New York and Silvia in Italy, immediately plotted murder in Sambuca. Lots of laughing and my Italian was improving.

A FEW QUESTIONS

Of course, my thoughts were constantly of Palermo. I wrote Alberto my questions about the property but he didn't answer so then I wrote Agata. She wrote back but didn't answer anything. I wrote again and her return email was evasive. Then she wrote how wonderful Alberto was and how he would deal with everything. I sent the following email to the notary, Agata, Alberto, Rosita in Rome who had given me so much good advice and to Sergio at Tecnorete.

To All of You:

I have supplied my birth certificate, my divorce decree, a copy of my passport and my codice fiscale to you but I have seen NO documents about the property.

I must have them as soon as possible or I cannot buy it on July 31st.

It is fine to send them to me in Italian.

1. annual taxes. I want to know what other city/Palermo/local fees must be paid

2. when was the property last occupied?

3. are there any liens or debts on the property? Have all taxes been paid?

4. how many people live in the apartment above the ground floor? Do they work at home?

I want to know how old they are. Details. I have had bad experiences with music until 5 a.m. and dogs left alone to bark for 8 hours a day. I work at home. Sono una scrittrice. I am a writer.

5. what is the condition of the electrical wiring? does it need repair?

6. what is the condition of the plumbing? does it need repair?

7. what is the condition of the gas lines? do they need repair?

8. what is above the false ceiling? what is the ceiling height?

9. I must have the plan of the property. The ground floor appears to have the only front door.

How do the other occupants of the building enter?

10. is the property zoned for residential use?

11. is there a condominio fee for the property?

I must have every document as soon as possible. You have my email.

These details are mandatory. I want no surprises. I want no future problems.

I cannot go blindly forward without all the information.

Thank you so much.

Clarissa McNair

Sergio at Tecnorete answered all my questions within a few hours! It was in Italian so I used Google Translate.

Good evening Mrs. McNair,

to follow the answers to her questions:

1) the apartment has not been inhabited for about 10 years

2/3) it was a pizzeria and closed about 10 years ago

4) the electrical system is present but is not up to standard

5) the plumbing has been recently redone but is not certified

6) the gas system is not present in the building

7) in the plan there is no balcony but rather an internal courtyard

8) the floor above is inhabited by a family of 4

9) the taxes to be paid depend on the cadastral income, and that of the property you purchased is: 134.80 euros.

Best regards, Sergio

Then I received an email from Agata who was utterly furious. She objected to the word mandatory. Fine. If she wouldn't supply the information then I had found someone who would. Again, she claimed Alberto was taking care of everything.

Alberto was out though he didn't know it yet. So was Agata's notary. Silvia's Gianni was in. At 28, tall, thin, with black-framed glasses, he wore tight trousers that were always about three inches above his ankles. He spoke English very well and I wished he had shown me vicolo della Gardenia and not Alberto. Gianni had a notaio in Sambuca who also worked in Palermo and Silvia was happy to sign for me in July. Wire transfers, all would be in order.

The notaio/notary fee was two thousand euros which shocked me as I was used to the notary in Astoria stamping my document then refusing my offer to buy him coffee. In Italy, it is a big deal to be a notary and you study years to become one. They are the ones to do the title search and check on liens, etc. so I don't have to drag my favorite Sicilian detective, Riccardo, into this.

A PRIVATE DETECTIVE IN PALERMO

On one of those mornings when I'd been in the hotel watching *Law & Order*, waiting for Alberto to call me back, I'd gone online and found private investigators in Palermo. There were a dozen and I called a few who didn't answer the phone and then thought, okay, this one has the most impressive ad. I called and a male voice answered. In my careful, bad Italian I told him I was un detective private da New York and could I come and talk to him?

It was a little office in a modern building down by the harbor. A pretty girl in a halter top and short shorts answered the door with a giant shar-pei dog observing. I was waved into the small adjoining room where a man about my height stood up from behind his desk to greet me. Dark hair, nice smile, tanned and fit. Low-slung jeans and a navy polo shirt. I was in my black T-shirt dress with high-heeled black sandals and my Panama hat. He grinned in approval, introduced me to Ercole (Hercules) who padded in and stared at me and then we all sat down. I apologized for my Italian but I talked. He said that it didn't matter and that the important thing was that we were communicating. His first question was could I ride a motorcycle? Inwardly wincing as I thought of all the huge, intimidating ones on the street, I said, "No, ma posso imparare." I can learn. This was to tail people and

I realized infidelity was the name of the game. I told him he'd be wasting me and that I could do interviews, deal with anyone who spoke English, that I had experience in France and New York. I told him I had contacts in New York, Miami, Paris, Philadelphia and dappertutto which means everywhere. He was nodding. No work permit? Don't worry about it. "I have contacts with the polizia and I'll tell them you work with me."

Riccardo told me he had twenty years of experience and he was 42 years old. I nodded and said that I, too, had twenty years of experience. I liked him and it was left that I would get in touch when I came back to Palermo.

There were a few texts between us and then I was in New York. I did ask him if he could find out who lived above my property and he did research and said it appeared no one did. I thanked him and said I owed him. He left friendly voice messages for me and then went silent. My website was very good, my reputation is impeccable so I suspect he found out my age and it put him off. What detective wants someone as old as his mother working with him?

Too bad, I thought. After a full two minutes of depression, I recovered and decided that I would bring work to him. Riccardo would work for me.

* * *

The July closing hit snags. I couriered the documents for the power of attorney to Silvia in Sambuca but the delivery man could not find her house so the papers never arrived and Silvia had to return to Genoa and could not sign for me in Palermo. The sale was then postponed.

The next few weeks Gema and I talked more than ever, always with the laundromat sound track, often interrupted by someone dropping off clothes or picking them up. Gema's doctor told her she needed more vitamin D so she came up to my terrace on her day off, arriving with margaritas, even the right glasses. The two of us sprawled on towels in our bikinis.

Birds had come to my terrace for the first time during COVID and I fed them. I called them my dinosaurs and Gema promised to feed them in back of the laundromat. Someone at the sandwich shop across the street gave her all the leftover bagels at the end of each day and she often gave them away because her freezer was full of them. Astoria recycling. These New York birds would eat bagels. Gema would look out for the Japanese sushi chef I tutored in English. He was shy, found friendships difficult. Since the library was closed, we had our lessons in the laundromat. Behind masks, I'd coached him in how to greet people, how to have simple conversations and he had practiced on Gema. Everyone knew her and Gema knew when a woman was pregnant before she'd told anyone, when a man was having a love affair, and she knew whose mothers still did their laundry. Everyone trusted her, everyone talked to her.

After watching the truck disappear with everything I owned, Gema and I drank tequila. It wasn't a celebration but more like the beginning of the end of my Astoria days. I would miss Gema terribly.

We sat on the curb in front of the dark, closed laundromat and drank out of paper cups, the tequila bottle between us. It was cooling off a little but the day had been smothered in that muggy city heat of concrete and traffic. I worried that my ship would dock before I owned the place in Palermo. Three weeks was the crossing time but what if some weird current drastically shortened the passage?

THE CLOSING

I bought my ticket to Palermo for arrival the weekend before the Monday meeting. September 20th was the earliest the much-in-demand notary was available.

Then it was COVID testing in Astoria and the worry over whether I'd have the results in time and always the twinge of fear that I might be a Typhoid Mary with no symptoms. I got on the plane and arrived in Palermo as scheduled.

That Monday morning the large conference table dominated a room with shutters open to green leaves and the twittering of birds. Sunlight streamed in. I'd been panicky when Gianni had been half an hour late picking me up at the hotel but it didn't matter. The rest of the cast drifted in with greetings and kisses. Sergio and another realtor from Tecnorete were there, a man or two I didn't know, a small, bald, sunburned man in his seventies accompanied by a younger man in shorts and a T-shirt. No sign of the notaio. We were all masked except Gianni who had the breath of a swamp creature. I offered him a mint but he refused.

Gianni told me the 4880 euros paid to Tecnorete was not right and said he would try to get it back. The stocky, red-faced Sergio wouldn't budge. Gianni was half his age and I thought he put up a strong argument. Later Gianni would tell me that he said that Alberto told him to charge me the money and that they would split it later!

The room was hot. There was the soft murmur of conversation as we waited for the notaio. I expected a large man in a very expensive suit, beautiful shoes. Instead, the notaio was a small, slender, blondish women in her forties. She was wearing a printed nylon blouse, nylon palazzo pants and white sandals. The emerald earrings, however, made a statement.

She took her place at the head of the table next to me. We were surrounded by masked men; perspiration shone on every pink forehead.

Any words in Italian deserted me and I sat mutely at the table hearing myself often referred to as "la Signora." It was a long ceremony with the notaio halting it at several points and leaving the room to confer with someone unseen and mysterious.

One time she re-entered and said the sale could not go through. Gianni was shaking his head, the other men were upset. I had no idea what was happening but the moment passed.

Another time she left the room to consult with a chief engineer. Gianni was keeping me apprised. I hated leaning towards him and kept thinking, of all the people to not wear a mask. I was told that vicolo della Gardenia, number one, at the present did not match the plan on file. This was extremely serious. All the men were passionate about the plan being exactly as the place was. The notaio zeroed in on me and pointed out that the plan showed quattro stanze (four rooms) and it is now two big spaces instead of four. I could never sell it if it were not exactly like this plan. I was thinking that the place was built in 1939 so, of course, it had been modified. I whispered to Gianni that I could put in room dividers if needed and he nodded.

The notaio stared at me very sternly and waited. I looked her in the eye and lied. I said the place was exactly like the plan. It was dramatic—the raised voices of the men, the quiet aura of power surrounding the notaio. She read every page aloud and there were times I wanted to giggle at the solemnity. I listened to all the back and forth in Italian I did not understand and thought, What am I doing here? What am I doing?

At last it was time to sign. Signor Orlando, the owner, the small bald, sunburned man wearing combat fatigues, came to stand between me and the notary. He was so short he didn't have to lean down over the table. There were many pages to sign and he drew his name very slowly. Time after time. The realtors grew restless. Gianni started reading and writing emails. There were audible sighs. One page after another was taken from him then turned face down. Finally, it was over. I felt so sorry for him.

Then the notaio said he had to sign his first name. Signor Orlando started with page one again and then hesitated. His pal in a white T-shirt and shorts stepped forward and helped him with the spelling.

The room was hot and Mississippi-muggy even with the tall windows open. We all wanted this over; the wait was excruciating. The notaio was like a third-grade teacher overseeing the drawing of the letters. My turn. I signed quickly, again and again. The notaio then asked my profession and I said scrittrice and she beamed. "Complimenti!"

I was becoming accustomed to this reaction. Writers are respected here.

I wrote the check on my Paris account in euros as the notaio watched. In black and not in my usual green ink, which always drives everyone in official situations to hysteria. She took it, examined it carefully and it was passed to Signor Orlando.

Keys were handed across the table and in careful Italian I told him I was happy to live in his house. He seemed to be a nice man and told me he lived nearby and I could come to him with any problem.

Going down the stairs, the notaio spoke to me and I smiled and nodded, unsure of what she was saying but then realized she was inviting me to her country house a few hours drive away, whenever I wanted to come.

Outside, in the sun on the sidewalk, the men all shook hands.

I NOW OWNED VICOLO DELLA GARDENIA, 1, IN PALERMO, SICILY

Gianni and I ate lunch together and later we drove to *my place* and met with his father who was short, stocky but not fat, with a handsome, tanned face. He wore a short-sleeved shirt and nice trousers which looked expensive; he had an air of confidence. I would later dub this arrogance but at that moment, I thought of Silvia's sigh of "I want to marry him." Maybe he possessed sex appeal.

Gianni and his father got the shutter up and we three left the bright light of the alley and entered darkness. After a few minutes, the two spoke in Italian that was too fast for me to understand. Gianni explained that I should have all new electrical wiring and all new plumbing. I agreed. There were the two disgusting bathrooms for what I was now told had been a pizza parlor. A pizza parlor in Palermo. Euphonious. Luca Iwanttomarryhim said he would do all electrical, all plumbing and would install the kitchen and the bathroom fixtures which I would pay for. I held my breath, waiting for the fee. I'd heard that renovating a bathroom in Manhattan was about $25,000. A friend had renovated a kitchen and spent $75,000. Renovated not created. Luca nodded as if doing math and I confirmed with Gianni what this would cover then I tried to hide my relief. There was the IVA tax of 22%. The euro was $1.20. My house had cost Euros 30.000 or U.S. $36,000 and Luca's fee was 6.000 euros or $7,200, which was reasonable.

THE CHECK

Back at my hotel I received word from Gianni that the real estate agency said my check was not valid because it was written with the wrong sort of pen. I had used a black fine-point, felt-tip pen and the notaio had examined the check afterwards. I texted Gianni that the check was fine and he texted back that they were lying and Orlando's bank didn't know what to do with a check from Paris HSBC. I was surprised to hear the word 'lying.' I said that the realtor could come to my hotel with his own pen and I would write a new check but that it had to be today as I was leaving tomorrow. Back and forth. I decided to call the notaio. I introduced myself and began to explain, she started to say something back. She giggled then I giggled and we were laughing so hard neither one of us could do anything but hang up. Gianni called her for she would have the last word. The check was fine.

But it wasn't. Signor Orlando claimed to have gone to every bank in Palermo and no one would accept my check. I still don't know why but I ended up wiring the money to Gianni's bank and Gianni then gave Signor Orlando the money. Suitcase of cash on a street corner? No idea. Somehow. In the next eight months there would be many details that I would not entirely understand.

Hello, Palermo

"Palermo isn't Paris . . . Palermo is Beirut, Palermo is Istanbul, Palermo is Jerusalem, Palermo is Tripoli. Palermo is a Middle Eastern city in Europe. The Mediterranean isn't a sea, it's a continent."

—Leoluca Orlando, former mayor of Palermo

Back in New York, it was address changes, a mailbox service, the dentist, a medical checkup, goodbye lunches and dinners. I had paid for my apartment up until the end of October and had things to do. One day I took a train to New Jersey to meet Anne Marie, a woman who wanted me to write her memoir. We spent most of the day in her kitchen going over photographs and talking. I would next see her on Zoom from my desk at the hotel in Palermo.

Those last days I said goodbye to people up and down Broadway. Many had witnessed the dramatic arrival of Moby Dick and the departure of the truck with International Air and Sea Shipping written on the side. Ingrid from Vienna who ran the thrift shop, the main Bosnian butcher, Harry, the limo driver, all threw their arms around me. Daisy at Retro Pizza seemed very serious when she said she would come to Palermo. The tiny Chinese woman at the post office said she would miss me. A few people said they saw me on my bike all the time and wasn't it wonderful to be going to Italy? Many asked when I was coming back and I said I didn't know. The words 'always,' and 'forever' stick in my throat.

I had another COVID shot and a flu shot, yet another COVID test and felt ready for anything. We were all still wearing masks.

My suitcases were in front of the laundromat and I was inside with Gema. The realization that we weren't going to talk every single day hit both of us at the same time. She knew me so well, read my expression and said, "Cici, you are doing the right thing." We embraced and she said, "I learned so much from you." Holding back tears, I whispered, "I think you taught me more."

Suddenly I was in the car with one of Sal's cousins. Sal owned the grocery store on the corner and was always reliable with getting someone in his extended Lebanese family to drive me to the airport.

Isabelle, who had been head of my HSBC branch, and her daughter drove out to JFK to say goodbye. I couldn't believe anyone would do that for me.

Suddenly I was on the plane with two suitcases containing clothes, my thesaurus, my dictionary, a few books, my computer. What I needed for the few weeks until the ship came in. I arrived in Palermo on Saturday, October 30th.

It was night when I walked into the lobby of the Hotel Joli. I'd found it online. Silvia had been horrified that I hadn't picked an Air B & B but the Joli was about the same price as it was low season and I like living in hotels.

My room was peach-colored, romantic with a very high ceiling and ornate brocade curtains framing a large window that looked out over Piazza Ignazio Florio with a statue of him in the center flanked by dignified palm trees. I grew used to the view but particularly liked being able to see when the grocery store across the piazza was open.

The room was lovely but small. It was during that first week that I asked one of the concierges if I could have a larger room and the answer was 'no.' But that was minor. The breakfasts were divine: lemon cake, chocolate cake, ham, salami, cheese, cookies and the usual cereals and yoghurt. Croissants called cornetti were either sweet or seemed soaked in butter. I had ham and cornetto sandwiches and chocolate cake every morning served by a young Sicilian named Danilo. My maid was Mariella. We tried to chat. She showed me photos of her glamorous daughter, her son; Mariella was always smiling.

On Monday, November first, I began to work with Anne Marie on her book. I sat at the little desk by the window early every morning reading what she'd sent from New Jersey as I slept. The six-hour time difference worked in our favor because I could read and write and send off what I'd written in the afternoon just in time for her to wake up and read it. She'd make notes, send me details which I would see in my inbox just before going to bed but I usually read them in the morning with a clear head.

My shipment was delayed. Now I would get everything December 8th which was okay. I could hold out in my summer clothes if it didn't get very cold here.

THOMAS

The Hotel Joli was a one-minute sprint from the church. Said to be the most beautiful Anglican church in Italy, the building itself could sit on a London street corner or in an English village but the interior with its gold mosaics was entirely Sicilian. I introduced myself to Father Thomas as having been sent by Philippa in Rome which appeared to make me instantly acceptable. Thomas was six feet tall with dark hair and an open, handsome face. His perfect smile was quick, he laughed easily, was entirely charming. In my eyes, he radiated conviviality. Thomas was American, gay, with a partner who has a farm outside Bologna; Marcello and Thomas go back and forth. Thomas was destined to become a best friend, confidante and ally.

• • •

We were still waiting for the permit to start work but another concern of mine was the permit to stay in Italy. I went to the questura and was told to return to NY for a document as I would be illegal in 85 days. Of course, I did not want to do that. I should have been quite tense but I wasn't. I thought all of it would be okay and I was happy to be here.

It was drizzling rain and November-dark at seven in the evening when Gianni arranged to meet at vicolo della Gardenia. The men were wearing boots and parkas whereas I was in my sopping-wet ballet slippers and shivering in the one sweater I'd brought.

Luca Iwanttomarryhim introduced me to a man I assumed was a contractor but I later learned he was a bricklayer. Well, whatever he was doing his big grey Mercedes parked in the alley meant he was making money at it. Giovanni was a hulking, blue-eyed blonde and looked as if he'd just stepped off a sailboat. I secretly dubbed him The Viking, at first, then called him The Norman and later learned he actually was Norman. I would never see him or any of the workers wearing a mask but with the doors open all day it was like being outside anyway.

With a great roar the metal shutter was pulled up and we entered a pitch-black space. It was cold and damp. By the light of cell phones there was a cursory inspection punctuated by quick Italian. Luca said all could be done in a month. The Norman stood in the doorway and told me I'd be living there by Christmas. I rejoiced.

A few days later Gianni came to the hotel with his fidanzata/girlfriend who was studying to be a lawyer. We chatted in a bit of English in the empty dining room under the elaborate ceiling and the Murano chandelier while Gianni talked on the phone to the electric company. It took nearly an hour to open an account with various documents read into the phone, questions answered, the call transferred from one clerk or department to another. My codice fiscale which is like a Social Security number was essential as was my passport information. I could not have done this on my own.

Another afternoon Gianni came to the Joli to talk about The Norman's fee. It was 15.000 euros and Gianni said his father and he both thought it should be ten. But The Norman would only drop it by one thousand. I took a deep breath and said 'yes' because he was willing to begin immediately.

The EU was giving countries money for building and Palermo was full of scaffolding and orange nets. I did not want to risk not finding anyone else. The Norman would remove the floor tiles, dig trenches so that new pipes could be installed by Luca, strip all the walls of the tiles, plaster the walls, build a loft, paint all the walls, do the kitchen backsplash, make a wall giving me a closed kitchen then power-wash, clean and paint the cortile/courtyard. He would also install a new bathroom door and a pocket door for the kitchen. I knew I was being overcharged but I was constantly considering the hotel bill and thinking I'd be out of the Joli before Christmas.

I'd been in Palermo about two weeks when I encountered the woman concierge on a quiet Sunday afternoon. She had a head of butter-yellow corkscrew curls which moved with their own independent sense of excitement. Her dark eyes were friendly behind the black cat's-eye framed glasses. She asked me to call her Maria but I would always think of her as Blondie.

Madly curious, she leveled a barrage of questions at me. Maria spoke not a word of English but I managed to tell her that I'd bought an old pizzeria and was going to live there. At the end of the conversation, she asked me in a very low voice if I would like a larger room. I said, "Assolutamente!" and she gave me the key to a room nearly twice the size of my original with the same piazza view. I went up and transferred everything before anyone could stop me and then ran down the stairs to give her the key to my old room. We were friends forevermore.

THE PIZZERIA TRIPLETS

One morning I walked from the hotel to my place and stood in the alley daydreaming. I had no doubt it would be splendid. I stared at the closed metal shutter and imagined what the front door would be like.

Three men approached me and said, "Buongiorno," in a chorus. They were probably in their forties and all the same shape and height, wearing the same uniform of sweatshirts, jeans and running shoes. They welcomed me to the neighborhood. One motioned that he lived upstairs and said to come to him if I needed anything. How nice, I thought. They told me they were opening a pizzeria next door. Molto buono, I managed as I thought, not so good as it would be noise at all hours and lots of people. It was explained that the tables would be outside and around the corner. I asked when it would open and sensed a flutter of unease. They shuffled their feet and looked at each other. Why did I want to know? I smiled, touched my stomach and said, "Ho fame." I'm hungry. They all laughed. They did not answer but it was a pleasant exchange and they strolled away. Yes, I thought, I already have friends in my alley. The Pizzeria Triplets.

THE WORK BEGINS

It was mid-November when we had the permit from the city of Palermo to start work. I assumed men would be there the next day but they didn't begin until the following Monday.

I arrived and saw that the doors were open and two men were chipping away with sledgehammers in the shadows. They had some kind of light propped on a pile of rubble. Giuseppe and Giuseppe, both with huge stomachs, dirty sweatshirts, trousers and shoes white with plaster dust. Palermo is filled with Giuseppes so I would number them, uno and due. We talked in my broken Italian. They told me they thought I was French and seemed relieved and maybe even glad that I was American.

One of the Pizzeria Triplets waved at me and motioned for me to follow him. He started unlocking his metal shutters around the corner of the building and then we entered an 8 by 5 foot area with a counter and a cash register. Then he led me to another room and another room. Each quite small but with gleaming stainless steel kitchen appliances. He said it would open soon and the hours would be 11 a.m. to midnight. Fine with me. I like pizza.

He paid 40.000 euros for the place and said he had to knock out walls, do everything. Then he asked if I would sell him my place! He told me he wanted to knock down the common wall and have an indoor restaurant.

All this was in Italian but I understood. I smiled and asked him what he would pay. He told me to name my price. I laughed and said I had just bought it, was going to make it beautiful and live there. He knew I'd paid 30.000 euros. I would learn that there are no secrets in the alley.

I told that Pizzeria Triplet that we should talk a year from now. We agreed if I ever wanted to sell I would come to him first.

I went back inside and measured. The ceiling is going to be nearly 14 feet high which makes me happy. It also means that the loft for storage will be higher than I counted on so I won't have to slither around on my stomach to retrieve anything.

Gianni did not arrive as he had promised. I left as I had to do the pages for Anne Marie before she woke up in New Jersey. Back at my little desk in the Joli, Gianni wrote me, "The Enel team of boys has come, the energy is active but there is a breakdown. Should they schedule an intervention?" ENEL is the electric company and an intervention, I discovered, is a "repairing operation" and is free. Do it, I directed.

Then he wrote that the gas line might cost 2 to 3.000 euros and encouraged me to have the bombs of gas delivered for six euros a month instead but since I was one person they might last two or three months. That word 'bomb' is discouraging but I agreed to it. If all I do is make popcorn and brownies one of those things might last all year. Then he asked me if I wanted a boiler or a water heater? I picked water heater because I'd had one in Philadelphia and because it sounded less threatening.

I was back in my alley at noon because one of the Giuseppes told me the postino usually came at midday. The other Giuseppe looked very comfortable in an armchair chuckling over something on his cell phone which rested on his huge stomach. It was their lunch hour and he was watching a movie. I wondered where he'd gotten the armchair and then realized he was relaxing in the wheelbarrow. I was hoping to see il postino but I didn't and then one of the Giuseppes said he probably didn't even come to this alley. Well, I thought, il postino had better start coming to this alley!

A FIRST ENCOUNTER

One morning while I stood in the alley writing a note to The Norman about the blacksmith this little grey car covered in layers of dust sped around the corner and stopped right in front of my doorway.

 Both Giuseppes Uno and Due knew him and came out and talked. I was told he was a proprietor but of what was unclear. He got out of the car. We bumped knuckles. He was under five feet tall, balding with some tufts of white hair in front in a tousled pompadour, maybe in his 70s wearing a black windbreaker with a sports team logo. Old clothes. Covered in dust. He looked like someone just pulled from a collapsed building in an earthquake. This man was very round, maybe as large in diameter as tall and had a serious limp so he rocked precariously from side to side. If he fell he would just keep rolling until he bumped into something.

 The first thing he said to me was did I want to buy his building. He pointed down the alley. The day before yesterday someone wanted to buy my place and now this man wanted me to buy his place.

 I said I had no more money, that I was giving it all to Guiseppe #1 who was standing beside me grinning with very few teeth. I pulled out one of my empty pockets. This didn't deter the man I later dubbed Trump of the Alley. He made me understand that he owns all the buildings from mine down to the end.

 The church next door is owned by the city of Palermo. His daughter lives on one of the top floors around the corner and he owns that building, too. Then he told me the entire thing was molto pericoloso or very dangerous and it was going to fall, people were going to die. I was confused. He wanted me to buy about five doorways and the two stories above them just before they collapsed and killed every resident.

 Historical district, great zona and I agreed. I did ask about my place and was told that my place and the pizza place were fine. They would not fall down, people would not die. He was waving his arms around talking and I was trying to follow when a horn started honking. It was a motorcycle behind his car that couldn't pass. He bumped knuckles with me, warned me about something I didn't understand, got in his filthy grey car and sped away. The motorcycle sped after him.

IF I had money, the entire clump of doorways and the two floors above them would be a good investment. A tear down unless there is something called a fall down. The area is really interesting and convenient; Lidl's supermarket is about a hundred steps away and via Roma is a main artery. I am liking the neighborhood more every time I go there.

I was trying to finish my note to The Norman holding the dictionary open to the word for carpenter which is impossible to say when he came purring up in his huge grey Mercedes. He parked so close to the wall I thought he'd never get out on the driver's side but he did. I averted my eyes. That man enjoys his food.

We walked in together and again I said how brutto/ugly was the false ceiling and was there any way to get rid of it? I had been told there were exposed beams underneath. I'd also been told the true ceiling would be higher. None of that was true.

I had been told the false ceiling would be ripped down. The two Giuseppes had told me 'no' and then The Norman told me 'no' and Giuesppe Numero Uno acted out being put in handcuffs and all of us being arrested and going to jail. The Norman was standing under the ugly ceiling waving his arms around to illustrate that the entire building would come down if he touched that false ceiling.

Okay. I surrendered. The morning was filled with dire predictions of collapse. The Norman squeezed himself into his Mercedes and left.

PIETRO

One day I was talking to Blondie and when she heard I was writing a book upstairs she insisted that I meet Pietro, the proprietor. He was a man of culture and would want to know that a writer was living in his hotel. I said, of course, I'd like that, never expecting her, quick as a cat, to dart from behind the big desk and disappear through the door marked Privato next to the elevator. In minutes, she was introducing me to a man my height with whitish hair and very kind eyes. Plainly excited, he motioned me to the dining room where we sat at a table facing each other. In my bag, I handed him my postcard with my eight book covers pictured and he studied it attentively. There were plenty of questions which should have been difficult to answer but I'd had wine with lunch and just added a vowel to the end of every word. The conversation seemed satisfying to both of us.

Pietro would become a dear friend and a great help to me in Palermo. A few weeks later when he heard, probably via Blondie, that I'd had no luck at the questura (police headquarters) which had been a very expensive taxi ride and a wait outside massive gates surrounded by young Africans in nylon track suits, he devoted half a day to taking me there. It was a long drive away from the centro and, again, a mad scene of mostly Africans waiting outside in a scruffy courtyard to be summoned to offices with doors open and men in uniform sitting at small tables. There were numerous women in saris and burqas with screaming babies. Pietro asked for his friend who was not there, my passport was examined and the answer was the same to us as it had been to me: go back to your home country to the Italian consulate. Pietro, ever polite, thanked everyone and we shook hands with one official, one guard, one policeman after another then went back to the car for the long, traffic-clogged drive back to the Joli.

Late the next afternoon, Pietro, dear man, called my room and told me to come downstairs with all my documents. We left the hotel and walked in near silence through the streets of Palermo as I was unsure how to ask in Italian where we were going without sounding rude. Like a child, I obeyed, following him into a modern building and up a flight of stairs where we faced a door that said CONSOLATO DELLA LITUANIA.

I was introduced with great fanfare as a writer and the air was full of "Complimenti!" The consulate staff and the lawyer were so gracious I was made to feel I was doing them all a favor to have come to their office. My papers were looked over but the advice was exactly the same. Pietro and I walked back to the Joli in the dark.

We entered the lobby together and there was Blondie looking calm. Usually when I came in she screamed about whatever I was wearing then tells me she got her little jacket on sale 15 years ago and what do I think? She has me inspect the neck label and the stitching on the pockets and I tell her—always true—that it is adorable. Then she inspects me and says, "Bel-laaaa!" She had a more extensive wardrobe than I did, of course, and was always overjoyed when I told her she looked chic.

Now she was calm and in the background. I thanked Pietro and he shrugged and said, "Niente," and I said, "No. Era qualcosa grande." It wasn't nothing. It was something big. Blondie was smiling, I was smiling, Pietro was smiling. All of us—pleased behind our masks. He left and I told Blondie he was molto gentile, bravo. She nodded, her yellow curls bouncing in agreement.

THE TWO GUISEPPES

Gianni finally brought a generator which meant light and threw the men's bulbous shadows on the wall. Today they wanted to know how old I was which is phrased as how many years do you have? This question I was destined to be asked dozens of times by all sorts of people. I avoided answering by pretending not to understand.

Both Giuseppes chain-smoke, are overweight and have heart trouble. I would learn they were in their fifties.

Giuseppe Uno was marginally less corpulent than Giovanni Due and spoke on the phone flirtatiously for long periods with someone who was probably not his wife. They took breaks to smoke, breaks to stand in the rubble to talk, cell phone breaks and a long lunch break. There were times when I wanted to grab a shovel myself.

MY DAYS

Living in that charming hotel was not entirely glamorous as I had to wash my bikini underwear in the bidet and then dry them with a hair dryer. I couldn't hang anything on the window sill—this was not Naples! This was a swanky hotel in the heart of Palermo! I didn't know why I had so many T-shirts and five pairs of sandals. I had the bathroom scales, sundresses and mysteriously I had two clocks. I had a wine opener. A huge ceramic pitcher I decided not to leave behind in New York was stuffed with underwear and packed at the last moment. One pair of black jeans and one black sweater. I remembered reading a novel by Nadine Gordimer about a South African family packing quickly in the middle of the night and running for their lives. Safe, somewhere else, they unpack and one of them had brought that little metal thing that removes staples. I felt like that.

At six every morning I awakened to the sweet scent of baking.

My days began early with reading whatever Anne Marie had sent. At seven I was downstairs for breakfast. Danilo laid out the extravagant buffet every morning and presented my bottle of fizzy water with a flourish. He knew that banana yoghurt was my favorite and put it way in the back for me so no one else took it. I would eat it at my desk later. In clear Italian, he told me his best friend was in NYC, worked in a pizza parlor, made a lot more money than here but all he does is work. I thought—that's it. New York was more about money.

The German couple I saw every morning in the dining room left today. I decided they were not married or not married long. There is a very slim chance that they were happily married because they talked at breakfast and enjoyed each other's company. The woman spoke to me in English as we both nibbled tremendous slabs of chocolate cake; she said it was a good thing they weighed the luggage and not the passengers.

By half past seven at the latest I was in my alley. The two Giuseppes had keys and sometimes had just arrived and were beginning work. My meetings with The Norman were scheduled, confirmed and I was stood up. Again and again. I had questions, I had drawings, I had memorized words for what I must say. Words like altezza for height, pavimento for floor. The meetings with Gianni were the same. Confirmed and then stood up again and again. He texts that he will be there at 10 o'clock and he isn't. Hours later he will finally answer his phone and say he is not coming.

THE EAGLE WAS MOVED

Every Sunday I dashed out of the Joli to church as Thomas gave thought-provoking, well-crafted sermons. Anyone who can quote Aristotle, Nelson Mandela and Sheryl Crow in the span of a few minutes has an interesting mind. The English women at the church, with few exceptions, were not nice to me. Most of them were small with grey hair and in their 70s, 80s, even 90s. I called them the Sparrows. My buongiorno or good morning would often be met with a stare. I was usually not acknowledged. Once as I was waiting for the service to begin, a Sparrow stood on either side of my chair. They were very, very close, an inch from touching me and conducted a conversation just over my head.

The first week of November, Thomas was "installed" as the vicar of the church. The word made me think of a kitchen faucet. He and his partner held a buffet lunch at a nearby restaurant after the ceremony. The Sparrows huddled in tight little groups but I barged right in and introduced myself. They appeared to not want to be there but they were and they ate the food, saw the flowers, drank the wine. I sat at a table with people from England, met Marcello, Thomas' partner, and had a super time.

I would later discover that the Sparrows were upset that the lunch was not held in the church nave as it had been in the past. Never mind that Marcello had paid for flowers, a photographer, wine and a veritable feast. There was also some mention of an eagle: Father Thomas had moved it. Shocking. The large brass eagle perched on a chest-high podium had been placed in the center aisle so that Father Thomas could rest the Bible on it and feel closer to the congregation as he read. The Sparrows were angry and claimed that the new position was dangerous as a person could bump into it and be seriously injured. Never expecting such acrimonious outrage, Father Thomas moved the eagle back.

MY FIRST PROSECCO WITH THOMAS

A few days later Thomas invited me for prosecco and we met at Spinnato's. He'd picked a table outside and a bit farther away from the others. I talked about life with the two Giuseppes and confessed that I sometimes felt silently livid at the way The Norman behaved towards me. "Is it because I am a woman?" I demanded.

Thomas said, "Yes, I think all of this would be easier if you were a man."

We decided that a sex change during the renovation was just too much to deal with and that I should soldier on. "I will," I said, taking a sip of prosecco.

"I mean, it can't go on forever," said Thomas. Then he laughed. "But this *is* Palermo so maybe it can."

"Don't even joke about things like that! I don't want to be talking about The Norman or the two Giuseppes or any of those men next year!"

"You will be," he said. "Next year is not even two months away."

"I am spiraling into depression so let's change the subject. Fast," I said. "How is everything at the church?"

Suddenly he was serious. "Now I am spiraling into depression. They want me out."

"What? Who? Out of what? What are you saying?" I was confused.

"They want me out of the church. The women, the council, most of them."

"But you only came in September and it's November..." my voice trailed off.

He swallowed and put his flute down.

"Is it because you're gay? Because you are American?" I was prepared to be outraged.

Thomas sighed and leaned back in his chair. "No, not that. The previous vicar was American but he was old and let everyone do what they wanted. I've been sent to enforce the rules of the Church of England and they don't like it."

"Are they breaking the rules of the Church of England?"

Thomas grinned. "Left and right!"

"But if—"

He interrupted me. "You are my escape. I trust you implicitly but I don't want to burden you with this. As I said, you really are my escape. You are my chance to think of other things."

"Okay," I nodded. "But if you want to talk about it, I'm around."

ANGLO SAXONS ON A MEDITERRANEAN ISLAND

That would be the first of our numerous meetings with prosecco for what I began to think of as debriefings. I had been here since October 30th and Thomas had arrived in late August. We trusted each other, we wanted to speak English and to be understood. At one point, we toasted, "Prosecco is the answer" and maybe it was. I could explode with frustration about my workers, we could both confess to great confusion over how the Sicilians did things, didn't do things and how complex their thought processes must be. I told him how I'd taken a simply glorious bouquet of lilies, roses and zinnias to a dinner and how my host took them very reluctantly and was disappointed that they were not artificial. Sometimes very little seemed to make sense. We were Anglo-Saxons trying our best to navigate the unfamiliar, mysterious world that was Palermo.

When I'm upset, the Italian language either leaves me or I level clear sentences like arrows and get my way. I'm getting pretty good on the 101 bus when heightened security won't accept my American vaccination card. That's happening more often now. I explain that the dates are different vis a vis the month here and the month written there. It's just a distraction to stall as the security man listens to me. I tell him I've been using it dappertutto/everywhere and by the time he orders me off it is my stop. Perfect. All this is just in case I haven't slipped unseen behind him.

November and December days were a blur of pouring rain, arriving at my place at half past seven, greeting the Giuseppes and waiting for The Norman or Gianni who had promised to come, had set the time and would never arrive.

Palermo was rain every day. Why was this island always yellow on maps? I bought leather boots which never got dry then surrendered to big, black, ugly rubber ones with tractor treads, stomped in puddles like a kid and realized I was crazy about them. Once I spent a winter in London and it felt like living in a basement. The street lights came on at three o'clock in the afternoon. This wasn't like that. I swear that the Sicilian drops are fatter than the English ones but suddenly stop and it's over like a tropical shower in the Caribbean; the sky would be a triumphant blue and the very air seemed to shimmer.

It was on the third Sunday that one of the Sparrows approached me after the service and suggested we meet for coffee. I hesitated because I'd been snubbed by nearly every one of the English women. "Yes, that would be nice," I said. Be optimistic, I told myself. Thomas was busy with guests who were raving about his sermon so I didn't tell him about the invitation. Americans always wanted to take him home to "our church in Baltimore." Or to Omaha. Or to Tampa. I would see this happen again and again. The visitors adored him.

THE UNDERCOVER SPARROW

The Sparrow and I met on Monday morning at eleven. It was raining, of course, so we sat inside a caffè on via Roma. She introduced herself but I promised to never reveal her name. Because of how our liaison unfolded, I won't describe her physically either. There were the usual questions about why I'd chosen Palermo, had I really bought a place and the renovation progress. I asked her why she was in Palermo, why were all these English women here at all?

"It is absurd that we are here! That all these years later we are still going to that church." She smiled and stared over my shoulder as if remembering. "We all married handsome, Sicilian men. Forty, fifty, sixty even seventy years ago. Of course, they were Catholic and our children were raised as Catholic. Now all our husbands are dead and that church is our little piece of England."

I steeled myself for any criticism of Thomas but it didn't come.

"You and Harold are the only Americans and I've picked you," she said.

"Picked me? For what?" I asked. I didn't know who Harold was but let it go. She was drinking coffee but I never drink coffee so a glass of orange juice was in front of me. I took a sip. Did I trust her?

As if reading my mind, she said, "I hope you will trust me."

I waited as she continued. "I am part of the old guard. Anyone will tell you that. But I am angry at what's happening to Father Thomas. It's disgraceful."

Red lights were blinking, bells were clanging. I pictured a railroad crossing. The train was coming and I was being warned.

"I know he is under stress," I said very carefully.

"It's cruel. What he is enduring." Her eyes flashed. "All of these women have run the church for years and they think he is interfering."

I stifled the urge to shout, but he is the vicar, he is in charge! Instead, I said, "Thomas won't talk about this with me. We see each other to talk about everything except the church. He puts it aside when we are together."

"If he won't tell you then I will. The persecution began immediately. When he arrived. He asked that the council meet once a month." She shook her head. "It's been meeting twice a year."

Keep quiet and listen, I told myself sternly.

"He told us this is according to the Church of England. It's the way it should be. So he asked every one of us eight to meet on a Wednesday. Every single person made it difficult. Oh, I can't meet at seven. Six is too early for me. Eight is too late for me. On and on. Back and forth. Mind you, not one of these people have a job or dependents or anywhere they must be. At last it was decided to meet at eight-thirty at the church." She pinched her lips together and shook her head, plainly angry. "Father Thomas went to the church and no one came because they all decided to meet at five." She spat out the last words, "Without him!"

"Now I'm angry," I said.

"This is what they do." She sipped her coffee then put the cup down "I have thirty examples." She frowned. "They look for things to complain about. They were upset that unrecycled paper was used for the announcements on the notice board."

"That's pathetic. I heard about the eagle which is . . ." I shook my head. "But If you are one of the old guard," I began, nearly calling her a Sparrow, "then why don't you do something?'

"I have campaigned on his behalf but I'm outnumbered. I'm getting nowhere and there is the possibility I'll be cut out of everything. I've decided to approach this another way."

"How?" I looked at this woman and saw intelligence. I also saw a glint of mischief in her eyes.

"I heard you are a private detective," she said, apropos of nothing.

"Yes, I am."

"I trust that you are discreet."

I nodded, waiting.

"I would ask you not to tell Father Thomas that we met or what I'm about to say. It will compromise him and that, above all, is what I never want."

I believed her. "What exactly are you proposing?"

"I will work from the inside. I want to change things."

"From the inside?" I asked.

She motioned our waiter for the check then turned back to me. "Yes. How do you say it?"

I waited, unsure what she was asking.

She smiled for the first time. "I'm going undercover."

• • •

Another rainy day. Expecting The Norman at nine, I waited until ten to contact him. Was it because I didn't want to be labelled a nag? I WhatsApped him and he wrote: 09:30. Tomorrow.

I felt like biting someone.

MOVING AHEAD... SLOWLY

"But Gianni, I don't need an architect." I objected but he insisted an architect had to do a final inspection of the work. We settled a few things on the phone then he said he himself was coming in to Palermo later in the day but he didn't know what time. Later, he wrote: around 1400.

I had a Caesar's salad at a place run by two nice women who were curious about me, seemed glad I was American and wanted to know where I would spend Christmas. I did not say Paris but said Rome. Even then, a few times when I'd mentioned Rome a person had said softly, in awe, "Roma." It was the way someone from Mississippi might sigh and say, "New York." Would I be with friends? It seems an underlying concern that I am not with family.

Family is very, very important. Anglo Saxons don't exactly eat their young but it's different. A close friend, English, was sent from where he was born in India all the way to school in England when he was six. When I caught him wearing my fanciest silk underwear I wondered about leaving his mother too soon. Like a puppy that had not been weaned. The closeness, the touching here. I remember going to London after living in Rome and being at a dinner party. I realized at the table that I was putting my hand on the forearm of everyone I was talking to. I guess life in Sicily will only make me "worse."

I was introduced to a tiny black chihuahua named Isabella who pranced in and out of the open doors of the restaurant. An entirely different personality from Hugo, the dachshund with the plaid vest who manages the hairdressing salon.

I rushed out to meet Gianni at 1400 but once there received a text saying "Maybe 1530." I sighed, watched the two Giuseppes for a few minutes with their big shadows on the hideous bright blue walls then left for Piazza Rivoluzione to sit in the sun and read.

Gianni did come but not at half past three. It was hours later. I bit my tongue and greeted him with a smile when I felt like screaming, "You wasted my time! And it's not just this one time . . . it's every time!"

ANOTHER SECRET MEETING

The undercover Sparrow did not want us to be seen so we picked an out-of-the-way caffè near Stazione Centrale and we always met inside at the same corner table. It was raining, as usual, and I came clumping in wearing my tractor-tread boots and a white slicker as she was hanging up a sodden navy blue raincoat.

The minute she'd ordered tea and I'd ordered prosecco, I said, "This is a bit insane. Really. Whenever I've gone anywhere, even for a few weeks, I go to the Anglican church to check out the English-speakers. And because I can count on the service. I've done it in Hong Kong, in Damascus . . ." my voice trailed off. "I thought that this church—I thought that I would like someone, maybe just one someone, and they would like me and it would make living here a bit easier. "

"All obvious to me. Good instincts," she said. "But this little enclave has degenerated into something aberrant, twisted."

"Very strong language," I said. "Tell me why do I feel actively disliked and why are we hiding the fact that we meet?"

"You are American like Thomas and we all know that you meet and talk. Everyone assumes that you know how they are treating him, that he confides in you."

"But he doesn't."

'I know," she nodded. "But you are his friend and not on their side. They want him to pack his bags and leave."

I felt a sense of outrage. "Thomas has a Ph.D. in, I think, religious studies and he speaks French and Italian. He has lived in Paris and Rome, Chicago and Washington. They are the places that pop into my mind. He is a sophisticated, highly-educated, kind, good man! His sermons are why I come to church. The Sparrows should be welcoming him with open arms and feeling lucky to have him!"

She blinked. "The Sparrows?"

I sighed. "I slipped. I call those women the Sparrows."

She nodded. "It's perfect. It's what we all resemble. Me, included."

I thought, well, that's out of the way. "So tell me why you are confiding in me? What is to be gained?" I hesitated. "To be brash and American—what's in it for you?"

She smiled and put her tea cup down. "I love the church. And I have a strong sense of right and wrong and all this against Father Thomas is wrong."

"You are consorting with the enemy, I guess." I took a sip of prosecco.

"I know I am. I've thought about this for many hours, many days. These women and I have been through the wars together. We were young English wives in what was then a very foreign country. We were without any relatives. We were coping with new ways of doing things, with new husbands and England and our families felt so far away."

"I can't imagine what Palermo was like for you women in the 1960s or 70s or 80s. I moved to Rome in 1981 and remember wanting to talk to my mother so much. But a phone call was about $7 a minute."

I grinned. "Who could talk for just one minute? A conversation with my mother would cost as much as a Super Bowl ad."

She laughed then her face grew serious again. "We all became mothers here. We went through our pregnancies together and raising our children. We had our husbands' families with whom to deal. The critical mother-in-law, the father-in-law we didn't like to be alone with."

"I think there are all kinds of bravery and you were all very brave."

She stared at me for a long moment and said, "We didn't feel brave. Lots of times we felt hopeless and homesick."

"I can understand the friendships. You have been close to all these women your entire adult life."

She nodded then said, "What you are not saying is you can't understand why I'm going behind their backs."

I sipped prosecco. "Right. You are taking a huge risk if they find out."

"Let's make sure they don't." She finished her tea and, taking a piece of paper out of her handbag, pushed it across the table. I read the email addressed to Thomas; the sender's name had been blacked out.

> *"Who do you think you are? This is a different time zone. This is Palermo. You should not be here. You have no authority here."*

"It sounds like the Mafia," I breathed as she stood and pulled on her raincoat.

"It's the Sparrows. You should hear the way they talk. Do you see why I can't stand by anymore?" Putting coins on the table, she took the paper back, raised a hand in goodbye and was gone.

SAMBUCA

The bus to Sambuca purred through grey and taupe mountains. I saw them as both beautiful and sinister. Gianni and his father (Luca Iwanttomarryhim) and I spent the morning picking out a bidet, a toilet, marble for the floor, a bathroom door. When I asked prices I was told not to worry and that if I bought everything in this one store it would mean a large discount. I worried anyway.

On the bus on the way back to Palermo, I got an email from the client I call Riviera Man who lives in the south of France. I met him ten years ago in the splendid lobby of a very grand hotel in San Francisco. I was doing a stakeout and he was distracting me. I gave him my card and basically said to please, leave me alone.

A few years later he contacted me as he was being blackmailed. I sorted it out without publicity and the resolution was very satisfying to him as he is tabloid fodder. We met in Paris for dinner four years ago and he has hired me for a couple of things. I investigated a crooked solicitor in England, located two scurrilous characters in Geneva and there are background checks of associates once in awhile. I like Riviera Man.

My other longtime client I dubbed the Beast of Barcelona. I picture him as a bull and thankfully work with his lawyers in Madrid most of the time. This man *lives* in the grey area. I don't work in the grey area so I am always pulling back, stating my terms, not doing all that is requested. When I get a call from Spain, I take a deep breath before picking up but the situation is, shall we say, always interesting. He once referred me to an associate who hired me to keep tabs on a Bulgarian in Moscow who had eight passports and was a money-laundering gunrunner. A super bad guy. You can't tail somebody during the plague. If it wasn't total lockdown in Moscow, it nearly was. Nobody was going anywhere. We knew where the subject was and there he would stay.

So Riviera Man and Beast of Barcelona called me with any problem and this made me happy plus I had small cases once in awhile. I'm charging an Italian actor in L.A. for an hour devoted to finding who owns the copyright to a book; he wants to make a movie based on it and has been running in all directions for a whole year.

In between cases I sometimes wonder if I really am a private detective. My days in NYC, Miami and Philadelphia are behind me. No more death penalty cases, no more wearing a wire for the FBI or Joint Terrorist Task Force so when I hear from Riviera Man or BB I know I am still a detective.

My bathroom in Astoria was covered with the book jackets that Mother had framed as a present for me. Sometimes I would go in there and stare at them then think, I am okay because I did all this. Money is the last thing that matters when I get a case. However, Riviera Man would question my capability if I charged him too little. At my present rate I could buy a bidet in Sambuca every hour and ten minutes.

* * *

The man in his tiny store devoted to maps spent a very long time with me looking for via Padua as my alley is shown nowhere but Padua merges into it. We unfolded about ten maps and went from one to the other with our magnifying glasses. At last I bought the map that showed via Padua. We were masked and alone and it was as if this were an absolutely perfect way to spend more than half an hour. Of course, he wanted to know was I French? Maybe English? Americana! His face brightened. Why was I here? Everyone was so charming. Every encounter was *an event*. I was surprised anyone wears a watch. Remind me of this when it's June and I'm still in the Joli.

Paying for the hotel, noting the accumulating pages of Anne Marie's manuscript, counting off my 90 days, I was very aware of time. As an American, I could be in the Schengen for 90 days at a time for a total of 180 days a year. Those two sets of three months each could not be consecutive. I knew Americans in Paris who rented a flat every year for three months and then went back to the States. But because I wanted to live in Italy, I needed a visa and then a permesso di soggiorno.

I wrote Gianni in Sambuca that I would do anything to move the renovation along. Because he spoke English, I depended on him and I trusted him. He wrote back that he hated asking me but he had to write two 280-word essays for his English class or he wouldn't be allowed to take the exam. Assolutamente. I've never helped anyone cheat before but I liked him very much. Both papers were due in a few hours, at 6 p.m. Easy. Done.

Thomas was away on Sunday and there was another priest, an Italian named Father Gabriele. He was tall, with brown hair and big brown eyes above the mask. Dealing with English was an ordeal for him. We all prayed hearing about Jesus-a Christ-a who-a came-a down-a from-a eaven-a. He was entirely adorable and doing his best. Someone announced at the end that we should thank him as he was from a place I'd never heard of which was three hours away from Palermo. After the service I went over to him and thanked him for coming. "Three hours each way!" I marveled. He took my hand in his and said, "I come-a by-a car-a" as if he did not want to take credit for walking. Sweet man.

ROSA

Rosa was sent to me by a mutual friend in Paris. She was a petite, very pretty, brunette Canadian who had started what Silvia told me was a famous cooking school in Nice. Writing a cookbook in Palermo meant many lunches together. Planning my kitchen dimensions, I thought aloud. "I would like to forget the kitchen. I am eating out so much now and it wrecks things aesthetically. Really takes up space." Rosa was aghast. "You must have a kitchen!" I told her I'd had a hot plate years ago in Rome and used it a few times for popcorn. Someone told me how expensive electricity was so I unplugged the fridge and put my white wine bottles out on the terrace. With only one lamp the place was very seductive. Well, actually *more* seductive. It was the pied a terre of Umberto Tirelli who designed costumes for Visconti's films. No kitchen was fine in Rome but I surrendered to Rosa, very reluctantly, and decided, oh, alright! I would have a kitchen.

I was cold all the time and felt vindicated when I saw how Arctic-worthy Rosa's parka was. If a Canadian was cold then I wasn't being a spoiled, weak American. The restaurants were not heated and doors were always open, sometimes an entire glass wall was open so one was always actually outside. We laughed about the weather. She told me she'd washed clothes, hung them out to dry and was leaving them there until they were. I pictured her, after every rain, wringing them out for the next round. Rosa called me when she had a mouse. I called her at seven in the morning when I thought Thomas was leaving Palermo. Rosa went back to France before Christmas and I missed her.

• • •

I went to a Tunisian place I liked for lunch and was all alone as usual. Surrounded by empty tables under umbrellas, I saw that a hole had been cut in one umbrella to allow an enormous tree to get through to the sky. My waiter greeted me, put napkin and utensils before me, took my order, cooked my fish, poured my wine. He was always wearing red and yellow trousers, a red shirt and bright yellow shoes. Sitting outside, the sole diner, I faced all the empty tables and paid in cash. Could this be a front for something else? Money laundering?

After lunch, I stood in the doorway of my place on vicolo della Gardenia and fantasized. This place will be designed only for me. I am being selfish. Bathtub, no shower, no sofa bed, no houseguests. All in one big room. Hotels are inexpensive so if anyone comes then they can fend for themselves and I won't feel guilty. No exceptions. Well, if a pregnant woman named Mary shows up on Christmas Eve, I guessed I'd have to deal with that.

HOW TO LEARN ENGLISH

In a driving rain, I went to the grocery store to buy detergent and came back to my room with cookies. No detergent. Maybe I was distracted by my favorite cashier whose mask was always slipping and showed his moustache. He is so young that I think he is quite proud of that moustache and he is pleased to speak English to me. When he asks how I am, I say, "I'm very well, thank you," and before I can ask how he is, he always says, "I am very glad."

"How did you learn English?" I asked.

"PlayStation."

MY BLACKSMITH

My first blacksmith! I expected a brawny, red-faced hulk with arms the diameter of my thighs but he was small-boned, diminutive. He knew this as his card read Il Piccolo Fabbro. The Little Blacksmith. Leonardo was his name and he had hair like my ex-husband's. I'd liked his hair. Maybe only that at the end. Behind masks, we discussed glass and the wrought iron design. I had photos, I had drawings, I had measurements. I took a deep breath and asked when the doors would be ready. This was two sets of double doors for the front which would be one pair of glass and one pair with iron bars for air, light and security plus one glass door and one wrought iron door for the cortile. Six doors. He said, "Una settimana," and I was euphoric. A week!

The piccolo fabbro did deliver the doors in one week but the iron front doors were six inches too short. The Norman dared to insist for ten minutes that they were meant to be this way. I stood my ground then drew a solution to that top space problem. The fabbro came with iron bars, a ladder and an assistant who wielded an instrument that shot out orange sparks and in an hour all was fine. It looked quite good!

Those doors—and my insistence on how they would be—were a great success. The exterior double front doors were not of a leaf design but simple squares. Each door had fourteen rows of six squares across. The interior glass double doors were about twelve inches away. To anyone outside they were mirrored but I could see out clearly from inside and remain invisible. At night I pulled my Thai screen across as interior light meant anyone could see in.

EARLY MORNING IN THE ALLEYS

I was out at seven o'clock yesterday and went to see Antonio at the ferramenta/hardware store but he doesn't open until half past. He closes at 1900 which is an 11 1/2 hour day. The streets were empty and quiet; the parked cars were sleeping. Via Garibaldi, with nearly every store selling the identical hat called a coppola, was deserted but there was one open doorway. Two men behind the counter at the electric store were joking with a customer. So much early-in-the-morning laughing. People are certainly having a better time in the little day-to-day interactions here than in New York City.

I peeked down one alley and saw two old men sitting in chairs. talking quietly, probably former Alley Men who don't want to stand up anymore. Vicolo del Forno. I wouldn't want to live in Alley of the Oven so I lucked out having an Alley of the Gardenia address. My alley a few steps away was sand-colored and silent. The motorcycles in their sheds were waiting for the day to begin.

NAMING THE OPERATIVE

My next two meetings with the defecting Sparrow were at the same place. The barman now knew us and brought our tea and prosecco immediately then left us alone. She thought it was way out of the way for any of the Sparrows but we were hyper-vigilant as to who walked in.

"You never call me by name," she noted as we were standing up, preparing to leave.

"I don't want to even think of your name as I don't want to slip with Thomas or with anyone."

"So," she said, sounding a little disappointed, "I am just another Sparrow?"

"Oh, no," I said. "In my mind, I call you The Hawk."

I had never heard such a delighted laugh from her. She put her small, age-spotted hand on my sleeve, her eyes were bright. "Oh! Thank you!"

• • •

One morning I went online looking at Media World (which sounded like a publishing conglomerate) and picked out a washing machine, dishwasher, oven and refrigerator. I'd asked Gianni about dryers and he'd shaken his head. "Not one person in Sicily has a dryer." Before I could react to this, he amended that statement. "Except me. I have a dryer because I am half American."

"You are?" The blonde that Silvia and I had plotted to murder, the wife of Luca Iwanttomarryhim was American? "Really? Your mother is American?"

"No. Not my mother. My uncle's second wife in Florida is American. So that is why I have a dryer."

I nodded slowly. "Okay."

CHRISTMAS

Christmas was days away. Paris or Rome? I had enticing invitations to stay in either city. I couldn't make up my mind but I couldn't lose. I picked both. I was leaving on the morning train to Rome for a few days then flying on to Paris. I didn't want to give up my big room so was going to leave all as it was and come back to it.

At ten o'clock that night I did the math, decided it was wildly extravagant and began to hurriedly stuff clothes in suitcases and shopping bags. It took several trips down to the storage closet in the lobby which was a few meters from the concierge desk. I'd bought lots at H&M to keep warm and I suspected my papers copulated at night and reproduced. I fell into bed exhausted but waked at six and opened a desk drawer and screamed. It was full of pencils and coins and the usual desk-drawer debris. I was on my train within a minute of it gliding out of the station and I was to have adventures in both capital cities.

Paris was cold and I wasn't dressed for it. As I was looking in a shop window, about to buy a black beret, I received an email from Diego, my shipping contact in Milano, saying that the ship had arrived in Napoli! I levitated right off Faubourg Saint-Antoine with joy! And I didn't buy the beret as *my* black beret was on land!

No more waking up in the middle of the night worrying about icebergs.

Back in Palermo the last day of December and I was delighted to be. Elated when the concierge handed me the big, heavy key to my same room. Very tired, I decided to deal with all my stuff in the storage closet in the morning. It had been four trips down in the little elevator. I opened my wardrobe and all my clothes were hanging there! The shopping bags, carefully labelled with my name, everything had been brought up! I ran down all the stairs and effusively thanked the concierge. He smiled and told me it had been Danilo.

THE NEW YEAR

The Joli was waiting for me but so was my house. Ground floor and front door made it feel like my house and it was called a house in Palermo. I was a little tense about any decisions made in my absence as I'd been told they were working every day except Christmas. I was anxious to see the progress.

There was no progress. Nothing had been done! I felt like checking the wheelbarrow for cobwebs. Now I knew that if I didn't show up every morning, the day would be lost.

January was much the same with the two Giuseppes slogging along. They took smoking breaks, phone breaks, long lunch breaks and often stood in the rubble, covered in white dust, and chatted like two men meeting on a street corner after a long absence.

There was a COVID scare and Giuseppe Uno was absent for

awhile. Gianni and his father tested negative but COVID was rampant in Sambuca, forty-five minutes away. The Norman continued to promise to come for measurements, to discuss the work but a meeting set for 8 a.m. usually meant a text at noon saying he was not coming at all. Writing the memoir with Anne Marie kept me sane.

The next step was organizing a truck from Napoli to Palermo. Now I only had the Straits of Messina to worry about. If only. The floor had to be done. The shipment could not be left in the alley. I showed The Norman the photos of the packed truck in Astoria, the packed truck leaving the warehouse in Philadelphia. I emphasized that this was not a few suitcases; the floor must be done before the delivery. Once all was inside, I would lock the door and go into exile. January was flying. At 8 o'clock one morning, The Norman said the floor took one day and it would be done today. I was very excited, came back at five and nothing had been done. This happened at least four more times. "Oggi. Si. Certo." One day. Today. When would I learn? Finally, a man named Francesco began to lay the black and white 24 inch-square pieces of marble. He was the only man not to opine that they were too big. In one day, he had done about 50 square feet. At this rate, I guessed it would take fifteen more days.

The Norman swore to me that the floor would be finished on Saturday, the 15th of January. The men did not usually work on Saturdays but Francesco would. I called Diego and said Tuesday, the 18th, would be safe. But then I had to call him and put it off until the 19th. And then again. Again. The fourth time I tried to cancel, Diego said he was sorry but the truck had been loaded and he had to pay the men. There would be a 250 euro charge and I told The Norman it was his fault and he agreed that I would subtract it from his fee. On the following Monday, the 24th, enough of the floor was done and two trucks arrived in via Padua and in vicolo della Gardenia at half past seven. Most of the stuff was crated or boxed and couldn't be seen. I watched as my Chinese Chippendale chairs were brought in. They had been with me forever. I grinned and marveled, all the way across the Atlantic. The pile of boxes and furniture stacked over my head I dubbed Mount New York.

A man in the alley who stopped to look at the progress told me it had never been a pizzeria but had been a Tunisian night club. That explained the strange lights and no pizza oven. La Tana had a rich past.

One afternoon I answered my cell at my desk in the hotel and confirmed that yes, I was Clarissa McNair. An Italian woman spoke quickly in Italian and obviously was waiting for my answer to her mysterious question. Again. I said, "Non parlo bene." I don't speak well. She said something else and I thought I heard vicolo della Gardenia. "Piano, piano," I requested. Slowly, slowly. Suddenly she screamed, "Water! Water!" Unthinking, I shouted back, "Acqua? Acqua?" She started laughing and I said, "Okay!" and we both hung up, laughing.

I would later realize that this exchange was the water company confirming my address.

January has 31 days and these were the final 31 of my 90 days in the Schengen.

Luca Iwanttomarryhim told me the bathroom would take two days and the kitchen half a day. We had eight work days left. At this point, the bathroom was only a giant hole with a huge red pipe reposing in it a few feet down. The kitchen was non-existent. I made it clear several times that I had to leave Palermo, Sicily, Italy and the Schengen on the last day of January. The Friday before my last week, Luca looked me in the face and promised to come on Monday and do the bathroom, hang the chandeliers, install the kitchen, finish all the work. With a bathroom and water I could move out of the hotel. "Lunedi," he said. I actually said, "Una promessa? Lunedi?" and he repeated it, looking into my eyes. A promise. Monday morning. Silvia had said Luca Iwanttomarryhim was so wonderful, so reliable that he would come in the middle of the night.

Maybe for Silvia but not for me. A plumbing emergency? I would be doing the breaststroke in the living room before he deigned to arrive.

That evening, I brought Silvia up to date and told her about my plans. I wanted to volunteer in some capacity with the Contra Mafia group. I wanted to take Italian classes. Silvia was very enthusiastic and complimented me on how many people I'd met but I felt I'd been a reclusa/recluse and only involved with the workers.

We discussed exile from the Schengen. She agreed that I could fly to Bologna and take a bus to San Marino and stay there for 90 days but a friend in Rome swore they won't stamp my passport and I'd be in jeopardy. Tunisia was closer. I could take a ferry there but I didn't want to struggle with French when I was just learning Italian. My brain is too small. I still liked the idea of San Marino because they use the euro and they speak Italian there. I could flip a coin: heads I go north, tails I go south.

I kept Maria/Blondie at the front desk au courant and she kept saying it would all be okay. Up in my room, I thought, take a deep breath, Maria is right. It's going to be okay and no matter what, there is chocolate cake for breakfast at the Joli. No matter where I am, forever, I like to think that.

Monday arrived but Luca did not. I waited in the cold of the alley moving inside which was just as cold but out of the rain. The interior was filthy with no place to sit. My chairs were wrapped in brown paper and way on top of Mount New York, over my head. Neither Luca nor Gianni answered their phones or texts. Tuesday, I waited. Wednesday, too. I thought he could still come and do the bathroom as there were two days left. Gianni called and told me his father had all under control. I said no, not unless he could install all kitchen appliances, a tub, bidet, toilet and sink plus an AC/heater, three chandeliers and two light fixtures in two days. As promised! I told Gianni that all I wanted was a working bathroom. No Luca on Thursday. He didn't come on Friday. I was quite angry. Angry at another no-show, at phones unanswered and another promise that meant nothing. Angry at myself for believing that these men kept their word. Luca, the father of Gianni, I had thought the most reliable. Grins and fist bumps and these men just said anything. They treated me like a child. A fool.

Now I knew that I would return from exile to the hotel.

I called Vivienne, a friend in New York, that night to wish her happy birthday and she said New York City was closing down. One in five New Yorkers had tested positive.

Anne Marie called from New Jersey and when I told her I had to go into exile and the plan of the moment, she started laughing. It was loud, out of control laughter even though I didn't think going to Africa was funny.

Exile

Saturday night I spent hours online trying to decide where to go into exile. Esilio. Dublin had not worked out. The hotel I could afford and wanted was full. It was right in the middle of town and I could go to the courts and listen. Bookshops! I called The Feathers Hotel in Ludlow but they did not want a writer in residence. I looked at the Cotswalds and Chichester. I'd last five minutes with those flowered bedspreads and little twee porcelain things on the bureau plus the mechanics of making tea in my room. A setting for suicide.

I thought maybe Cairo would be good as I'd been several times and from the age of eleven on I'd wanted to be an Egyptologist. That idea had been derailed when I discovered that I must be fluent in German. My aptitude for learning a language is so nonexistent that I think it is a miracle that I speak English and am not sitting on the floor in a corner of an institution, drooling. Maybe I could take courses at the American University. Finding a reasonable place to stay in the center of the city appeared impossible.

Sidi Bou Said in Tunisia was a village of blue and white houses on the coast. I made a reservation for the maximum number of nights but then checked the temperatures. It was the same as Palermo and with nothing heated. I don't mind cold weather but I mind being cold *inside*. Then I found a place in Kenya, outside Nairobi, with a swimming pool. A good price and I booked it knowing I could cancel the Tunisian place within 24 hours of arrival. Kept filling out the reservation form and there was some problem every time. I started over. Maybe this was a sign to go to Tunis. I saw online that the U.S. State Department advised *not* going to Tunisia. There was the threat of terrorism and it was a red zone for COVID. I rolled my eyes. I'd arrived in plenty of places where the U.S. had closed the embassy the day before. I'd be okay. I booked the ferry leaving Palermo at 2:30 in the morning on the first of February. Then I began filling out the Tunisian health document but I was tired and went to bed without finishing.

The next day was Sunday the 30th of January. I was rather dreading Tunisia, had sprained my ankle and had hobbled from the pharmacy to a restaurant for lunch. Outside, of course. Marcello, the partner of Thomas, called my name and invited me to sit with him and a woman with a pixieish white haircut and a big laugh. I joined them when I finished eating. "What happened to you?" demanded Marcello. I winced. "I was up on Mount New York which is my pile of stuff from the States and stepped down the wrong way. I guess I sort of fell. Wine will help."

The woman introduced as Edith thought it was wonderful that I was having two glasses of wine at lunch because I was in pain. Marcello left to fish Thomas out of a terrible meeting with the Sparrows and left us two alone. Edith was in her sixties, was English and told me she was an Anglican nun and never married. "What would I ever need a man for!" Giant guffaw with head thrown back.

She was working on immigration issues and human trafficking, spent lots of time in Africa, had worked in the Congo. I told her I spent most of a year traveling in Africa and several weeks in Kinshasa. We got on so well that she wanted me to work with her and told me she would be in Palermo until April. Thomas arrived without Marcello then went off to find him. At last, all four of us were all talking in a mix of Italian and English. It was sunny but we were all in parkas at an outdoor table under one of those giant cellophane tents which makes no difference in the temperature whatsoever. I guess we pretended. Edith's huge laugh was the sort that causes people to turn in search of the source. It sometimes finished in a snort of delight. Edith seemed to enjoy life in a rich way.

I left them to pack. Late in the afternoon, a two-minute voicemail from Edith exclaimed how great it was to have met me; she advised ice on my ankle. I was busy sorting the papers on my bedside table. Maria said the hotel had no ice but she found it from somewhere and sent it up in a plastic bag in the elevator. I hobbled out in the hall to retrieve it. I hadn't been able to fill out the Tunisian government health form, was unsure if I had a ticket for the sailing tomorrow night or actually half past two in the morning as my credit card information kept bouncing back but I did have the room at Sidi Bou Said. I fell asleep wondering what to do about this exile thing.

The next morning, the day I must leave, Edith texted that I could have her house for five weeks. It was too late. If she had told me yesterday or even last night I could have cancelled the hotel in Tunisia.

I was to meet the water man (after weeks of negotiation and phone calls) at nine at La Tana. As I entered my alley, Giuseppe Due shouted my name. He was there to get more of his stuff left behind. Last week I told him very clearly several times that I was leaving today and that all would be locked up and to take his tools on Friday. The men didn't seem to believe me. They didn't take me seriously. The Norman arrived. I thought of the floor, the promises and couldn't stand the sight of him. He said to call the week before I come back. They left. The water man materialized on the nose of nine which was stunning, amazing, incredible.

I unlocked the little steel door outside with my new cluster of keys. But no, he needed the bolleto, the invoice, the receipt, something. I said I paid 150 euros but he had no record of it. Gianni had me wire it to him to pay and never gave me a receipt. Back and forth. The man insisted, I insisted. My ankle hurt. My COVID test was this morning and this man wanted me to go to the AMAP office and pay them 147 euros and come back and show him the paper and then he would give me water. I explained that I had already paid. My ankle hurt. The man was speaking so fast and I said, "Lentamente, per favore," again and again. "Piano, piano." I got tears in my eyes.

I called Gianni and he did not answer. I called Pietro and he did not answer. Then I called Luca Iwanttomarryhim and he got on the phone with the water man then the phone was given back to me and he said something I don't understand. The man was jabbering at me.

I hung up with Luca. Then the water man dialed his son who speaks English. My ankle was throbbing. It was explained to me that I must pay this money and blah blah which is exactly what I understood before. I don't want to pay it again but I have no proof of payment and Gianni won't answer his damn phone. I called Pietro and Gianni again.

The man gave me the address of the water company and told me to walk on via Roma to the first semaforo/traffic light and then keep walking to the right, on and on. I set off limping, nearly crying. I showed a woman the address and she said it was very far away. I kept walking. No taxis. No buses. I was limping on via Roma. Pietro called. I explained the situation to him and he said he would call me back. He did and he talked to that woman—the one who screamed "Water! Water! at me—and I didn't have to pay anything and I didn't have to go to the water company. I hobbled back to La Tana and padlocked the outside door to the water pipes as the water man was long gone. I felt defeated. I had been told it was not easy to get water turned on but dear Pietro had intervened. He knew someone at the water company, he would deal with it and I would not wait weeks, maybe months. And now, on THE day, the water man had come and gone. I was unsure if I felt like lying down in the alley and bursting into tears or screaming in rage. Maybe both.

Edith had called three times but I had been in no position to answer and at last she was on the phone offering me her house and I told her it was too late. I couldn't cancel the hotel reservation now. I could have yesterday but not now. We were cut off, we were reconnected. My ankle hurt. She said we'll work this out, we should meet for coffee. I told her I was at the corner of via Roma and via San Cristofero. It was 10 o'clock and I told l her I must have the COVID test at 11:30 as they are very rigid about it and busy. She said she was leaving Piazza Marina right then.

I stood on the street corner waiting for 25 minutes then I texted I was going back to my place to get my winter coat. I went back and as I was trying to lift the shutter which is very difficult, Luca Iwanttomarryhim arrived. I didn't even look at him, he helped me with the shutter and I grabbed my black cashmere coat which was unbelievably right there in front of the pile and I locked up the new doors and we lowered the shutter. I said grazie then hobbled away as he got into his car. I felt like shouting, you are a liar! You said it would take two days to do the bathroom and you would come last Monday and you never came! Not on Tuesday or Wednesday or Thursday or Friday and I waited for you! Every day! For hours! You kept saying the bathroom would be done!

I hobbled back to the corner and Edith arrived and we sat at a caffé at a tiny table outside. I hadn't seen her stand up yesterday and now I saw that she was wearing very wide culottes to mid-calf and I so obviously stared that I had to comment and all I could say was how comfortable they looked. She said she made four pairs, she sews. This woman was low to the ground and wide. Thick torso, broad shoulders, wide hips. She sat with knees wide apart; red and white striped socks circled very robust calves and disappeared into tan suede, very sturdy mountain boots. She ordered coffee and I said, "Please, a glass of wine," and put money on the table. Oh, no, she wanted to pay. It was 10:30 and I was exhausted, my ankle throbbed, and I had been near tears of frustration until Pietro took over.

I draped my coat over the extra chair, sipped my wine, looked at my watch. This house in Cambridge. Well, it would be wonderful to speak English, to be in a city, to have bookstores and go to the movies. Maybe I could take Italian classes at the university. I took another gulp of wine and leaned back. Her coffee arrived and she said, "I thought the first time I saw you, now there is a woman who deals in options."

I nearly laughed. All options are on the table. Tunisia, I think. The ferry after midnight. I'd had so many problems with the internet I still wasn't sure if I had a ticket or not. I'd wanted Ireland then I'd wanted Egypt. Ludlow had seemed good initially. San Marino was a thought. Kenya had fallen through. Options.

"The stock market," she said.

I was barely paying attention to her but responded. "Sure, I used to buy stocks."

Edith leaned forward. "And you had a bad experience, didn't you?"

I said, "No. Actually every stock I bought made money. I sold them all to stay in Paris."

"Oh, but options are different."

I sipped my wine and listened. Those culottes were huge. The gist of this was she wanted us to go into something together with this man who had had a spectacular year. "I've been watching him. And you start off small. Just two thousand euros. That's nothing."

I smiled. "It's not nothing to me."

She was enthusiastic. Shining blue eyes. I was thinking of the water company and Tunisia. I had to go back to the hotel and get a ticket on the Grimaldi Lines. Maybe a concierge could help me fill out the health thing. Or was I going to her house? Was that why I had my long black coat on the chair beside me?

"The house is in Cambridge. I have the nicest scientist staying in the downstairs apartment but you can have my bedroom. There are clean sheets on the bed, the cleaning woman was just there. It's all in order." I listened. I really didn't want to go to Tunisia and wrestle with French when I was just getting along in Italian. "When Graham leaves you can decide where you want to be. I usually have someone paying 700 pounds a month but I want to get someone compatible with you or else I won't let it at all."

I said, "I don't want you to lose money because of me."

"Oh, no, it's fine, if it's only you."

I had to go or I'd miss my test at the farmacia. She could even arrange a plane ticket for that night by simply changing the name. I said, "Yes. Okay. Thank you." Just like that. Settled. Cambridge. I stood up, grabbed my coat, rushed away. I jaywalked with a limp across via Roma and a bus pulled up like magic.

A white tent was outside with people standing in line obediently distanced. I got my test—negative. And I finally got the Green Pass! Had tried apps for ages and nothing had worked. When it was handed to me I wanted to fall on the floor in gratitude. The farmacia had a woman's name and there were three attractive women in white coats who ran it.

I limped back to the hotel and then back at my desk I went online and canceled the hotel in Sidi Bou Said. Amazingly I would only be charged for two nights and not the entire reservation. Edith texted me that to change the ticket we should meet. Yes, I thought, and maybe an address and a key would be a good idea. I texted back that I needed food and to meet where we met on Sunday. My ankle was better.

I arrived there and it was closed but I saw Edith sitting outside at a nearby restaurant. I said, "Oh, this one is pricey. Let's go just across—" She claimed it wasn't expensive at all in a grandiose way. I hesitated and then reluctantly sat down. Edith exuded charm talking to the Nigerian waitress. Suddenly she diverted her attention to me. "I hope you aren't allergic to cats." I shook my head. "I let them come in the house but they live outside. I think they should be free so they go anywhere they want." I wondered how many there were but she was on the phone dealing with the ticket change. All during lunch. We split the check but she left a very large tip which is not done here and I was glad she was not American.

We started this endeavor at 2 o'clock and finished it at my hotel in the dining room because her battery needed charging at 4:45. It was passenger locator form, COVID test, on and on and the name change. I had to pay an extra $100 and had to read my debit card number to her. I hesitated and then thought she is in the Anglican church so, of course, she is an honest person. I sat there as she did all the work but I had things to do. She said I could do a bank transfer to pay her for her ticket. I wondered about the $100 *and* reimbursing her as Ryanair was always cheap.

Then she said, "Okay, I have this man in Palermo who will take you to the airport for 25 euros."

She was texting him and looked up. "How do you say tonight or this evening?" I said, "Stasera."

"How do you spell that?" I was astonished and spelled it for her. He was to pick me up at 6:15. Then she said, "I have to arrange for you to be picked up at Stansted. You won't get a taxi there at midnight and it'll be one in the morning before you get your luggage."

"Okay," I said. "How much is it?"

"It's only about 75 pounds." I winced. She said, "Well, come on, Clarissa, you're staying rent-free." She wanted my credit card number once more and I reluctantly read it out again.

I told her I had to take things to be put in storage at the hotel, had to finalize a few things and I thanked her profusely. Her last words were, "I'll tell Graham to leave the front door unlocked."

THE HOUSE IN CAMBRIDGE

I left the hotel feeling a bit sad and asked one of the concierges to tell Maria that I had changed my piano and that the woman he saw in the dining room had given me her house in England. I left a thank you note for Pietro. The driver came in, masked, smiling and genial and asked for Clarissa. I sat in the front seat and we talked politics. Berlusconi, Trump, he loves Obama. Just when I'm starting to talk, I leave. Back in 90 days. Is speaking Italian like riding a bike?

Off the plane at Stansted into the bitter cold of England, I was glad for my long black coat. As I turned the collar up, Edith's text apologized that she forgot to tell me that Richie who lives in one of the vans uses my bathroom to take a shower every morning early—4 a.m.—and she hopes it won't bother me. What can I say? One of the vans?

A Pakistani driver arrived, took my suitcase and helped me into his car. He was without a mask which surprised me. He fumbled in the glove compartment for one and put it on when I asked him to. I opened my window thinking, I've been so careful and am not going to sit in this closed metal container and get sick. Three friends had written me in the past week that they tested positive.

We drove for nearly an hour into pitch black darkness. The darkness seemed thick. No lights anywhere. Deep into rural England. Where was the city of Cambridge? He turned into a dirt lane then he backed partway down it again. I said, "She mentioned vans . . . ." I think this is English for trailer. "Let me get out and look."

"No," he said. "I don't think you should get out." His voice sounded worried.

I didn't want to get out. The headlights were showing overgrown grass, weeds. All sorts of debris. Tin cans. Broken terracotta pots, old, torn, half-filled bags of fertilizer, pieces of metal. There was a rotting wooden fence that was falling down.

No house in sight. Pens for animals which seemed empty. We backed out and down the road aways he stopped the car and called to confirm the address. The dispatcher said that was the place. Back we went, up the rutted driveway. We stopped. In the headlights a gaggle of geese went hurrying by.

"I don't want to leave you here," he said. His voice was quaking. I felt like saying, then don't leave me here! Take me home with you. I will live with your family! Instead, I said, "It's uhh . . . it's . . . probably okay. It looks like there might be a house back there. She said the front door would be unlocked. So, let me find the front door and then we'll know."

I saw a grey car parked way off to the left of the driveway. Edith did not mention a car. Then I saw a small trailer but could barely make out a shape that might be a house. I got out, stumbled in the dark, found a door then a doorknob and pushed. Stench hit me like a fist. There were yowls and jumping bodies in the air at face level. I gasped and stepped back. It was a small shed, full of cats, cats that seemed huge. The driver called, "Are you alright?"

"I'm okay," I called back, wondering if I were.

The door was unlocked so this must be the place. If it's not I guess

I'll introduce myself to whoever lives here tomorrow morning. I went back and thanked the driver then pulled my suitcase over the ruts, through what was like a junkyard. I looked back and saw the driver in the light of his open door, watching me. He asked, "Are you sure?" I told him I'd be okay. He seemed reluctant to leave me; I wanted to go with him.

The smell was gag-worthy. I stepped inside feeling uneven boards under my feet then opened another door and stumbled into what might be a kitchen, rubbing my hand on the walls for a light switch. I found one and gasped. There were pots, pans, dishes for 100 people stacked on every surface. I dragged my suitcase in and closed the door.

I found another light and went up a narrow, crooked staircase. The house was meat-locker cold. What might be a study was across the hall from a bedroom. I took a hot bath, thankful for that. There were no sheets on the bed, just a blanket covering the mattress so I got into clean clothes and slept in them with my winter coat over me. There was a duvet without a cover and I pulled it over my legs but didn't want it to touch my face. I did find pillowcases on a chair but wondered if they were clean. It was 4 o'clock Palermo time.

Next morning. Edith talked me through the internet password. I told her it was a sunny day and the fields were green, the cats welcomed me and I was happy to be here. I was staring at myself in the bedroom mirror thinking, so this is what I look like when I'm lying. I would still be on the Mediterranean at this point; I was on the plane before the ship had sailed. More details from Edith. The linen closet was behind a chair in her study piled with dirty sheets. "The cleaning woman comes on the ninth."

I found the linen closet but it was as if the door were painted shut. "Oh, just use a butter knife to get it open." A butter knife? I couldn't find a butcher knife or paring knife or ANY knife in that kitchen. The heating mechanism was complicated and she was worried about oil being expensive.

"You might want to make a grocery list. I've called this nice Cypriot doctor to come by and take you shopping. He's just retired."

"Okay," I said, trying to sound cheerful. "Where is the grocery store?"

"He'll take you. Don't worry."

"I mean, well, couldn't I just walk?"

Edith suddenly said she had to hang up and would call me back.

About half an hour later a man was at the front door. Not the door with all the cats. I assumed he was the Cypriot and got in his car and went with him. He was plainly not happy about this favor but he lit up when I asked what he missed about being a doctor. We had time for a conversation; the store was not near. I mentioned staying in Edith's house while she was in Palermo and he corrected me quickly. "It's... well, it's not her house. She... uh... rents it."

I thought it was an odd thing to stumble over. So, she rents the house.

The conversation swerved away from his statement and I told him I was a private detective and asked why the tops of my hands would tingle when I was in a car chase. The Cypriot doctor explained it was about adrenaline and carbon dioxide and were my fingertips tingling, too? I didn't think so but I was clutching the wheel so tightly that I probably didn't notice. He advised breathing into a paper bag when I experienced this.

I tried not to smile. There had been times with Mickey, my closest p.i. pal, and the cops when I had felt a bit of panic, of I don't want to screw up, I refuse to be the weak link. The men would have been falling out of their cowboy boots if I'd said, "Hold on. I need to breathe in a paper bag. It'll just take a minute." Who has a paper bag anyway while driving 80 miles an hour on the NJ turnpike tailing somebody in the Born to Kill gang?

In five minutes, I had gathered all I could think of at the Co-op. McVitties milk chocolate digestive biscuits, tuna fish, lettuce, two bottles of wine, salmon in a can—I was not overly inspired. The tab was 34 pounds. Gaspingly expensive compared to Palermo. The house was chaos and I bought toilet paper. Later in the day I saw a roll of it on the hall table with the mail.

I told myself I'm here and I am warm. On the phone that morning Edith had given a long monologue of how to turn on the heat and it's now on. The sitting room was warm and reasonably neat except for a contraption festooned with male underwear. I looked online for places in Cambridge. Very expensive.

An email came from Anna who is Thomas's mother. She wrote that Thomas told her I was going to Africa and she was praying for me. Someone is praying for me in St. Louis; it's sweet. Pietro sent me a poem. Translated courtesy of Google. It's sweet, too. Later he wrote in Italian that he was sending a video of his property outside Palermo and wanted to know if I knew anyone who would want to buy it. I wrote back that it was beautiful and I will think about it.

At about five, I heard water running in the kitchen. I stood in the doorway and saw a man washing dishes. I called out to him and he didn't turn so I waved at him and finally he saw me. Wearing ear plugs. He's Richie who is getting a divorce and lives in the white van. We stood in the kitchen and talked. I opened a bottle of wine as he finished washing dishes then offered him a glass.

We moved into the sitting room. He was leaving because things were not good between him and Edith. His soon to be ex-wife lives in his house, the house he built, and he is in the van. Edith charges him to use the shower which is not 4 a.m. but 6 a.m. "She was wonderful. At first. I'm a builder." He sat across from me on the sofa. He had an open face, ruddy from being outdoors, looked physically very strong and was wearing jeans, a black and blue plaid flannel shirt and work boots.

"Edith introduced me to a woman—American—who bought a house around here. I bought lots of material, there was lots of work to be done. I was glad for the job." He took a swallow of wine. "I did the billing and Edith said she'd take care of it. The woman went back to Detroit and Edith said she hadn't paid."

I sipped the wine as a very bad feeling swept over me.

"It was over 3,000 pounds and I kept asking Edith and she kept saying the woman hadn't paid. I called the woman and she told me she had paid Edith months before and then she sent me the proof." He sighed. "Edith kept the money."

I was shocked.

"She told Graham someone was coming and Tim and I thought she'd sent you as a spy."

I burst out laughing. "I only met her the day before yesterday. In Palermo."

Richie looked stunned. "The day before yesterday? Palermo? You came here from Palermo?"

I nod.

"So you don't really know her?"

I shook my head. The absurdity of the situation was hitting me.

"What are you doing here?" he asked.

"I had to leave the Schengen after 90 days and Edith offered me her house."

"She offered you her house?"

I nodded. "Yes."

"Well, it isn't her house. Edith does not own one thing in this house except some photographs and some books. She owes the farmer who owns it over 10,000 pounds."

I blinked. This rang true. I'd thought it odd that the doctor mentioned her renting it.

"Honestly, every single person in the village now knows to stay away from her." He named person after person she had bilked.

I listened, feeling breathless. "But she is an Anglican nun," I said.

Richie said, "Or was. We don't know. To tell you the truth, she says she is and everyone trusted her."

I looked at Richie. Obviously, today, I felt I was not a particularly good judge of character but he seemed refreshingly honest. "How far is Cambridge?" I asked.

"If you start walking now you can get there in about four hours."

"So much for her house in Cambridge," I said.

Richie exclaimed, "She's got you here in the middle of nowhere where you'll go mad with boredom and there is no way to get groceries, nothing!"

I said, "She offered to put me on the insurance for her car and let me drive it," and he laughed. "Oh, four weeks ago she offered that to me, too, when I had a problem with my car. We searched the entire house—six of us—and no one could find the keys."

He stood up, left the room and came back waving the mail in front of me. All from collection companies, bills unpaid, taxes unpaid. "Bill collectors have come. The bailiff has come. The sheriff knows about her." He handed me the three-inch stack and I looked closely. Bold, red font demanding attention. FINAL NOTICE.

Richie said her father made loads of money and she was an only child. "Truthfully, she's torn through that inheritance. Used to spending money, I guess." He took a sip of wine. "Even when it's other people's money."

What made me queasy is that she insisted she change the name on her plane ticket and had to have my debit card number again and again. She was on her phone for nearly three hours changing this with Ryanair and then there was the COVID thing to enter and the passenger locator number. I was watching her but I didn't know if she had written my debit card number down on her phone or not so I was moving every single cent except for a few dollars out of my checking account, just in case.

Richie stated, "To tell you the truth, she is a charming con artist. Very heavily in debt. She might be waiting, leading you on for some reason. She must think you have money."

"Well, I told her that last year I bought a Tunisian nightclub and I'm spending every cent I have on the renovation."

Richie was looking at me quite intently. "A Tunisian nightclub," he repeated slowly.

I said slowly, "A con artist Anglican nun."

Suddenly I wanted to laugh.

Terrorism in Tunisia, the Red zone for COVID? Easy stuff. Maybe Thomas' mother in St. Louis could forget Africa and pray for me in England.

"I don't want to leave and have her accuse me of having broken anything."

Richie said, "Honestly, the cats break things. Never seen such huge cats. Feral. She lets them roam around inside."

I cringe, remembering those bodies flying past my face in the dark last night. Or was it this morning? We agreed to block them into that squalid little room where I first encountered them.

"I don't want her to send me a massive bill for heating."

Richie showed me how to regulate the boiler for one hour and advised to use the electric radiator I can actually move to where I am sitting. He will also bring me some logs for the fire in the sitting room.

We went back to the sitting room, kept talking. "The trouble is that people who don't know her, trust her."

I laughed. "Yes, they do. Me, included."

Richie drove me to an ATM through miles and miles of nothing but darkness. This is a new kind of darkness. I'd had no money except euros and now I had some pounds.

I asked again about going into Cambridge and he said the ten-minute walk to the bus stop was not good as the road is very narrow with no shoulder. "To tell you the truth, you really have to come back before dark as the pikeys are about."

"Pikeys?" I said in confusion.

Then he called them travelers or gypsies.

"Also," he said, "be careful and don't go near the geese. Don't run away from them either."

He told me what a farmer advised. Hold your arm out straight and walk towards them. "Never run away or they will run after you and attack. Their wing can break your arm."

I started laughing and said, "So I shouldn't try to pet them?"

Ritchie then told me drugs were a huge problem here. Coke. "Truthfully, it's everywhere. At a pub there's always a line in the men's room to get into a stall and do coke. They call it pubgrub."

A friend of his is 35 years old and has had twenty heart attacks. Meth, crack. Epidemic in Manchester, up north of here.

Richie kept talking. He has a seven-year-old son who would be over the moon to meet an American and he has custody on Saturdays. Of course, I agreed to meet him but I wondered if I would still be here. He said he'd drive me in to Cambridge whenever I want (it is half an hour by car) and I could take an Uber back for 20 pounds. I thought I'd do it once and then . . . I didn't know.

His phone was going wild and he was not answering. "To be honest, my wife is going after everything and Edith owing me that money hasn't helped." He disbanded his company and now works as some kind of foreman. He had 80 men and charged his phone twice a day. Richie lifted my 23 kilo suitcase up the stairs very casually and said it was nothing compared to a bag of cement.

I've now heard snippets of his life story. Parents divorced. Studied to be a stone mason like his uncle. One day next week he was taking a day to drive four hours to some village in Wales to see his uncle's grave. His uncle carved his own tombstone with a picture of himself and his wife on it. The funeral was in Dubai months ago but for some reason they had to have it without a body. Now he was in the ground in Wales. On the average, at any given moment these days, even in English, I was only understanding about 80% of any situation.

Richie took a shower and came down and kept talking. Just dying to talk. Drank only three sips of wine, said his phone needed charging again and he hadn't eaten all day. Tim arrived. A short, thin, small-boned man in his 30s wearing a wool cap pulled down over his eyebrows, appearing meek and generally beaten by life. Narrow-shouldered in his windbreaker, he stood with his feet apart as if to maintain his balance. Never moving a muscle as I leaned on the sitting room door and Richie stood on one leg and the other in the kitchen doorway. Richie had told me that Tim has a horrible family, has had a terrible time. "To be honest, he was homeless but don't say anything." I said I wouldn't. Tim was now a Buddhist so I will hear chanting. He worked at Sainsbury's supermarket. They left together.

Then Richie came back, worried about my being safe. I don't have a key to the front door so he suggested a system of locking the other door to the kitchen when I'm here and leaving it unlocked when I go out. He said, "I know that's the place for the cats and it smells. It's because they bring the dead birds in there. Sometimes they are still alive."

This man then gave me his entire weekly schedule.

He will take a shower at six tomorrow and be back here at 3:30. "Tim and I are just outside if you need anything. And don't be worried if you hear great thumping in the middle of the night. It's the horses." I had no idea there were horses. Where? I decided to let it go.

At about 9:30, the front door opened and a tall, slender twenty-something blondish young man walked in. Graham. He sleeps in what Edith described as the downstairs apartment which I thought meant basement but there was no basement and it was just a bedroom and a bathroom on the ground floor. He was a scientist/mathematician doing research, about halfway into his Ph.d. Black T-shirt, muscular arms, black jeans. Quite tall.

Richie said he was not a talker and to never ask him anything, that he was not easy. "He keeps to himself, does not talk." But he talked for over an hour, asking me about being a writer, a detective, and I heard all about his work and how he does not know what to do next.

Didn't want to be a professor. Academia. No tenure here. Can't see himself teaching.

He is researching something to do with ageing. I brought up Hester Ford. Loved her obituary. Died at 117. We talked about fasting, genetics, diet.

So attractive, so earnest and so intense. Graham talked and talked and talked. I stood in the doorway as he asked me questions. I watched him make soup and eat it, always talking.

I will be entirely alone next week when they all go. Graham goes back to work in London where he was before COVID. Richie was getting out because of the bad blood between him and Edith. Tim might be moving to Wales.

Maybe this was the perfect place to write. Maybe it was time for a novel about a con artist who happens to be a lapsed nun and floats between this run-down farm and Palermo pretending to have loads of money. And maybe she does. As Richie said, other people's money. She's very intelligent, has two master's degrees and a Ph.D. Richie thinks Edith picked me for something long-term. We cannot figure out what but we agree I should get out of here. This woman was desperate for money. He suggested that she might say I owed her some huge amount. I said, "Then if I refused to pay, she'd tell people in Palermo that she had given me her house and that I had taken advantage of her generosity." Richie agreed. She claimed to be a woman of God. People trusted her.

A long con? Maybe. But right now, I had to be careful of the pikeys, the killer geese and to not worry in the middle of the night if I heard a thumping horse or a chanting Buddhist.

ALERTING THOMAS

Second day in The House in the Middle of Nowhere. I was thankful to be warm and to perch in the sitting room and deal with emails and the bank debit card. My checking account now had $5.31 in it and the bank said nothing would be paid over that. Anne Marie called, was horrified, said to cancel it but I can't because they'd want to send me another card and I have no address. So I've essentially made it useless. Luckily, I have my French bank debit card and some money in Paris.

Anne Marie's memoir, *IMPERFECT GEMS*, was now on Amazon. She insisted my name be on the cover which I never do for a memoir. It was very nice of her.

Since so many friends were curious about my life in Palermo I had been sending out a running commentary and everyone knows The Norman, Luca Iwanttomarryhim, all about the Joli, that Giuseppe Due takes naps in the wheelbarrow. I sent off my dispatch concerning The House in the Middle of Nowhere and several friends got in touch. All had the same advice: GET OUT.

Edith texted me that she was going out to raise money for an immigration project. That was when I thought I'd better call Thomas. Palermo and Sunday lunch seemed years ago. He answered on the third ring and I began tentatively. I told him the conversation could only be between us and Marcello. I don't need enemies in Palermo. I already have Agata. "I thought you were great friends. I mean, I met her with you and Marcello and she is a nun and she does all this work in Africa and . . ."

"Oh, Clarissa," he sighed then suddenly exclaimed, "Oh, no, what is happening? I can't . . . I can't believe . . ."

"What's wrong?"

"I'm out on my balcony and across the way is this naked woman. No. Wait a minute, she isn't quite naked . . ."

"What?" I shouted from The House in the Middle of Nowhere.

"She's across the street on the second-floor balcony of this building and wearing, well, not very much and these men . . ."

"What? Men? What are the men doing?"

"These men are holding cameras and that big, reflecting aluminum foil thing and I . . . I think it's a porn film."

"Shooting a porn film outside in broad daylight? In Palermo?"

Thomas said, "I think it's over. They've gone inside." Without missing a beat, he said, "Sorry. What were you telling me? Where are you?"

I said, "I am in Edith's house in Cambridge but first of all, the house in Cambridge is not in Cambridge. It's 97 miles from nowhere. I am in the middle of fields. Just fields. And it isn't her house at all because she owes over 10,000 pounds to this farmer in back rent." I told him that all the bills were overdue, that no one trusted her because she was a con artist. "I was warned not to take a walk because the geese are dangerous and the place is swarming with gypsies . . ." I burbled it all out as Thomas exploded with laughter. Then I started to laugh.

When we stopped thinking the situation was entirely hilarious, Thomas said, "I've been waiting for a story like this. I had bad feelings about her. I met her three months ago and she was too buddy-buddy. And I'm not sure about her working with the Palermo police on human trafficking."

"She can't work with the police because she can't speak any Italian. When she was ordering my taxi to take me to the Palermo airport, she texted the driver and asked me how to say tonight and then how to spell stasera."

"No! She's been coming to Sicily for ten years!" he exclaimed. "When I heard you were going to England to live in Edith's house," he said, "Pardon me, as a priest, but my reaction was 'Holy fuck!'" He barked with laughter when I said I thought the huge culottes and the knees wide apart were a bit masculine. "She might be interested in you."

"She's a lesbian?"

Thomas was laughing as he elaborated. "She has a lover in Palermo that she is fighting with right now but maybe she is hiding out in Palermo as things are so bad in the UK and it's cheaper and she can live with her lover here as long as they are not fighting."

Palermo is very small, I decided.

Thomas kept laughing on the phone. "The bailiff?" he shouted.

"Or the sheriff. Or both. I'm not sure who's who." I sighed. "The thing is everyone believes her. She is charming and high up in the church."

"I don't know about that," said Thomas. "She wanted to start a mission in Palermo in conjunction with me, with the church and I smelled a rat and said 'no.' I had a bad feeling about her right away."

There was a pause. "You have to get out of there."

"I know. All the men are leaving next week so I'll be a—"

"All the men? What men!?"

I felt so much better being able to laugh with Thomas. I told him to be very careful about anything to do with money. He said, "Well, that's easy. The church has no money!" Then he said, for the second time, quite seriously, "You must get out of there. I'll see if where I stayed in London, near St. Albans, has a room for you."

I wondered if all those priests would let a woman live with them.

"I don't check for texts all the time but Edith is a constant texter. When I do receive yet another one from her I send 'ok' or a stupid little face. She texted she was in the bathtub reading Goethe."

"Oh, no!" cried Thomas. "And you sent her a little happy face back?" More laughing.

"She texted the names of all the feral cats who are the largest cats I've ever seen and I don't want to see them again. Edith texted me to look for a book on cats written by Doris Lessing."

Thomas was laughing.

"Doris Lessing I'm not crazy about. She and I had the same literary agent in London and I sat next to her for a very long dinner. She was chilly and aloof and I was made to feel that I was not worthy of her attention. Maybe I wasn't but she could have been a tiny bit nice to someone young, having her first novel published and making an effort." Thomas agreed.

"Edith texted me about lovely walks in the fields which Richie said were not a good idea because of the pikeys." Then I had to explain what a pikey was. I was feeling quite sophisticated having known what one was for an entire 24 hours.

"You must get out of there," insisted Thomas and I agreed. He said he'd make some calls and then he said, "Clarissa! A lesbian, con artist, Anglican nun?" Laughing, we hung up.

Suggestions came via email from friends. I knew I must leave even though I was warm and liked the bathtub. Liz, an English friend in

NY, had found a site to join so I could peruse ads for housesitting. I admired how direct and practical and "let's get on with it" she was.

Richie arrived back at about five but was called away on a water emergency. "I don't have a plumber's license and all my men are licensed but I have all the experience. I wonder how they get dressed by themselves."

Edith kept texting and I always answered hours later with emojis or Oks. A text arrived with directions about filling out a form and going out the driveway and turning right then left then proceeding on to a certain village with a post box. I didn't answer it. Then another one said the cleaning woman would come on Monday and Wednesday and I was to pay her 100 pounds each time. I ignored that.

Third day in The House in The Middle of Nowhere. This morning, I saw Richie in the kitchen. He'd worked till four a.m. and was here to take a shower. Graham was in plaid pajama bottoms, bare-chested, very white, making tea. The most perfect male body I have ever seen in my life. Nicer than David in Florence or anyone by Bernini in Rome. I think he is in his early 20s.

"This is lunacy. You cannot stay here alone," said Graham.

I read the text aloud about mailing that form and they had no idea what she was talking about. "A poste is miles and miles away," they agreed.

I asked if a cleaning woman came and they said never. Richie shouted, "Blimey! It would take an hour and it's 8 pounds an hour! Tell her you will clean and she can pay *you* a hundred pounds!"

I said, "I think this is only the beginning. I am afraid I will be accused of breaking something priceless."
Graham said, "Yes, I would be careful. I am paying her 700 pounds a month and she is charging Richie to take a shower and yet she is not paying the owner any rent."

"I talked to a friend of my mother's who is in the police department to see if she has some kind of record," chimed in Richie. "She is checking."

Graham was more circumspect than Richie but standing in the hall, he said, "You really cannot stay here alone."

Richie and I wondered aloud why she needed money. Gambling problem? Drugs? Blackmail?

A text came from Thomas in capital letters: RUN!

An email from Bettie in Rome brought the most welcome news: a room in London! She owns a house there and her daughter lives in it. Never met the daughter. The bedroom was empty and she hadn't visited for two years because of COVID and she was happy it will be used! As long as I want to be there! Other people in this house: A Sicilian bus driver has been there for 15 years. I didn't ask what a Sicilian bus driver would be doing in London. Better to just let it go. There is also the ex-boyfriend of the daughter who is "into drugs." Bettie's daughter is Jamaican and said to be difficult to get along with. I was told she also keeps the house quite chilly but maybe I'll buy a little heater and chip in for electricity.

It will be okay.

London was easy for me. I have lived there so many times for months at a time.

I would leave tomorrow or Friday. Whenever Richie could drive me to the Cambridge train station. Look on the bright side: I wasn't kidnapped by gypsies or attacked by geese. I was warm but I did want to get out of this house before the electricity was turned off.

It was a revelation to learn that the high-spirited, white-haired Anglican nun had actually stolen money from Richie, was mired in debt and enjoyed the reputation of a swindler and con artist in this corner of England. I pushed Richie to report the missing money. He groaned. "This divorce is already killing me! Every time my lawyer writes a letter it's 500 pounds." I said, "Forget the lawyer. Go to the police. You have proof the Detroit woman paid her." He did this and he thanked me. The local police actually contacted the Palermo police. I know nothing more.

Seen in daylight, the grounds around the house were strewn with broken pottery, plastic bags, a falling down trellis, tall grass and weeds. Neglected flower beds were littered with plastic bottles, glass bottles, tin cans. A clothesline had clothes and towels hanging on it and some had fallen on the ground and been left in the mud. Articles from some weeks or even months before. The oddest thing I saw were huge leather golf bags with their top openings and pockets crammed with woebegone plants. Rained on and generally destroyed by weather. Six of them in different colors in a row beside a fallen fence. Each one sporting dying vegetation. An orange one leaned beside the front door and was where I was directed to leave my keys except I never had keys. An injured black umbrella with broken spokes stuck out of the top.

I got to know Graham, the physicist, rather well as we talked for hours. Both of us interested in World War Two and British politics. Comparison of US politics. Quite good looking, terribly bright, very curious about everything, so many subjects. He said that in the UK, you decided on the subjects for your A levels and that was the path towards university and all your study. A person who wanted to study physics and took the A levels for that would probably not ever know very much about English literature. It was one track you were on for the rest of your education and it was decided at about age 18. He said he never thought he would be admitted to Oxford but he was. His father is a lorry driver and has a small farm and his mother he didn't describe at all. He is the first in his family to go to university, his father thought it was a good idea but hadn't counted on Oxford or a Ph.D. and always harps back to the farm waiting for him. Not a chance, Graham told me.

He had a long explanation of why he left Oxford which people never do and went on to Imperial College which is considered up there with Oxford and Cambridge. One cannot go from Oxford to Cambridge or vice-versa. Not ever. He said whenever he is interviewed he worries that the missing year between Oxford and Imperial College will be asked about and he does not want to say he left Oxford because usually the person interviewing him went there. He didn't want anyone to think he was asked to leave and had no idea what to say. "Oh, that's easy," I said. "Tell them you were in jail." Graham, though quite serious, burst out laughing.

We skipped from subject to subject. We talked about love and sex more than anything else. How do you know if you are in love? Had I been in love? How many times? What were the signs? How to be sure? What is the best thing a man can do for a woman? The worst? My worst love affair and why. The unforgiveable in a relationship? When is the right time to get married? It was plain that he wanted more sexual experience before settling down. I urged him to sleep with several women. I described what the 60s were like as opposed to now. I told him I had experience but had made hundreds of mistakes. Thousands. I was Mrs. Robinson to his Benjamin except we never touched.

It was a bubble of time in this House in the Middle of Nowhere. Richie was gone on plumbing emergencies so Graham and I were alone together in the kitchen for hours, each of us leaning against a kitchen counter or we were in the sitting room all afternoon then in the dark and turning on lights without missing a word. I was entirely honest, told him things I'd never told anyone. At one point, he said, "You are the most interesting person I have ever met in my life." That was an enormous compliment but he is very young.

No internet connection for the last three days, no television. It was fine, though looking out at fields and hearing the honking of geese is not for me. I tried to lose myself in the books I'd bought from Thomas's little church library but couldn't concentrate. I didn't care if they were nominated for the Booker Prize, nothing held my interest. I'd read ten pages and think I was wasting my time. Graham would arrive from Cambridge and we'd begin talking again.

I felt in transition. Leaving on Saturday. Enough food until Saturday. I was devouring McVitie's digestive biscuits at a dangerous rate. Richie would drive me in for the train. I was packed and ready and at 10:30 that morning had heard nothing so I walked out through the sodden grass past the overturned buckets and general debris and banged on the trailer door. He didn't open it but called out that he'd been sick about five times that morning. I asked if I could bring him anything and he said no. Then I said I hoped he felt better and if he did, we could try for Sunday.

This meant hours and hours of talking to Graham. He'd stand in the doorway of the sitting room or the kitchen as if it were going to be a quick conversation and it never was. Richie came in to take a shower and Graham heard his coughing. Richie later took a COVID test, said it was negative but he knew the home ones were often not accurate so he drove into Cambridge for another one. The day passed and Graham went off to the gym in the dark and then was back again when I was ready to go to bed. We began talking once more.

I told myself I was warm and safe but couldn't wait to leave.

On Sunday morning Graham said that even if Richie wanted to drive me to the station, he didn't think I should get near him. It might be COVID, might be stomach flu. We had not heard the results of the 2nd test. Graham's idea was that he and I would share an Uber to Cambridge and he'd go on the train with me and drop off some of his stuff at his friend's house in London. He'd go in with the rest on Tuesday.

Graham and I took the COVID tests together in the sitting room on Sunday morning.

Then he checked his test and mine. One line meant we didn't have COVID. I gasped with relief. The possibility of quarantine *here* was unimaginable.

We stood in the kitchen talking until the very last minute of getting my suitcase down the stairs. The driver called to confirm that this was the place and Graham went outside to wave him up the drive. It did look bad.

The driver wasn't wearing a mask—Graham and I were—and seemed surprised when I asked him to. Most on the train were wearing masks but a few weren't and there was certainly no one asking for a Green Pass. The train was fast and suddenly we were at Kings Cross and Graham was hugging me goodbye and saying to call him if I needed anything.

LONDON

My refuge would be a three-story powder blue house in north London, specifically Golders Green. Bettie's daughter, Ella, opened the door to a large and lovely ground-floor bedroom painted a Roman coral and then offered to turn on the heat, to do all to make me comfortable. So welcoming, so hospitable. Keys, internet, towels. Ella and Chris, her boyfriend, were on the top floor and Ettore, the Sicilian who drives a bus, sleeps on the second floor. I had my own fridge as did Ettore in an immaculate kitchen. Bathroom immaculate, too. I shared this on the second floor with the Sicilian. Ella told me lots about the dog who is a rambunctious half-beagle and half-Lab called Daisy. She saw her online and paid for her to be delivered all the way from Romania.

That night I fell asleep feeling safe and happy; the hum of traffic on Finchley Road preferable to the occasional honking of geese. I had been rescued.

I was relaxed in London. The Tube. I knew the routes, the lines, the Oyster card (tube pass) was in my pocket, the crowds seemed reasonable, and I was easy leaping on and off vertiginous escalators. The unmasked on the subway were all in their 20s and 30s, I noticed. There was an announcement that one must be wearing a mask but no enforcement and nearly half of the passengers were not. After Palermo, I was surprised. I also noticed how grey and tired people looked. More like New York City than Palermo.

Monday, the day after my arrival, I immediately went to the British Museum to check on the Egyptian collection. On Tuesday, I set out for the Old Bailey. Northern line to Tottenham Court Road and then the Central line to St. Paul's. I was there at 9:30 talking to a guard who directed me to Warwick Passage. Then I remembered to walk to the travel agency and drop off my phone. I paid them two pounds and tucked the little stub in my wallet.

The Central Criminal Court of England and Wales, known as the Old Bailey, is on the site of the old Newgate Prison which was built in the 12th century and in use until 1902. Two years later it was torn down. Since my last visit to the Old Bailey years ago, enormous modern buildings now surround the area.

I was alone for a few minutes under a sign that said, "Public Gallery" and then a down-market version of a Kardashian with poofy lips, dyed black hair and false eyelashes arrived with a man about her age. I asked if they were here for a particular trial and she said, "Yes, it's my son. It's a murder trial."

She's divorced and she and the new husband standing there live two hours away by train. Her son who will be twenty-two on Friday is accused of murder but I listened to their description of the situation and thought the charge should be manslaughter. Initially solemn they became animated as we talked. They were excited that I was a private detective and peppered me with questions. Especially excited that I had been at El Chapo's trial.

The son's crime or accident occurred in 2019, and I said, "Oh, a delay because of COVID," and the woman asked, "Do you believe in it?" and I said, "Yes. My cousin died of it." She gasped and I thought, don't you read? I was masked, they weren't.

We waited for about ten minutes until a burly guard with a full head of white hair wearing a bullet proof vest opened the door and motioned us up a steep flight of stairs. My bag was taken by a policewoman, I was wanded, explained about my two hip replacements. I'm actually glad they set off a buzz as I know they are still there.

There are three floors of courtrooms up many flights of stairs. I went to their courtroom and sat behind them. Imagine being in a theatre, up in the balcony. It's a better view on the top row; there are just three rows. The front row of every gallery is off limits with yellow police tape saying Do Not Cross looped over the railing and the chairs. I found out that no one can ever sit on the front row again because some rapper was being sentenced and his pal jumped over the railing right into the courtroom below.

Wigs but no masks. The judge, they told me, was presiding over the last case of her career. She may have been the first female judge at the Old Bailey. I could barely hear her tinny little voice and thought, yeah, maybe it is time to hang up your wig. There was no jury and all was adjourned to discuss legal questions.

Another courtroom, another case. Now I knew two more horrible ways to die: being beaten with a wrench as someone else stabs you OR being dragged under a car. The female barrister for the wrench-wielding Sudanese drug dealer rather weakly tried to introduce testimony of the defendant saying "I only meant to hurt him." The jury was out and the judge was not having it. Manslaughter? Not happening.

The second Sudanese indicted in the murder of the drug dealer was on the stand, just as brain-dead as the first one. No remorse and it seemed no realization of what a terrible thing he had done. Why am I here answering these questions? Yes, I hit him again and again with the wrench as hard as I could so why are we still talking about it?

I found myself phrasing questions as the prosecutor did. I loved the game of citing the details and painting a clear picture of events in perfect order and then saying, "This is what happened, yes?" There are no objections in this court. Not even when a prosecutor addressed the defendant with, "Are you still lying?" I had to stop myself from leaping to my feet to object. I was pulled into the entire cross and enjoyed every moment of it.

The Old Bailey is the most famous criminal court in the world and I went at least three times a week. Looking down at the wigged judge and barristers, witnesses on the stand, the defendants in the dock, I heard testimony from lots of cases, saw a few all the way through. People talked to me: standing in line in Warwick Passage, women in the ladies room, the guards in the hall, family members waiting on the stairs to go into the courtroom.

Today, in courtroom 5, the down-market Kardashian was not there. I think yesterday was too painful for her and she and her new husband do have a two-hour train ride. I felt sorry for her so should not call her that. She told me that her son had gone to live with his father in London for the summer (2019) and had just gone "roun' to the pub" and he'd hit someone with a car and didn't stop but "they wuz chasin' 'im with bats an' knives." That was Tuesday standing in line and maybe it was the story he had told her.

Yesterday's testimony of witnesses who heard shouts and screaming was chilling. It seems her son hit someone with a car and didn't stop and the person was caught underneath and dragged to his death. Witnesses were wakened by his screams so the son, whose surname is Eastwood, knew and kept driving. Kim was crying as we left the courtroom. Maybe this was the first time she had heard that version of events.

Today I listened to an expert giving testimony about the injuries suffered by the victim and the findings of the autopsy report. I could see the son below behind a wall of glass. Head in his hands, elbows on knees, staring at the floor. I saw him reach down, again and again, and then wipe his eyes with Kleenex. He is tall, slender, nice looking with dark hair. Today was his 22nd birthday.

The newspaper story I read online described an argument at the pub and later Eastwood went looking for this man and, when he saw him, ran him down on purpose. In a stolen car. Then he ran away and his girlfriend arranged for a train ticket for him in another name. She was indicted for helping him.

The defense would soon start for Kim's son. Alcohol? I thought I'd try to go with the frontal lobe. It's not fully developed, the latest I read, until about age 25. In Miami, I recommended a shrinking frontal lobe defense for an older man, a chief executive, who'd stolen millions from his own corporation. I couldn't believe the three lawyers hadn't thought of it as they were considered Miami's best and the expensive suits they wore and the cars they drove represented their enormous fees. In our meetings to discuss the case, they were never more than slimily condescending to me. When I spoke up to all three of them with my idea, they'd never heard of what I assumed was a landmark case. I toned down my explanation, didn't want to seem like a know-it-all, wanted to appear appropriately respectful facing their arrogance. They never bothered to tell me that they used it as a defense and I think they got the accused off.

ONE MOMENT, ONE DAY

The date, July 26th, 2019, echoed again and again across the courtroom. One day in his 19 years of being on earth. Or was it? Was this the culmination of who he is, how he has always behaved?
A life could spin on one day or even one hour of one day. Or one minute.

I thought of stepping off a curb in London that summer of 1966 as I looked the wrong way. A man yanked me back. One moment and I would never have experienced all that has happened since. My life would have ended at age 19.

My death penalty clients in Philadelphia: all male, Hispanic or African-American, from 18 to 30, and every single one of them had reached for a gun and fired. How many minutes or seconds did it take to grab the gun from the front seat, to run into the house and find it, to pull it from the waistband of jeans? Later, I would meet with sobbing mothers, crying sisters, weeping baby mamas and tell them I would do my best to help the lawyer fight against the death penalty. What was I fighting *for*? Life without parole. Never another Christmas or birthday celebration. All of that swept away.

I met with forensic psychologists who tried to discover something in their childhood, in their parents' lives, anything that might explain what they had done in a sympathetic light. The two women forensic psychologists were afraid to go into the dangerous North

Philadelphia neighborhoods and would sometimes ask me to ask mothers, aunts, grandmothers questions. Their interest went back to breast-feeding, back to the previous generation. I found it fascinating and didn't mind.

One minute could change your life forever. Of course, there are two sides to this.

In New York I had a sign scotch-taped on the wall that proclaimed: EVERY MOMENT IS ANOTHER CHANCE.

And it is.

• • •

One morning a guard greeted me with, "You missed it! You missed it!" The previous afternoon I'd skipped and the guilty verdict was read and the sentence handed down. Not like the States where the edicts are months apart. Twenty and twenty-four years to two knife-wielding, murderous gang members.

The guards seemed to all know I was a private detective and presented me to any police officer in the hall. Guard Dreadlocks was my favorite. Stocky in her black uniform, with a corona of dreadlocks, an open face and a bright, white smile, she introduced me with such pleasure that I felt like her discovery. I talked to everyone. The guards asked how a man can be sentenced to 125 years plus life. George Floyd? Why do the police shoot so soon? I asked questions and learned about the rules of prosecution, secondary DNA and joint enterprise.

• • •

One afternoon I was about to follow a guard down the hall when a young woman stopped him, said she had to do a paper for "Uni" and could he please advise her what case. The guard shrugged; she looked quite forlorn. I told her I would pick the simplest one and that was courtroom ten. "There is one defendant, no doubt about the identity of the perp and a defense plea of insanity so it will be expert opinions you could write about. Probably pretty straightforward." She was nodding, pleased, and off she went to courtroom ten. I loved helping her. Mygod, what a case. A man with a machete on the tube at rush hour going towards Charing Cross.

* * *

One morning I went up the stairs intent on going into courtroom five. The guard told me and a man—tall, well-built, in his 40s—to wait outside in the hall so we did. A big sign says not to discuss the cases but we were alone and it was tempting. I asked if he were family and he said he was the father of the girl in the case. I hadn't seen her yet but she was required to be there and he drove her in from outside London on Monday and Tuesday and her mother did it every Wednesday, Thursday, and Friday. I knew that she'd gotten a train ticket in another name for Eastwood who ran down the man who was dragged to his death. I said, "Poor judgment," and he spat, "Bloody stupid!" She was 17 then and now she is 19.

We were allowed in and sat two seats apart as the only ones in the gallery. She was in the dock sitting about four feet from Eastwood. The former lovers never exchanged a glance. They may as well have been strangers on a bus. Her name was Jasmine, a lovely brunette in the quiet way of Jennifer Connelly. Slender, wearing a black dress with a curtain of long, straight dark hair falling below her shoulders.

The text messages from Jasmine to Eastwood were read aloud. Jasmine remained expressionless. These were filled with fucking this, fucking that but actually seemed to convey the voice of reason. She told him he had "fucked all our dreams, all we talked about, by being stupid, doing something stupid which would wreck your life." Pages and pages of text messages written a few days after the July 26th event. At that point, he was on the lam.

As the father and I trooped out, I asked if she were still in love with him and he snorted, "Of course not! She was 17!"

A quick lunch and at five of two I was first in line at Warwick Place which is like a tunnel. Everyone waits by the door to be allowed up the stairs. It opened and a guard called "Family," and four or five people went in. The rest of us watched the door close. A white-haired woman and her son who had their phones, were asking if they could turn them off. No. I told them to take them down the block to Capable Travel and check them as I did every day. There was someone else asking me if we should ring the bell. Somehow, among ten people, I became the authority. One tall man in his 60s said he'd wanted to come here all his life and now that he was retired he could. He wanted to know if I had done this before and what I recommended. I told him about three cases I knew and gave the courtroom numbers. Someone asked if I came every day. Why was I coming? A short woman with brown hair and glasses said she'd been a court reporter in Australia, had been there during the dingo case. I remembered that movie and Meryl Streep saying, "A dingo ate my baby!" The court reporter and I were just starting to talk when the door opened and since I was first in line, I went up the stairs.

I went to courtroom 16 in time to hear the prosecutor I liked give his closing statement. The Sudanese drug dealers. Horrible physical details. I was glad not to have seen the film footage that the jurors and barristers saw. No denying anything as CCTV is everywhere. This was a street scene of a murder. "Clothes appeared to be dipped in red paint . . ." On and on. The Australian court reporter slipped in quietly and sat a few seats away. At 3:20 p.m. the prosecutor was finished. The jurors filed out and the judge said he was starting at 9:45 in the morning. I assume the defense will defend the indefensible.

I talked for a few minutes to the black female guards when everyone had gone. There is a new case starting tomorrow in courtroom 18. Arson. Guard Dreadlocks kept calling me "luv" and asked if she'd see me tomorrow. I said I didn't know though I would like to know how the defense will deal with the case.

The court reporter was in the ladies room and once we confirmed we were alone we exploded with our thoughts on the Sudanese drug dealers. She told me she had worked with the Home Office in immigration dealing with people who had committed crimes and were in danger of being deported to their home countries. We talked about these men on trial. I used the word "animal" and she said, "Yes, feral." Completely desensitized. The devaluation of life, inflicting pain. She said, "I am so relieved that my job is over. Certain people are . . ." She didn't finish the sentence. I found the Sudanese on the witness stand to be scarcely human. I asked her if the people she had interviewed had actually committed crimes and she said, "Oh, yes, but it is so difficult to deport them. They'd get six women pregnant and the women would come and cry that the father of their child could not be sent away. You have no idea of the ploys they used and yes, horrible crimes." She asked me if I were coming tomorrow and reminded me it was 9:45 so now, of course, I must come.

As I fell asleep in my warm bed, all these characters paraded through my mind. Kim and her son, the girlfriend, Jasmine, and her father, the seven brothers and sisters of the murdered drug dealer, the Sudanese killers. Dread and grief and fear must haunt them, keep them awake or give them nightmares. I was sad for each one.

* * *

Of course, I could not stay away. At 10 o'clock the guard opened the door and we stumped up the steep stairs to empty our pockets, have handbags put in a metal box like a safe and to be wanded. It's embarrassing that everyone knows about my hips now. The guards, in black uniforms, are friendly, good-humored.

Courtroom 5 was not sitting today as the judge is ill. I was a bit relieved as I was looking forward to the closing statements of the drug dealer murder trial and now I wouldn't miss anything in the Eastwood case.

Courtroom 16 was already in session as the judge had said he'd start at 9:45 and he did. The female lawyer looking ridiculous with dark hair showing under her white wig was doing her best but her best was not very good. She soldiered on but made no progress with me. At last, she flumped down in her chair perhaps feeling relieved the show was over.

A break. Then back and the barrister for the other Sudanese stood up. Tall, black-robed and also looking ridiculous with the white wig perched on dark hair. A barrister once told me that starting out they never want the judge or anyone to see them as inexperienced by their wigs so they put them in the washing machine, do all kinds of things to make them look worn. However silly he looked, he managed to make points. But nothing he said could make me forget yesterday's description of the victim's clothes "looking as if they'd been dipped in red paint."

The Sudanese killers lounged behind glass. It may as well have been a terrarium for lizards.

I walked to a pub a block away noting that no one wears masks in the stores or restaurants. Lunch was a beer and chips and appalling but I just felt like it. Back and up the stairs. The guard took the family inside the glass doors on the landing and prepared to open the courtroom door. He was talking in a quiet voice. There were five of them. Another murder via machete. He saw me, pushed the glass doors open and motioned for me to come in and join the group. "The judge said only the family. But I know you and you can go in."

What a treat. Oliver Glasgow, my favorite prosecutor, was giving his closing speech. Literate, eloquent. Beautifully prepared, beautifully delivered, he laid it out. I'd been there for the discussion of intent, when he'd hammered away at joint enterprise and when he had waved the machete at shoulder-height. We six spectators sat there like birds on a wire, not breathing as he spoke. The judge said we'd return on Monday at ten.

Out on the street having left the building I heard calls of goodbye. I turned to see two of the guards standing in a doorway in their black uniforms and bullet-proof vests on the site of what had been the old Newgate Prison. We all grinned and I wished them a nice weekend.

PREPARING FOR THE CONSULATE

The health insurance drama continued. I needed it to present with all my other documents in New York at the Italian consulate. My appointment there was for March 22nd and had been made months before. A man from CIGNA called me on Friday with the strongest Scottish burr I have ever heard and offered me a policy for E 8000 a year but with nearly E8,000 deductible. It's all hospitalization so I will only be happy about it if I am near death.

HCI, the UK firm I used when I lived in Paris, is offering the same thing for $8,000 a year but I must pay it all at once.

Pietro, the owner of the Joli, was my champion and, back in January, when I confided in him about needing health insurance, he'd called me in my room an hour later and said to come downstairs. He and his friend who owned an insurance company were waiting for me in the dining room. Marcella was Pietro's friend's daughter and I felt a personal connection, as if she cared. She was offering Italy for 1600 euros and still checking on coverage for the EU which was critical. A friend in Paris said, by all means, get the EU coverage so you can come to France if you want to. Best in the world, of course, and I have already experienced the marvels of French healthcare. I had wine with meals in the Paris hospital when I had my hip replacements done but Italy is excellent, too. I await Marcella's news.

I wonder if stress is beneficial. Maybe it courses through your body, invigorates your circulation, revives your cells and improves your complexion. Yesterday I missed the Old Bailey because of phone calls using Skype and actually the time here at Ella's was well-spent. Not so easy getting a COVID test here in London. One nice man at a pharmacy last week said he also worked at another pharmacy that did the test. I called to confirm that I could come on the way to the airport on Wednesday for my Rome flight and the good news was I could have an appointment and the bad news was it is over an hour and a half away by bus!

Then it was calling Boots, the pharmacy chain, one after another all over London. Discovered Covent Garden branch will do the COVID test and I can take my suitcase then I will get the result at the boarding gate. This will be okay for the flight to Rome and on Thursday to the U.S. The time frame for the COVID test will work.

Preparing all the documents required for presentation at the Italian consulate in NYC was a logistical nightmare. I made lists, I drew a chronological map of what was required and when. My flight was London to Rome to Dublin to Kennedy. Honestly, I cannot remember why I went via Dublin.

I needed a second passport as I could not leave my present one at the consulate for as long as three months while they made their decision about my visa application. Where would I stay all that time in the U.S.? But I could not call the National Passport people until 8 a.m. EST on Wednesday which was 1 p.m. for me at Heathrow. I must prove I am traveling within 14 days. When I leave Italy, my Italian phone would only work with WhatsApp and emails so I will have to borrow a phone from some stranger at the boarding gate. This was for an appointment no sooner than five days before my international flight back which is the 22nd March a few hours after my appointment. AND I was told that there is no guarantee they will have an appointment available! I dared not wait to call them when I arrived at seven p.m. in Rome at the airport hotel. If I don't get that appointment at the National Passport office then I won't have the secondary passport to leave with the consulate.

The day after I arrive in NYC is Friday, March 11th, and I will go to the post office at Rockefeller Center and get fingerprinted. That will go to the FBI who may or may not return my Police Clearance certificate within 48 hours. It's the weekend. I'll check with my p.o. people to see if my birth certificate has arrived from Mississippi. I had some more photocopying to do and right now I was waiting for Marcella to tell me that her policy can cover the EU along with Italy. They seemed to believe I am a resident of Italy and had waived the 65 years old cut-off for new clients so I was being optimistic about this last hurdle.

I had my letter saying why I need the secondary passport and my letter describing why I want to live in Italy and my codice fiscale. I had photocopied 27 months of bank statements and I had the property documents for La Tana. The expense of this photocopying in London was outrageous. I had photographs of myself with such high cheekbones and such piercing eyes that I would frighten little children.

This will be a cinch, I told myself. I simply need that second passport, birth certificate, the insurance that covers the EU and police clearance from the FBI. Easy. But nothing matters if I don't have that appointment for the passport.

In 1985, when I came back to Rome after the publication of *DESIRE AND DENIAL*, I was no longer with the Vatican and had no permesso di soggiorno which is permission to stay. A friend of mine who had once been crowned Miss World and was the mistress of a Roman prince often came to my penthouse apartment on Piazza della Rovere in the afternoon. She'd go through at least half a bottle of Smirnoff as I sipped a glass or two of wine; every visit was alcohol-soaked and meant I would hear yet another version of her childhood. Appalled to discover I had no residency papers, she announced she would take care of it. This woman was gloriously beautiful. Blonde, voluptuous. Anita Ekberg-luscious with a sweet, soft voice. She was kittenish.

About a week later she handed me my permesso di soggiorno. I was speechless. "Oh, it was easy," she shrugged, batting her big blue eyes. She'd been very, very nice to the general in charge. A true friend.

But now it seemed the EU has the last word and the rules must satisfy the Germans. For Italy this means no more shrugging, winking or sleeping with generals for documents. So even if I were platinum-locked, well-endowed and dazzling—it's too late.

I am tense. My skin is *glowing*.

THE UNITED STATES

Thursday, March 10, 2022

I flew from London to Rome to Dublin to New York and arrived at JFK at night. There was construction and not the usual taxi line so another woman and I were directed outside and around the building to a dimly-lit desolate area strewn with trash. We stood alone, wondering if we were in the right place. She took the first cab. A few minutes later a cab with a bad muffler whoofed to a stop and a scruffy-looking turbaned driver put my suitcase in the trunk. The backseat had slid off its moorings and the bulletproof glass was opaque with the filth of shouted directions from the breath of hundreds of passengers. I had never been in a taxi like this in Paris or Rome or London. What must the new arrivals to the United States think?

Astoria. Directly across Broadway from my old apartment, I rang Gema's doorbell which didn't work but a neighbor came downstairs and, convinced I was not dangerous, let me in. Two apartments on each floor and Gema was on the top one, the third. Everyone who lives there is Hispanic. A scream from Gema and Paul was grinning when I pushed open their front door. They never lock it. Paul went down to the landing to bring up my little suitcase.

The reaction to my appearance in the next days ranged from shy, "We haven't seen you in awhile" to open-mouthed amazement. Everyone had questions about how I was, how was Italy, and why I was back.

I explained about the visa and the Schengen. The secondary passport was possible if I were traveling within 14 days. I could only call the National Passport office for the appointment 14 days before the flight and I could not have an appointment sooner than 5 days before the flight. I was told not to arrive more than 15 minutes before the appointment. I felt strangled by the rules.

That call for the appointment had been made. Betty, my best friend in Philadelphia, did it for me as I was leaving London and arriving in Rome that day and I could not phone at 0800 EST. She started dialing at 7:59, busy signals again and again and finally a clerk answered. Betty went through the code words, my unique identifier, my appointment number and then took the only appointment offered. Eight-thirty on the 22nd. However, my appointment with the Italian consulate on Park Avenue at 68th Street was at 0930 and I'd never make it from Hudson Street uptown in time. The clerk had told her it would take about an hour. The moment I arrived in NYC I called the National Passport office to reschedule the 8:30 appointment, went through the code words, my unique identifier, my appointment number and was told no other appointment at all in NYC. None in D.C. or Philadelphia or Boston or Connecticut or New Hampshire. She then said, "I have one in Buffalo at 12:30 on the 21st."

I took it. Then began the search for how to get there on the 21st and back in time for the morning Italian consulate appointment on the 22nd. Amtrak was 8 hours 24 minutes. Same for Greyhound. No trains in the afternoon coming back so it would be a bus arriving at Port Authority in NYC after one a.m. on the morning of the 22nd. Should I risk that? I pictured mechanical problems, flat tires, unseasonable blizzards even hijackings.

My fingerprinting at the Rockefeller Center post office had taken two hours and I had been first in line when they opened. A form to be filled out online with no internet in the basement of the building or the lobby or even outside. What? Even Palermo has internet in the street but New York City does not? Back and forth up and down two long sets of stairs. Four times. Finally, I WhatsApped Ron, a dear friend who is always dependable, and he filled out the form and submitted it. I was now registered with the post office. I had only registered with the FBI not knowing the p.o. registration was necessary. Two obscenely obese black women whose thighs were so big they could barely walk were in charge.

One woman in line with me had come *four* times to be printed for her Austrian visa. Prints too light. Machine broken. Prints not sent to the FBI as they should have been. Closed early for the day. She was in a pink-faced rage and when one of the women would not answer her questions, stomped out muttering, "Fucking imbeciles!" They did my prints three times, had to call for help in operating the machine, and the same woman who did the prints waddled over to another window to take my money as everyone in line waited for her. I've been printed in ink at least 12 times and it's an easy procedure—even accomplished by an ex-cop with a cigarette dangling from his lip, the radio going, a dog barking and a conversation about the next location.

I paid $50 for the fingerprints along with my $18 sent to the FBI. Done. I was told it would take 48 hours to generate the document.

My post office people on Fifth Avenue had received my birth certificate from Mississippi. That was good.

The application for the visa was in Italian so I was looking up words I did not know and going over it carefully.

On Tuesday, Marcella in Palermo sent me the policy to sign and the bank transfer directions. It was three days of trying to transfer the fee to the assurance company because the name on the account was six names and HSBC would not accept it. Marcella sent other names. Names in a different order. I tried at least 15 times entering the 27 letter IBAN, the Swift code, all of it over and over again. I was tense. I met my friend, Liz, at the Oyster Bar at Grand Central and hated myself for not being able to relax. I needed internet and there was none. That was Thursday. Liz suggested we go upstairs to her husband's law firm and use their internet. We did and the money transfer was made!

Friday, March 18, 2022

I arrived in Philadelphia to see friends on Friday which meant calling Marcella at one in the afternoon and asking her to send me a letter saying I had paid for the assurance the day before. It was seven o'clock in Palermo and she said everyone left early on Friday, no one was in the office and the letter could not be sent until the money arrived. That would be Tuesday. Tuesday was my day at the consulate. I'd already told her I was a resident of Italy (well, I am mentally and emotionally and surely will soon be legally) so I couldn't tell her I desperately needed it for the consulate meeting for the visa. I said, "Tuesday will be too late. I need the letter sooner." She thought for a moment, a very short moment, and then said she would pay the company and write the letter for me! Sixteen hundred euros is over two thousand two or three hundred dollars and Marcella had never met me. We'd talked a few times and WhatsApped many times but for her to do this for me, a stranger thousands of miles away?

Marcella took the money from her savings account, paid the company and sent that important letter in the next hour. Eight o'clock on a Friday night in Palermo. I will never forget this. We wanted to meet each other anyway but I wrote that we were going to drink Champagne when I was back in Palermo.

Astoria, Astoria. You changed me. Most of the people I know there work two or three jobs seven days a week. Every single one loves the United States and is so happy to be here. I used to see someone dozing on a morning subway train and stupidly think, too much internet late at night. Now I know that he or she is very likely on his way home from working all night and will shower and go to a day job.

I ran into Lewis's office on Broadway to get him to notarize the bond to renew my p.i. license. Lewis is a small, trim man in his 60s, with grey hair and glasses. He had a client and the client was speaking Italian to Lewis's wife and the entire scene was merry. The client, bald, bespectacled, heavy-set and grinning, said, "Take care of her and I'll take a percentage." He called Lewis Luigi.

Lewis arrived in New York from Lucca at least sixty years ago and somehow—it must have been a geographical mistake—his ship docked in Palermo for one day. He was five years old but his strong impression all these years later was that it is violent, criminal and dangerous and that I should move to Lucca instead. We chatted as he filled out the form and had me sign. The client was making jokes in Italian and Lewis's wife who was now platinum blonde was laughing.

I told them I was going to the Italian consulate and there was groaning and general sympathy. I wanted to pay but Lewis never let me pay. I had to hurry to the post office before it closes and am rushing out as the client calls, "I want my percentage! I am going to get my percentage!" and I turned and shouted back, "You'll have to find me first!" Lewis and his wife were smiling. The bell on the door jangled as I closed it.

Last September, Lewis sent me to Angie, at the Italian American Federation, to help me with the papers for Silvia to sign for the deed in Palermo. A great many people have been involved in The Palermo Project.

I decided to fly to Buffalo and do the round-trip in one day instead of telling myself I could read on the train and take a bus back after the 12:30 appointment at the passport office. The plane fare was more than my round-trip flights from London to NY: eight hundred dollars. Sunday night I realized I could not use an Uber to LaGuardia as my phone was Italian and Gema had no credit card so I WhatsApped Sal and he couldn't do it and his son could not but he located Mohammed who had taken me to JFK before. From one man after another there was universal reluctance to pick me up at 6 a.m. but Mohammed said he would.

That night I woke up on Gema's sofa with this tightness around my ribs, like a vise. It hurt. I told myself to not be ridiculous and to lie still and think good thoughts. I lay on my back, pretending to be wearing an emerald green bikini on a beach beside the ocean. I closed my eyes against the bright sun, imagined the sound of the waves, the cry of seagulls. A few minutes later the pain was gone. Then I slept and dreamt I died. I was walking around behind a small crowd of people as they talked about me. No one saw me; they were saying nice things but it was a very small crowd. I was in the coffin a distance in front of them and didn't see myself. Filled with rage was I. I was so angry. I stood there behind everyone and thought, what about Palermo? I didn't finish La Tana and I don't speak beautiful Italian yet! I have books I have to write! This is not fair! I can't be dead now!

Mohammed came on time. It was dark at six o'clock. He told me he was so worried about oversleeping and disappointing me that he had never gone to bed!

LaGuardia was easy. The cab from the Buffalo airport to the passport office was 30 dollars. The driver left me off at a building with a glass storefront and an American flag. Manning the security X-ray machine was a chatty guard, interested to hear that I was from New York City. To my horror, he said, "Oh, you won't make that 3 o'clock flight. They do all the passports at the same time at the end of the day."

A room of chairs in rows filled with people. Maybe 100 of us. Masked, some in burqas, some in blue jeans. I was there at 10 as no one was paying any attention to the admonition not to come sooner than 15 minutes before your appointment. My number was called and I told the very nice clerk the situation: the flight, the visa, the consulate, the flight to London. She called her supervisor who said, "Don't worry. We'll take care of you. You'll have your passport by 12:30." The man who took my information on my second visit to a window asked if I wanted to not only have a secondary passport but did I want to renew my old one which would expire in December? Did I have another photo? Absolutely!

After lunch I returned at 12:30 for the passports. The same uniformed guard was at the front door in charge of security. As I retrieved my pocketbook from the plastic bin, he said, "Alec Baldwin was here the other day." He elaborated, "Since you're from New York." I smiled uncertainly as he added, "You must see him all the time." I sort of nodded and smiled as I was opening the door to the main room. Should I be complimented to have this man from Buffalo assume I travel in such circles? I think it is so adorable of him to think that Alec Baldwin and I would see each other all the time. At the drugstore? At the bakery?

Buffalo to LaGuardia was a snap. Back to Astoria and to Gema and Paul in mid-afternoon.

THE ITALIAN CONSULATE

Tuesday, March 22, 2022

THE day. I was up early as usual. Gema and I chattered in the kitchen as she wasn't due at the laundry until two. I would get on the subway at nine for my 9:59 appointment. Oh, yes, the Italians changed my apptment from 9:30 to 9:59 meaning that maybe I could have kept the NYC passport appointment for the passport and not flown all the way to Buffalo.

Thomas warned me to have copies of everything. They had demanded a third copy of something from him and then smugly said, "We don't have a photocopy machine." He had to go to the Italian consulate three times for his student visa and by the time he had it summer school was over.

I was buzzed in at the locked door on 68th Street when I said my name on the intercom. Directed downstairs to a basement room I handed over my cell phone to a uniformed woman behind plexiglass who then gave me a locker key. I was the only person in the bare room. My idea was that I'd meet with someone behind a desk in an office and he or she would read my letter which I thought was pretty persuasive about why I wanted to live in Italy and we'd have a pleasant conversation as my application was looked over. A disembodied voice told me to go to window one.

An American woman with grey hair escaping from a messy chignon and I exchanged good mornings. From there it went downhill. Behind plexiglass, there was a sort of lever she pulled down which opened a slot and enabled me to slide papers through. I thought, my god, it's like visiting someone in prison. I gave her my passport. My application was "Unacceptable. Here. Do it again. Sit over there and fill it out again." I had no choice but to fill it out exactly as I had before and went back to the window. It was now inexplicably acceptable. I said, "I have my birth certif—" She said sharply, "Don't tell me what you have. It has to be in order. I will tell you what to give me in order."

She asked for my last two years of income tax returns. I said, "I don't have them. I didn't know I needed them. The website—"

"It is on the website." She pushed two stapled pages through and in yellow highlight it said 'last two years of income tax returns.' I had memorized the website and was jolted to see that it wasn't this one. Then she abruptly said, "Tell me what you have." My birth certificate was scoffed at. "Who told you to bring that?" My Social Security card. "You don't need that! Where did you get that idea?" All the priority mailings, all the extra fees, all the tension over documents arriving on time and here was this woman, rude and hostile for no reason I could comprehend, saying I didn't need them. I tried to tell her that I was concerned about the country of residence question on the application. She brusquely cut me off and said we'd deal with it later and then asked me for proof of address. I said, "That was my question. I have purchased a place in Palermo and don't know if Italy should be listed as my residency or if—" She told me that if I wasn't a resident of New York then "this office cannot help you" and she scooped up all my papers in both hands and made as if they were going into the wastebasket beside her. I quickly became a resident of New York and tried to give her my voter registration as proof. Unacceptable. Where was my driver's license? Well, I wasn't going to tell her that I was meant to be in Tunisia, didn't think I'd need it in Sidi Bou Said and hadn't packed it. Every question, every demand was snapped at me. I offered my Police Clearance Certificate from the post office and the FBI and was sharply reprimanded. "What is that? Who told you to bring that?" I didn't answer—another website, of course.

I was told to email my two tax returns to her when I got home. Very generous, I thought. I told her I had insurance. She took the pages and the letter from Marcella. Then she said she wanted two more things: a self-addressed priority envelope and a money order for $133. Of course, I had neither. I said I had a credit card and a checkbook. I didn't say it but the website had told me either one was fine. Unacceptable. She told me to go to the post office so I retrieved my phone by giving back the little key and raced out. I found an ATM, practically ran the few blocks to the post office, stood in line, got my envelope, got my money order, hurried back.

I crossed Park Avenue gulping in the fresh air and wondering why someone could show such animosity towards me, could radiate disdain even contempt. I thought of Thomas who is the most attractive, personable person in the entire universe and his description of how downright nasty they were to him. So, it wasn't me as a person.

Back at the building. The intercom. Buzzed in. Handed over my phone again, was given a tiny key. Window number one had these little Venetian blinds down. I waited. The blinds were yanked up with a snapping noise and I slid the envelope and the money order through the opening in the plexiglass. I told this same tight-lipped, frowning woman I had been very careful to stay out of the Schengen and only in Italy for less than 90 days. She took my paper which listed the dates, studied it and scowled. "You overstayed. This is not legal." I said, "You can see for the first period starting in June ending in September that I was there for 81 days not 90." She grabbed a calculator, punched in numbers as if angry and saw that I was right. Then she pointed to December 4th which was the start of my second 180-day period and asked if I'd left and I said no, because the new period began on that day. It was very clear on the page but she seemed eager to accuse me, to catch me in an error. Math is math and she couldn't argue. Unwilling to admit a mistake, she sniffed, "You overstayed but we'll let it go this time."

My question about the next 90-day period was unanswered; she was irritated, dismissive. Then she told me that it would be three months until I received my passport back which meant I could not leave the United States for three months. I thought, oh, yeah? Those nice, decent people in Buffalo! I thanked her very sweetly then she scowled at me for the last time and snapped down her Venetian blinds.

I raced out, anxious to escape that horrible room. On Park Avenue, I realized I'd left my phone. I'd had to check it with the nice

Latina guard in her plexiglass booth who had this alarmingly blonde hair. She had actually smiled at me once. I'd retrieved it to run to the post office then checked it again. She buzzed me in and I gave her the little key and she handed it over. "You left so fast," she said and I told her I was a bit tense, that I wanted this visa very much. She said everything would be okay. Then I went out and zipping my folder saw that I had not handed over the February 2022 bank statement. The website said to bring "at least two years of bank statements" and I had spent a fortune in London at a print shop and had 27 months as if the extra three would give me extra credit. However, Window One had only wanted the final three months. I rushed back to the door, got buzzed in, and the guard behind plexiglass said she would give it to the woman in window one. I asked if I could go to the ladies room and she said sure. I did then went back to her in the booth and said, "You've been very nice and I promise you will never see me again." She grinned.

Then I left, was on Park Avenue once more and wondered what mistakes I'd made. Okay. Over. I had to go back to Gema's and send the income tax returns but Peg, my accountant, would send them instantly. She was great about that sort of thing. Actually, great about everything. I walked into this shop in the 60s on Park and thought of Lynn Chase whose artwork on china is my favorite. The place was crowded with pillows for $385 and bamboo chairs, place settings, framed prints, all with a jungle theme. Nothing of Lynn's. The clerk said that the pieces out there fetched very high prices as she was not making any more. Of course, I knew this. I browsed and then, for some reason, I bought two green candles for $8. For my house. A positive statement. Because I would have the visa and live in Palermo. I left the shop with a little white paper shopping bag but on the subway realized I no longer had it. I laughed out loud.

Gema was waiting for me in the kitchen. She took one look at my face and threw her arms around me. I felt like crying. Stupid, I know. "Gema, I've dealt with murderers. I've ..." I murmured. We talked and came to the same conclusion: It was power. That woman had power over me and my visa.

Peg sent me the tax returns and I sent them to the email address on the bottom of those printed website pages with information entirely foreign to me. There was no mention of insurance.

Then at 4 o'clock when I was being picked up by Mohammed at 5:30, an email came telling me that I must mail the first page of my tax return to confirm my address. They already had two complete returns. I downloaded it onto a thumb drive, literally ran to FedEx on Steinway, printed it then ran to the post office which had about ten people in line. I approached the first person and said I needed one stamp and was hurrying because I was going to be picked up to go to the airport. I asked if I could go before her. She said she was in a hurry, too. The Asian man behind her said, of course, I could go ahead of him and I thanked him and said I hoped no one else minded. The woman behind him said, "Please, go in front of me!" and then other people down the line echoed this. The little Chinese woman clerk was surprised to see me, said she had missed me. As I rushed out of the post office there were calls of, "Have a good trip!" "Be careful!"

Astoria, Astoria.

Victor in the Verizon store waved at me from behind the shop window and wanted to know why I was back. He is from Trinidad and we used to talk a lot when the store was empty. Politics mostly. His Indian boss is mean as a snake and maybe he was jealous. He was filming us talking and laughing and so I was banned from the Verizon store. After that we developed a system where I was out of range of the security camera. Of course, Victor was on camera, grinning and animatedly talking to himself like a lunatic.

I embraced Gema in the laundromat as Mohammed loaded the car. On the expressway, he told me he was looking at houses as he wants to leave the city. "Thinking of Buffalo as real estate is cheap." I smiled and said, "The people there are awfully nice."

LONDON

My flight back to London was easy. The Virgin flight attendants were all in red uniforms and rather hilariously popping out of them. Every woman was packed into a skirt and jacket two sizes too small. Confusion at the dry cleaners? I took the tube in from Heathrow back to Golders Green on my Oyster card. Bright sun. Ella opened the front door with Daisy, the dog, at her side.

Upon arrival at the house, I received an email from the Italian consulate announcing it was a Visa Rejection Warning. I was to send them my last two income tax returns and explain this and that and supply a "duly registered in Italy" deed to my property. I had sent the income tax returns and had handed over the deed. Gianni amazingly answered his cell in Sambuca and said the deed I gave to her *was* duly registered. He called the notaio, called me back and said all I needed was on the first page so I had given them the right thing. He sent one other thing called a visura catastale.

The letter said all requested had to be received within 10 days and had to be sent by regular mail. If it did not arrive or the documents were not acceptable or there was anything sent that was not requested then the visa would be denied. Regular mail? There was no mention on her website sheet of insurance and I wondered if I had not supplied her with the policy if the rejection warning letter would have asked for it. I'd handed over the insurance document which had required so much effort on my part and on Marcella's. I would never have gotten it within 10 days! And via regular mail? From London? Of course, the consulate thought I had no passport so I was still in New York.

That evening, I met Stephen, my English midwife to the sheep/opera critic/gourmet tour guide friend who always picks marvelous restaurants.

The next day the panic began again.

Liz, my English friend in New York, told me her husband had

dealt with a lawyer in Sardinia who was wonderful. I called this Sardinian lawyer and she said not to involve a lawyer as the consulate did not like that and there was really nothing she could do for me as she dealt with citizenship. She advised getting advice from an elective residency visa lawyer. Was there such a thing? I looked online. $ 280 for a 30-minute consultation on the phone.

I called Ron in New York who called his Italian friend who met me once at dinner and she said to call her friend, an Italian cooking show host who supposedly had contacts at the consulate. I called her and she offered to make a complaint that I was treated badly. Oh, no! Then she said she didn't know anyone who dealt with visas.

Ron came to the rescue making the outrageous offer to print out what I needed and to deliver it to the consulate. The consulate had stipulated regular mail so hand delivery wouldn't do. I sent everything in files and he went to Kinko's to print them and sent me photos of the way the documents would go into the envelope and how he'd addressed it and even the receipt from the post office. Ron is an amazing friend. I wanted to know exactly how much everything cost but he told me, over my protests, that it was all an early Christmas present. I will send him a check for a good bottle of wine. At the least.

I look back at this New York trip and think of all the friends who helped me. Of all the people I love, of all the favors, all the ideas, the enthusiasm, the advice. I felt that everyone wanted me to live in Palermo.

I told Ron he had a future in crime as he forged my signature on the letter for the consulate perfectly. An hour later, Thomas in Palermo wrote me saying he hoped I didn't mind but he'd forged my signature on a document saying I'm now registered in some way with the church.

Of course, I didn't mind. It is the first time in my life I've had two men forge my signature in two different countries on the same day.

YET ANOTHER POSSIBILITY

Late one afternoon I received a message from Thomas who said he was in an airport drinking prosecco out of the bottle. For some reason the airport won't supply cups. He must be on his way to see Marcello who lives near Bologna; those partners commute. If all goes haywire, he said, then he and Marcello will hire me as their housekeeper.

I wrote back that I would adore to be their housekeeper. Even their maid. I want a frilly apron, a little white cap and a huge feather duster. The hell with the consulate. Whatever happens—I can't wait!

* * *

Minda who headed the All Aboard charity shop said, "I like you. I want you to work here." I was auditioning to be a volunteer and the vetting was scrupulous as it was a Jewish neighbourhood and there was worry about a bomb being hidden in a donation bag.

One day I went to the Westminster magistrates court and after court was adjourned, I approached the three magistrates who were very interested in my background as a private detective. As I had experience on both sides—the defense and the prosecution—they were certain I would be approved as a magistrate. I would fly back for my few days of duty per year. Best of all, it didn't matter that I was American. Here and at the charity shop I felt assessed and appreciated which was particularly delicious after my time at the Italian consulate when that woman had treated me like gum on the bottom of her shoe.

I remember that, in my twenties, I could walk into an office, introduce myself and be hired. Just like that. Job after job. Actually, it was necessary to get job after job as I was usually bored after the second week and quit job after job. I treated job interviews like blind dates and blind dates like job interviews.

* * *

It was April the second. That night I lolled in the London bathtub, closed my eyes and pretended to be in my new Palermo bathtub. My

Venetian pineapple chandelier would be shining brightly over me or maybe the thrift shop Philadelphia one I'd painted green. Glistening mountains of bubbles, hot water, silence, luxury. A year from today, next April second I would have a birthday party for Casanova; I had compiled a guest list already. My cortile will be filled with geraniums and we can float out into the alley if there's a crowd.

Last year at this time I had not yet seen La Tana. I was online wondering when there'd be flights to Italy. La Tana was dark and deserted, languishing. It was waiting for me to walk down the Alley of the Gardenia to discover it.

MURDER AS A DIVERSION

April 13, 2022

I will be okay if I don't get the visa. I told myself exile every 90 days could be fun. Maybe next time that place in Kenya with the pool. I was steeled for disappointment but ready to celebrate, too.

On the Thursday before Easter, I received an email from my mail box people in New York saying they had an 8 by 11 envelope for me from the Italian Consulate and should they send it Priority mail or would I pick it up in person?

They won't open it and told me DHL/FEDEX, whatever would be more than $50, maybe $70 and they add another ten and I thought, I can wait til Tuesday and spend the money I saved on a celebration. If it is bad news then why pay all that to get the bad news sooner? With the post office in the UK closed on Friday and Easter Monday, it will be Tuesday or Wednesday at the latest. Okay, Priority.

Wednesday came but no visa came. It seems if you put something in a special big cardboard envelope from the U.S. Post Office, label it Priority and pay extra then the U.S. Post Office puts it in a special place and forgets about it for awhile.

This afternoon I thought there was the slender chance that the envelope might be delivered but I didn't want to brood about it. A murder trial was the only thing to divert me so off I went to the Old Bailey. One of the guards told me my favorite prosecutor was in Courtroom 12 then held the door for me.

When I arrived, the defense attorney was saying, "Now, if you don't understand something, tell me. It is my fault, not yours. If there is a word you don't understand, tell me and I'll try again. This is my fault, not yours."

In other trials, the judge has leaned forward, asked if the witness needed a break, needed a glass of water. So solicitous. Next will be to ask if the accused would like a cushion or a footrest or maybe a massage during the cross.

There he was, my man, standing up and approaching the witness. Oliver Glasgow. Graduated from Oxford with honors. I could never see his face, just that wig and the back of him under black robes. Glasgow began. I was familiar with his style by now, knew he often didn't expect answers.

"You were swinging the machete at his head to get him to back off, is that correct?"

"We have you on camera swinging the machete twice. Look, there you have it over your head, bringing it down with great force. And missing. Twice. So, you swung and missed twice *on purpose* and that was your way of saying stay away?"

"Swinging a machete is not a sign of aggression?"

He held up the machete which struck terror in me. Huge. Serrated teeth.

Then we watched the defendant's own video of his knife collection. Glasgow had him relate how he put one knife he particularly liked on the wall as decoration. We were told that he never left the house without a knife because South London was a dangerous area and this was for protection. "Are you often stabbed? What is it about you, Mr. Habib, that makes people want to stab and kill you?" I imagined hands shooting up in the courtroom as we probably all had ideas.

"How many knives do you own? How many knives is enough? Five? Ten? Twenty? More?" There was a mumbled answer of "I dunno."

"All these knives and machetes are to cause bodily harm, correct? They are not to cut fruit."

"You always carry a knife? How do you decide which knife to carry on which day? A machete is Monday, the Rambo knife is Tuesday. How do you decide?" Muffled answer. "You say it's instinct? You instinctively felt you needed the protection of a machete stuck down your trouser leg on that particular day?"

This was a gang war with several people injured and at least one death. The witness claimed not to know the name of his gang or of the gang his friends were in.

What a day. Glasgow was in great form and I have seen the evil glint of a machete waved by a man in a wig.

I took the tube back to Golders Green.

The Priority envelope was propped against my bedroom door. After eight days in transit. I tore it open in excitement. My second passport slipped out and I held the page which began: "We regret to inform you . . ." I was shocked.

The visa rejection hit me hard for about fifteen minutes and then I took action: I wrote back.

Immediately began thinking about what next. All I wanted was to be in La Tana with my black and white marble floor, my books and my paintings. Okay, regroup. Plan B. If that fails, there will be Plan C. I always have ideas and can work my way right through the alphabet. I am out of New York which is the first step. I am in Europe which is positive. I found a place in the center of a city with high ceilings. I bought it, I own it. No one is taking it away. Nothing is as I imagined. I pictured a terrace with a view of church steeples and clouds but I can wheel my bike in.

I never thought I'd buy a Tunisian night club in Palermo. Life is a constant re-shifting. Like sailing. Pay attention to the wind and let out the mainsail, pull in the jib and keep your eyes on the horizon.

LAST DAYS IN LONDON

In early April, I made my calls, sent my messages to Palermo and alerted The Norman, Gianni and Luca Iwanttomarryhim that I would be at La Tana on Thursday, May 5th at 0800. Francesco who'd laid the marble floors would come on Saturday to put together the dozen bookcases and the kitchen cabinets. The armadio men who were making my closets would come. Armadio means closet. I wanted to unpack my clothes, some of which had been packed for nearly a year. I'd been warned of mildew on the ship and I wanted those closets.

The Italian consulate letter was postmarked April 5 and I needed to file the appeal within 60 days, which meant by the first week of June. I must hire a lawyer to file the appeal and it was specified that he must be a lawyer in Rome.

All these demands and deadlines fed my frustration of being in London when so much should be done in Palermo. But days were passing. My 90 days of exile were ending.

London was getting to know and admire Ella. She is a personal trainer and the doorbell rang every hour with a client who was taken to the studio/gym in back of the house. This was a structure of glass and wood that made me think of Scandinavia. Ella worked hard.

London was the Old Bailey. Every morning I'd think I really should go to a museum. I really should get tickets to a play but the Old Bailey was my theatre and I couldn't stay away.

London was spending a day at a magistrates court and seeing a man named David Smith, who looked like every whey-faced, middle-aged Englishman, in the dock accused of spying for the Russians.

London was lentils. I had this craving for them and ate them for breakfast and any time in the day when I was even slightly hungry. I ate them cold with a spoon and couldn't get enough. I must have eaten hundreds of McVitie's digestive biscuits, too. Amazingly, I stopped wearing reading glasses. It was lentils or those cookies.

London was Sundays volunteering with Damjana at the charity shop. She knew everything about film, we both loved mysteries and we had a good time. Located in the Jewish section of Golders Green, the clientele with side curls and long black coats who came into the thrift shop fascinated me. Women wore wigs and pushed baby carriages.

London was the British Museum, the V and A, the Wallace Collection, the Tate, art galleries, bookshops, so many newspapers in the morning and two plays. My afternoon at the House of Commons was spent hearing about Partygate when top political figures ignored COVID restrictions and caroused like teenagers as their constituents suffered. I went a few times to the Everyman Theatre with the plush seats and the popcorn and prosecco delivered to you right before the movie. There was dinner at Brooks Club with a Canadian who had become more English than any Londoner of the 19th century.

Lunch with a producer, friend of a friend, at Sloane Square who asked if I'd had trouble finding the restaurant and I said, "No. I used to live at 82 Cadogan Square." I explained that I'd been a maid in a men's boarding house in the summer of 1966. "Later I found out everyone made bets on how long the American would last. But I did. I was the mascot of the cricket team and was carried on the players' shoulders through Sloane Square on a Sunday afternoon." I gestured out the window. "Right there."

Jane was excited, "You must write about it! You already have the perfect title! 82 Cadogan Square!"

I shrugged. "Maybe. It was an outrageous summer of the Beatles, the Stones. I wanted to look like Jean Shrimpton. Kings Road was wild. London was wild. Seven of the boys wore their pajamas on the tube and nobody blinked. My God, it was fun!"

My last week in London, after years of sporadic searching, phone calls, the internet, English newspapers, I would find my great love of that summer. Fifty years evaporated; he was exactly the same in my eyes. Slender, quick-witted. Brian came to London with his very beautiful, blonde wife called Vi and Simon, his effervescent son. It was all I had wished for him. The four of us had a hilarious, exhilarating five-hour lunch.

The next afternoon, shivering in my little black leather jacket from Rome, I walked to Cadogan Square which was outrageously lush and green, the garden neatly surrounded by tall, black iron pikes. I used to climb that fence with Brian in the middle of the night. My thighs in my miniskirts were always decorated with bruises. We'd sit on a bench in that private, forbidden place, arms around each other, talking. Kissing until we couldn't breathe.

Numbers 82,84,86. Those three houses had connecting doors and countless stairs. We four maids were on the fifth floor; I woke one morning with a pigeon on my chest. A hundred and ten men and two sour man-hating wardens with dark pasts. Miss Anne E. Dight was a hunchback and rarely seen. Mrs. Woodruff was never married at all and had her own bitter story. I avoided her teenage son who was big and strong and would grab me on the kitchen stairs. All the residents were Irish, Scottish, English, Welsh, "from the provinces." The shouts, the constant slamming of the front door from five o'clock on and later the boys streaming into the dining room in their coats and ties. All those young men with dreams of making enough money for a flat of their own and becoming a success in the grand capital.

Did they?

What happened to them?

82 Cadogan Square, S.W.1. The most elegant postal code in London.

I do wonder if traces of us, if whispers, if sighs and smiles, if traded secrets linger in the mews and float over the square from long-ago summer nights.

If they do, then I will always be there.

Extortion, Fraud, Threat of Bodily Harm

The Joli embraced me. I opened the door to my old room, put my suitcases inside and walked to the window. The postcard-blue sky, the piazza, the palm trees—my sentries—still there.

I arrived at La Tana at eight the next morning and no workers showed up. I know because I waited. All day. My messages from London, the promises made in Palermo meant nothing. Is it because I am a woman? Is it because I'm struggling with the language? Is it because I am alone here? I never *feel* alone but I must *look* alone.

That first afternoon back in Palermo I contacted a Roman lawyer to handle the appeal to my rejection by the Italian consulate. A friend in Rome gave me his name, said he was good but warned he had a bad temper. He was brusque on the phone but I sort of liked that. When I said I needed an immigration lawyer he'd snapped, "There's no such thing." I begged to differ but I decided not to fight about it. I sensed toughness and no nonsense and that's good in a lawyer. Besides, how many rude lawyers have I dealt with? At least a hundred and we never failed to end up getting along. Michael is an American which may be a plus or a minus; I shall see. He needed all communication between me and the Italian consulate in New York and the deed to La Tana and I said he'd have it right away. He wouldn't promise he'd get that visa for me saying, "It would be unprofessional."

I asked how much he will charge me and he barked, "An arm and a leg!" I winced as I walked on via Roma, phone to my ear, trying to hear above traffic noise. A siren screamed then faded after tearing past. "How much is an arm and a leg going for these days?" He quoted a price and I said, "Wow. I hope you're worth it," and he barked, "I'm worth more."

The next morning at eight my mission was to find the water company which was called AMAP. If anyone showed up at La Tana they could wait for me for a change. Pietro had prevailed upon a Dottoressa Germana Spera to help me. Dear Pietro. Blondie told me one could wait months for water.

The hotel scanner wasn't working so I would present my contract to her in person. The water company is a building on a tree-lined street just off Piazza Verdi near Teatro Massimo. It was easy to find as the theatre is my North Star. The guards out front, all smoking, told me she was late. The fat one read my email from her on my phone as if he were studying the Rosetta Stone. After ten minutes or so of standing around with these men, a young slender man bounded out of the building and down the steps motioning for me to follow him inside. Sliding glass doors, the cool breath of air conditioning then up some steps we trotted to a high-ceilinged office with two desks. He was Spera's colleague and wanted to help. The walls had several depictions of Jesus and crosses. Her side of the room especially. At eye level there was a portrait of Jesus looking a lot like Johnny Depp. This Jesus might have been appealing to a jury.

The colleague and I were chatting about my situation when another man joined us. I do my best with the Italian but I know I get things wrong. Something was said about night and day and twenty-four hours and I thought he was talking about appointments so I may have asked in Italian, "A man will come to me in the night?" They exploded with laugher. Enter the Dottoressa who looked a lot like Claudia Cardinale as I'd just seen her in *The Leopard*. Black hair, gorgeous face. She read my card and oohed, 'Una scrittrice?" I am catapulted into the stratosphere when I say I am a writer. Suddenly I am a force, I am respected. She wanted to know if I had anything published in Italian. We talked. My Italian was embarrassingly bad but she was kind. Then Claudia Cardinale put in a call to someone, couldn't reach him but said she thought I would have water on Monday or maybe Tuesday. Favoloso!

I left and went to my hardware store and they still had no answer about the chandelier bulbs. I'd carefully packed two dozen that did not work here and had to be replaced. Then I saw a place to make keys and I had two copied. Three men were animatedly discussing something and wanted me to weigh in. I couldn't understand what they were disagreeing about and finally realized, just before the 2nd key was made that it was *tomatoes*. They were very upset about some situation involving *tomatoes*.

I still had no bathroom and had to deal with the piccolo blacksmith who was asking for money he should not ask for. He told me, in clear Italian, that there was no charge for changing the back door glass from opaque to the same front-door mirrored glass. That was the end of January. I was surprised as I had the euros in my hand. He was thanked profusely, we looked each other in the eye, we shook hands and now it's May and he says I misunderstood, you owe me 250 euros and I won't do any more work for you because I am offended that you are disputing my word. Gianni becomes involved and says he will get the fee down. "But, Gianni, he is not telling the truth!" This is teeth-gnashingly familiar.

Emails and phone calls from far away friends sustain me. I have allies.

Happy to attempt unpacking. I was lifting and slicing open boxes, pushing and pulling them and I stood all day as any chair seems to have been swallowed up in the chaos. No shelves, no closets, no place to put anything away so mostly it was consolidation, getting rid of empty boxes, attempting to shrink the footprint of Mount New York.

Some mornings I would take something from the hotel storage—a suitcase or a shopping bag—and get on the bus with it. Today The Norman was to come at 10:30 as were Luca Iwanttomarryhim and Gianni. The Norman showed up briefly at about noon and left. Blonde hair mussed, face very pink, he seemed flustered. Huge stomach preceding him; he is starting to look like a Macy's Thanksgiving float. He should be installing the doors to the bathroom and the kitchen but insists it's Luca's job. Luca is an electrician and plumber so it is not. The two men loudly bicker about this.

Every detail of La Tana is in Italian. Every word, every centimeter. I spoke badly but clearly. I drew pictures. I bought a ruler and drew things to scale. I had a dictionary. As the detective said, we are communicating.

I noticed fist-sized blisters on the wall which adjoins the thousand-year-old church. Wonderful. The Norman who was a bricklayer pretending to be a contractor should have treated the wall for moisture before painting it. I negotiated for a second wall to be built with a five-centimeter space between the two. There was plenty of scowling about it but it must be done. I was polite but firm. I did not say, it's your own bloody fault!

I was at a very low point and told myself to snap out of it. I should have felt rejuvenated by London but I didn't. Every day began with the constant off-balance feeling of 'will they even show up?' It was daily confrontations about the work not done properly. There was the waiting and the unanswered phones, unanswered texts and broken promises. Every evening was full of WhatsApp messages arranging the next day with what was to be done which very likely wouldn't be done. I was quite happy in Geneva and maybe Palermo was just too dramatic a leap for me. London was a recess but I've returned to exactly what I left.

It was facing these Sicilian men and saying, No, this is not okay. Sometimes I think the only things I have going for me are 1. Knowing I am correct and 2. Usually I am taller.

Glad to see them when they arrive, if it's morning I bring them coffee from Stefania, aka Miss Blue Glasses, across via Roma. A tiny paper cup of amaro or dolce. I praise when it's merited and am ever-polite when asking that something be done or redone. I must be careful as I need them to finish and there is plenty of work in Palermo. Bruno, the concierge at the Grand Hotel des Palmes told me how lucky I was to have any workers at all.

A minute's walk from La Tana is Matteo's tile store with terra cotta pots for sale out front. I squinted and saw my future trees in those fat and perfect pots. I decided on green and white tiles for the kitchen backsplash.

I was weary. One afternoon I went to the big German supermarket, Lidl's, paid for my stuff and walked away. All these people were shouting, "Signora! Signora!" I had left everything there by the cashier. I turned around, put the groceries in my bag and then pushed open the Emergency Only door and all the sirens shrieked. I pulled it closed and impassively walked past the guards, through the crowd, as if I did this all the time. Like a zombie, I left the store.

On this all-important morning that Luca Iwanttomarryhim had scheduled for a visitation I went to the hardware store and bought green outdoor paint for the big star to go over my front door. On my way back I passed a small man maybe in his 80s with those round Harry Potter glasses wearing a coppola. It's what I call an English newsboy hat. One of the Alley Men was nearby just standing, gazing into space. It's as if they are on the bridge of a ship alert for whales or maybe in Africa scanning the plains for lions. It was a geographical mistake to be surrounded by parked cars and laundry hanging from balconies.

About to enter my vicolo, I heard "Clarissa?" and turned to face the man with the glasses. He said his name was Harold and "I thought that was you. Thomas talks about you and said we should meet." Harold from the church. Hawk mentioned him as being the other American. We chatted. He glanced at my alley and said, "You live in the best neighborhood." I smiled because Antonio at the hardware store told me it was a bad neighborhood. When I remarked to the fabbro that I felt safe with the iron doors, he laughed and said that thieves would take the doors off their hinges and the police would arrive in four hours. So far, Harold was alone in his opinion.

He was a retired psychiatrist who grew up in Tennessee and told me he's been in Palermo for 18 years. I said, "You must like it here," and he responded, "My partner is Italian so that limits us."

"You've been here a long time and know the ropes. I'm fumbling along. Do you have any advice for me?"

Without hesitation, he said, "Trust no one." At that moment, I thought, how cynical but his words would ring in my ears later.

We chatted then said goodbye as I looked at my watch, thinking, mygod, I've waited so long for this damn Luca Iwanttomarryhim and he is coming at 10:30 and I must be there. Father and son arrived at 11:30. I was reminded of my friend, Lynn, writing about Mercury in retrograde and how things will go wrong. Maybe that planet got stuck in retrograde at the start of this renovation.

Luca Iwanttomarryhim and I didn't speak. I loathed him for not coming that last week before I left for exile when he said it would take two days to install my bathroom. Every day for five days I was there waiting. Every dark, cold, miserable, rainy day. All day. That last week in January I could have had a bathroom and a kitchen. I could have had water if Gianni had given me the receipt or answered his phone and talked to the AMAP man. It was all so typical. They were the reason I was back at the hotel.

There was a white-haired man with him. Antonio? No, he is called Nino. Big smile. Lots of nicknames here. Giovanni is Gianni, Salvatore is Sal, Giuseppe is Peppe. I saw Gianni for the first time since before I left for England and we went over the payments. My records plainly show that I only owe The Norman 1900 euros as I have sent him money every single time he has asked. I asked Gianni not to tell him that as I am afraid he will walk away from so much work to be done.

That evening Gianni called me. The Norman said he is quitting unless I pay him the rest of his fee. I told Gianni that I had sent him 500 euros only last week but did not want to pay everything until he finished. Gianni had no idea of this and the news seemed to have an impact. I thanked him as I always do and we hung up. I felt a bit sorry that he must be the liaison for this. Gianni was a tall, slender young man with black-framed glasses and those trousers two sizes too small, tight and way above his ankles. Soft-spoken, a mediator. He was so different in looks and personality from his father that one would never connect them.

The Norman preferred communication to go through Gianni even if I had seen him that day but there'd been no sign of him for at least three. I wish I could have told Gianni to tell him to quit but the unbuilt loft kept me from doing that. No word from The Norman and no sighting. When I was told he was fuori/away and had left Palermo, I experienced a twinge of worry.

Another bright and glorious May day. Expecting Luca Iwanttomarryhim any minute but I refused to call or text for an update. I went to Caffè 48 and took a little bottle of Pinot de Pinot out of their fridge then brought it back to La Tana and poured it into a beautiful green goblet that had survived the Atlantic crossing. Actually, it was a wedding present and it had survived much more than traversing any ocean. After three sips I didn't care about anything: a missing bathtub, the armadio men who promised to come but didn't, The Norman whom I learned had reportedly scampered off to Milano and no one knew if he were ever coming back, a lying blacksmith and a thousand-year-old church that I thought was romantic until wet bubbles the size of baseballs began to appear on my wall. I toasted myself, finished the little bottle and thought, who cares?

* * *

I liked the weekend when I was alone and could open boxes and find things. Without noise, without men. Masses of books, 42 boxes of them, are a problem. Looks like many I bought for research. *BONDAGE ON A BUDGET*? I remember that case. Should I keep the life stories of Trujillo, Hussein, Peron, Anwar Sadat, the Ceausescus? Books on Africa and the Arab world, on interiors and dessert-making? Should I keep my crime books and my spy collection or should I just remember how much I loved tearing through them, one after another?

When I pulled away the wrapping on Mother's Haitian painting,

I knew I was going to love living here.

* * *

On Monday morning I was at La Tana like a good soldier, waiting, and no one came. On Tuesday morning I was there at the agreed-upon hour of eight and Gianni sent a message at noon saying we are not coming. Media World had delivered all the kitchen stuff after two months and about ten calls from Pietro so I wrote why don't you come and do the kitchen? But, he answered, the kitchen does not take much time so they were writing off the whole day. I had a pedicure, tense about how long it was taking then rushed to be back at three for the appointment with the fabbro/blacksmith but the fabbro never came.

Accessing one plastic bin after another seemed endless. Sheets and towels had to be somewhere. Reaching up, digging down, trying to remember what had been put where as I'd packed on my sunny terrace in Astoria nearly a year before was true exercise. My sprained ankle of January was the result of stepping off a crate onto a box at a bad angle. Worse than pawing through boxes was stacking it all up again on Mount New York. Tremendous sheets of plastic were then pulled over it to protect it from the painters. When they decided to show up.

* * *

Trumpets! Ticker tape parade! The bathtub was carried in by Gianni and Luca and installed. The bidet, the toilet were put in place. Whenever Luca was there discussion centered on the height for the bathroom sink. I wanted it one meter high, was tired of bending over to wash my face at the Joli. Absolutely not possible, stated Luca. I looked at him and said I was tall and I was going to live here and wanted it that high. Back and forth, for several days, he told me I could never sell the property, no architect would allow it, it was never done this way, etc. The kitchen counter the same. He refused to make them higher. Francesco intervened when Luca left, marked where the pipe would be and said that now it must be a meter high. Same with the kitchen. At last, the basin was installed and Luca said he was ashamed.

I looked at it and proclaimed, "Perfetto."

All this talk was accompanied by the screaming and shouting of the couple in one of the five apartments above my cortile. They fight in the morning, the afternoon, the evening and at night. A man and a woman going at it like tigers. I picture him, brawny with big arms in a white wife-beater, and her, messy hair pinned up, pink-faced from the steam as she drains the pasta. Someday I'll know what they are screaming about—money? A mistress?

The Norman came in his huge orange truck wearing a huge orange T-shirt and did the grouting on the bathroom marble piece installed the day before. The attempt to install the toilet paper holder had cracked the marble so the huge slab had to be taken out and replaced. I asked him and his worker to help me with the heavy box spring. I'd gotten it out of its cardboard box but now I needed another person to lift it with me. The Norman would later complain to Gianni about this request! On my own, I worked like an ant lifting and moving what I could then I put a towel under anything heavy and pulled the item along the little path I cleared. Sometimes I arranged for a large box over my head to tip itself onto my shoulders and before I actually dropped it from the great weight, I bent my knees and let it sink to the ground telling myself that I loved gravity.

I made a path from my bed to the bathroom and because it was an obstacle course I planned to sleep with a flashlight under my pillow after I moved in. On the other side of Mount New York was another path from the front door to the cortile.

I couldn't wear anything but trousers as my legs were covered in big, purplish-grey bruises. Arms, too, actually.

How tough was I? One face-off after another. I could look at every corner of this place and remember demanding The Norman remove his ridiculous plaster patch over the hole in the front door, remember demanding Luca raise the bathroom sink, remember insisting the front door was six inches too short with The Norman insisting it was meant to be like that, on and on. One confrontation after another.

I never said I am paying you but I did say I will live here not you.

Most of the time the men weren't even there but when they were and when I dared go out to grab a panino, I'd often return to see a hole the size of a saucer in a wall. No one had asked me about this; they just decided. I'd ask why it was there. It was for a light over the front door which I did not want. Another time the hole was for an emergency light which they said was necessary. It was the law. No, it wasn't because I checked. Not unless you are in a public building. So, I'd say that the hole must be filled. The men would look at me and one would slowly, very slowly mount a ladder and fill the hole. If reluctance were a noise, it would be screaming.

Tomorrow I get wifi. The man is meant to come between 8:30 and 10:30. It was time for The Norman to do the backsplash tiles in the kitchen as was agreed but he'd been so awful about the bathroom door I was ready to call Francesco and pay him instead. The black and white marble floor was fine, detailed work so the tiles would be easy for him. Then I must go to Matteo and order enough tiles for 300 centimeters by 49 cm. The painters were meant to come but they were meant to come on Friday then on Monday as was the mason and none of them did so who knows?

PAYING FOR WATER

May 17, 2022

Tuesday arrived. All I wanted was to be able to flush the toilet and take a bath and I could leave the hotel at last.

The AMAP truck pulled into the alley and I handed over the key to the padlock on the little grey metal door at the corner of the building. It took one minute and he closed the door, clicked the padlock closed and handed me my cluster of keys. I was delighted until he told me that my idraulico/plumber had to perform a second operation. No La Tana tonight but tomorrow Luca Iwanttomarryhim was coming.

At least, he said he was.

I thanked the AMAP man and then went inside and positioned my desk so that I could see out the front door. The diminutive fabbro/blacksmith had done an excellent job. The iron doors may have looked a bit prison-like but the bars allowed light and air in and made me feel safe. The second set were glass and meant I could see out but no one could see me until after dark if my lights were on. Anyone outside in daylight saw only a pair of mirrored doors just inside the iron ones. My idea was to keep the iron doors locked and the mirrored doors open if the weather were right.

MAY 18, 2022

The next morning, I was at La Tana at seven. Luca I wanttomarryhim said he'd arrive in the morning and, of course, I always believed him. However, this time he did. I greeted him effusively then went inside and was at my desk when I heard shouting in the alley. There were often arguments but never gunfire as I experienced in Astoria so I paid little attention to men's raised voices. This shouting was different. My cell phone rang and Gianni said that his father had told him to call. "You must pay 800 euros, Clarissa." "What are you talking about?" I asked.

"For the water. You must pay 800 euros."

"Where are you?" I asked.

"In Sambuca. You must pay 800 euros for the water," he repeated.

This went back and forth with my saying I paid AMAP, the water company, that I had an account with them. But no, this was different. The man outside said he owned my water, he had installed it, it was his building. I said, no, but Gianni was insistent. I must pay.

More shouting. I went outside with the phone to my ear. Gianni told me to give the phone to his father. The Norman and Luca Iwanttomarryhim were bending over on their knees beside my front door. They had hacked away a few feet of the wall and exposed a horizontal grey pipe. I assumed this had something to do with my having water so didn't question it. I handed the phone to Luca who snapped in staccato Italian at Gianni. Behind Luca was the short, round man I'd named Trump of the Alley. The one who'd disembarked from the dust-covered car, covered in dust himself and asked me if I wanted to buy any of his buildings. He glared at me and stated loudly, "Otto cento euros!" Eight hundred euros.

A small crowd had gathered in the alley, all men in jeans and T-shirts, and they were saying, "Paga!" Pay!

Luca handed the phone back to me. Gianni said, "Clarissa, you have to pay for the water. The line was paid for and you must pay your share." I objected, said no. "There is no condominio fee and I own my place. When one buys property, one pays the water company for water." I went inside again wondering if I should lock the iron door or would it look as if I were afraid. I just closed it and stood over my desk.

Gianni argued some more and told me that this pipe had been paid for a few years ago and I owed money for it. I said that I had nothing to do with his paying for it. "I was probably living in New York or Paris or Santo Domingo when he paid for it. It has nothing to do with me." Gianni was exasperated, acted as if I didn't understand. He told me to go outside and give the phone to his father again. I did. Then Luca Iwanttomarryhim handed the phone to Trump of the Alley who stood with hands on hips supervising. The Norman was hacking away with his slipped-down jeans exposing quite an expanse of rear.

Trump of the Alley shouted into my phone and then he handed it back to me. Gianni said, "Good news, Clarissa! I have gotten the price down to only five hundred euros!"

My response was, "I'm not paying five hundred euros or one euro. I'm not going to talk about this anymore." I hung up then took a few quick photos of the scene. Trump was shouting at me, Luca, who spoke a bit of English, said very firmly, "You must pay." The cluster of interested bystanders had grown. "Devi pagare! Devi pagare!" You must pay! I went inside. Gianni called back and kept telling me that

I didn't own the line and that they would cut the line if I didn't pay. I was concerned as the exposed pipe made that look easy to do. Then Gianni said, "If you don't want to pay you can ask the water company to install a private line for you but that means digging up the street and it will cost thousands of euros." I was silent. "You can call the water company but they won't tell you how much and it could take months." I said nothing. Yes, anything here can take months. Gianni kept on. "Clarissa! Five hundred euros is better!" I said I was not going to pay.

I stepped outside. The crowd of men started shouting again. "Devi pagare! Devi pagare!"

Trump of the Alley wanted the phone again. I handed it over, hating him to touch it. He shouted at Gianni for a minute or two then gave the phone to Luca Iwanttomarryhim who shouted at Gianni for a minute or two. The phone came back to me. Gianni then shouted at me, "You have to pay him! Just pay him and all this will be over! He says you will never have any problems with the water after this! Pay him!"

"Devi pagare! Devi pagare!" insisted this Greek chorus in the alley. Blue sky, bright sun and this was all wrong.

I stood there, greatly outnumbered, and thought, one turn of the dial or knob or whatever and I'll have water and I can leave the Joli, I can live here, start my life here.

I told Luca I had to go to the bank. I told Gianni the same thing on the phone then hung up and went inside to get my bank card. Walking on via Roma, I kept thinking I don't want to do this. With every step, over and over again. I don't want to do this. I put my card in the ATM. Punched in international transaction and then the tab that said 500 euros. A message flashed on the screen. That amount was not allowed. I tried 400, then 350, then 300. Same message. I withdrew 250 euros then went to the next machine and tried. No, I could not withdraw a second 250 euros.

I walked back to via Padua and turned into my alley. It seems those men had nothing better to do than stand around in the sun for this drama. Before I handed over the money, I went inside and took a piece of typing paper and, in green ink, wrote: Ho ricevuto 250 euros from Clarissa McNair on Maggio 18, 2022, and here I drew a line for a signature. (I received 250 euros from Clarissa McNair on May 18, 2022)

I took it outside where I handed the paper and pen to Trump who signed it on the hood of a parked car. The signature was illegible; Luca Iwanttomarryhim took my pen and helpfully printed 'Di Lauro Luca" at the top of the page. Reluctantly, hating it, I gave the bills to Trump of the Alley and said my bank would not give me five hundred. "Domani," I said. Tomorrow. Trump was stuffing his shirt pocket. "Domani," he said gruffly. I did not know it then but HSBC not allowing me to have 500 euros would prove very beneficial.

I went inside and a few minutes later, Luca came in and said I had water but I had to pay the other 250 euros or the line would be cut. I looked at him and didn't answer. I trusted him. I trusted Gianni. Were they right about this when it felt so wrong?

I called Claudia Cardinale at the water company. No answer. I emailed her.

Then Michael, my lawyer in Rome called. I told him I couldn't send anything yet as the internet man was meant to come but never showed up. He suddenly said, "I read you bought a nightclub. That got me." That made me smile. "I was told it was a pizza parlor but I found out it was a Tunisian nightclub. I wondered why there was no pizza oven and now the weird lights make sense." Then I sighed and said I was having water problems with a demand for money. I filled him in and he erupted in "Bullshit! The oldest trick in the book! Don't pay anything! Don't give him a cent!" I said I already had.

I must reach Claudia Cardinale.

NON PAGA!

Claudia Cardinale called me the next morning and was vehement. "Non paga!" Don't pay! I told her I already had but they want more. She says if they ask for money again then call the police.

All my instincts were correct. I hung up and when I saw The Norman I told him I'd talked to the water company. He did not say anything. He had hacked out my wall but I noticed that he had been silent when the others were shouting at me to pay.

I was sitting at my desk beside the open mirrored door at midmorning when I saw Trump of the Alley standing outside smiling. The iron door was locked, of course. I suppose he was thinking about his next 250 euros. He is a comical figure, short, with his pants worn so high that the belt is under his armpits allowing his watermelon-huge stomach freedom. I kicked the door closed and he walked away.

Luca Iwanttomarryhim arrived and began to install the kitchen appliances. Later as he was passing me on his way to his truck I told him I was not paying the other 250. He said that the men were Mafia and I must pay. I exploded at him in Italian. "That's why there *is* a Mafia! Because people pay!" He stared at me with no words. I told him that I had been told if he asks again to call the police. It wasn't even four minutes later that Gianni called. The usually calm negotiator was shouting that I didn't understand, kept saying the same things all over again and that I *had* to pay. "You are calling the police and you will get my father in trouble!"

His father in trouble? I calmly said, "I never said I was going to call the police." More shouting. "You must pay!" Screaming! I said quietly, "Stop shouting. If you can't stop shouting you can hang up and call me back when you are in a better frame of mind." He was then shouting, "I'm not shouting!" Over and over again. Then he lowered his voice and said I didn't understand and I had to pay! Then he insisted I should ask the water company about the independent line. But this would cost thousands and mean a bricklayer and the water company would not know how much the real cost was." Pay these men! It is cheaper to *pay* them!"

I said I didn't want to talk about it anymore, said goodbye and hung up.

FIRST NIGHT AT LA TANA

At the Joli, I was down to one bag as I'd taken one or two at a time on the bus to La Tana. My last night at the hotel was Thursday, May 19th. It was bittersweet leaving for the last time. Danilo I saw every day at breakfast. Mariella was usually the maid who cleaned my room. Maria comes on the front desk in the afternoon but Friday was her day off so I'd stop in tomorrow and see her. She will love the newest chapter. I have been gone every day to be at La Tana at seven or eight so haven't seen Mariella often but I left her an envelope with money, a note of thanks and my card with my address. When I left for Christmas, I extended an envelope to her and she put her hands behind her back and shook her head. I insisted she take it.

I went to the stationery shop with Rosy and Diego where I like the dog so much. They scanned the property documents Michael needed and sent them off to Rome. I was in my old neighborhood so I walked to the grocery store which is just across the piazza from the Joli, the one I could see from my window. The young butcher wearing his trademark coppola was behind the counter behind the big glass case. He knows me. I asked if there were roast beef and he didn't understand me. An elderly woman, tiny, white-haired and masked, understood me. I tried saying it several ways then said it was meat from a cow (mucca) and he didn't seem to understand that either. I actually mooed a few times and then he thought I wanted cheese. The woman was trying to get him to understand and then a young woman came over and she said, in English, "oh, you want roast beef. They probably don't have it. It's too hot for roast beef." I told the young butcher I had bought it here two weeks ago. The three of us were all trying to break through to him as he stood in his long white apron and wool cap looking blank. Then a burly man came over and I swear he said it the exact same way we were all chorusing "roast beef" but he put all his fingers together, turned both hands with fingers facing up and at waist level moved them up and down as he said "Roast beef!" The butcher sighed with recognition and we three women started laughing. I did the same with my hands, all fingers together and then up and down motion and said, "Roast beef" and all five of us laughed.

Now I know how to say it with my fingers locked, with elbows bent and I also know May is too hot for roast beef in Palermo.

Luca had not yet put covers on any wall outlets so I couldn't put bookshelves in place or move furniture into position which meant I couldn't hang paintings. Bob, a friend in Paris, told me how easy it was so I went to the electric store, bought them, snapped them on. I can't hang up my clothes until I have closets and the armadio man said he will come on Wednesday but he has postponed several times then cancelled two firm appointments. I was a bit anxious to unpack suitcases as I was haunted by the idea of mildew.

Claudia Cardinale called me on Friday afternoon which was a surprise as I felt I was becoming a nuisance. Again we stammered to each other but the message was clear: if he demands money, call the police. I did ask that burning question: does he have control over my water? The answer is no.

Gianni called. "I am sorry for yesterday." I said, "Okay." He said that he was not mad at me. "But the men threatened to cut your line if you did not pay and he also said he wanted to gouge out your eyes and my father's eyes with his car key. These are bad men, Clarissa."

I said the dottoressa at the water company had called me just moments before.

Gianni immediately asked, "Is she in Palermo?" I told him I didn't want to discuss it any more. I knew that he would insinuate that if she weren't in Palermo she could not understand the situation. If she were in Rome, forget it. I did not want to defend her or her advice no matter where she was. I did not want to be badgered as if I were a stubborn child.

Michael wrote and said the PDF file with the lease had not come through. I took the bus back to my old neighborhood and Rosy scanned and sent the file again and did not charge me. Then Michael called me as I was walking back on via Roma and told me, "What you have means squat. It does not say that you own the property." I thought, that's wonderful. "Well, I paid money. A bank transfer for something." I sighed. "Actually, this is just perfect because if I don't own it, I don't have to worry about water anymore." I told him about the eye-gouging thing and he was confused as to who was who and I had to explain the identities of the gouger and that I was the gougee. Again, he insisted that I not pay them.

"How do I call the police here?" I asked as I stopped at a shop window to look at a spectacular green satin evening dress.

Michael wasn't sure how it was in Sicily. Everybody in Rome acted as if Sicily were a foreign country. Sirens wailed on via Roma as Michael explained that all my visa application documents would be translated into Italian, submitted to a magisterial court in Rome and then there would be a hearing but I don't have to be there. "You understand this could take six or seven months but we might be able to speed it up." The good news is that I have all the documentation and this pending action takes precedence over my having to leave every 90 days. I was elated. "I don't care if it takes a year if I don't have to go into exile." He said, "The Italian consulate in New York is notorious for this stuff. Everyone knows that." I hung up with Michael then wrote the notary about that legal document for La Tana. I smiled thinking of all our giggling on the phone and all that consternation over the uncashable check.

My first bubble bath at La Tana was that night. I watched the water pour from the gleaming steel faucet and told myself to clear my mind, to think of nothing. Sublime. I love the tub and the high sink and I laugh thinking of Luca being ashamed. There was a barking dog for awhile. My cortile could not be uglier with each story having an air conditioning unit and pipes sticking out. The occasional clothes line is actually pretty in comparison. A situation of Don't Look Up. I'll get an umbrella to put out there and yank anyone under it immediately but maybe it's easier to drink ourselves blind.

Happy to be in my French sleigh bed for the first time since last September 6th. The iron doors in front were always locked but now and every night I pulled the tall Thai screen behind the mirrored doors so that no one could see in. The iron door in back opening onto the cortile was locked but I left the mirrored one open for fresh air all night. And for the barking dog. And for Whitney Houston. Someone was getting over a bad love affair. "I-I-I-I will alwaaaaays love youuuuuu . . . ." again and again.

The next morning I wakened and realized I was in my own bed which had crossed the Atlantic plus the Straits of Messina. I was now living in La Tana. In Palermo. In Sicily. In Italy. Doing my sit ups, I said aloud, "I did it."

That day was much the same: Luca Iwanttomarryhim didn't come, The Norman wanted money, Trump of the Alley banged on my door and wanted money and Whitney Houston wailed. But I had water, I lived here, I felt renewed.

RANTING IN THE ALLEY

That evening, I called Sarah, a friend I met in Rome in 2015, but it's as if we have known each other for years and years. I told her about the threats as I talked in the alley for better phone reception. "That horrid man was at my door this morning and demanded his 250 euros! I just kicked the mirrored door closed so I could see him but he couldn't see me." I stopped and shook my head. "And how am I supposed to know the word for 'gouge?' I mean, I know eyes but cavare? Nobody learning Italian knows that! Throwing away 250 euros to Trump of the Alley who wants to gouge out my eyes, the cracked marble because of the silly toilet paper holder holes, the armadio men may not even exist so I can never hang up my mildewed clothes, the internet man calling to say he is not coming as he was due to arrive at that moment. He said, 'C'e un problema.' I think that unless you are dead there is not a problem. Get over here and give me internet!" Sarah was laughing. I was explosively frustrated. "AND with all of this I am about to pay this lawyer in Rome 2,500 euros because I want to stay here!" It was so good to laugh. I went on. "Gianni keeps saying that I have used the best material and that everything will last without repair for at least 25 years. Why do I care? Am *I* going to last that long?" Laughing, Sarah said "My father would say 'let my heirs deal with it!" We both giggle when I ask, "Will I outlive my bathtub?"

Sarah had a good plan: if Trump comes to me for money I will say let's go to the water company together. I will tell him to take his receipt for the work he supposedly paid for and his carte d'identita and we will go together. To Claudia Cardinale. But, of course, he won't go. A scam. It does not matter if he paid or what he paid. I was living in Beverly Hills or Cyprus or who knows where at the time and I have nothing to do with it. Sarah said, "Ask him what his mother would think." I found that quite wonderful and hilarious, too, after the car key threat. What would his mother think of that? Unless, of course, she is tougher than he is and taught him all he knows.

I was living in La Tana. That phone conversation in the alley was very good for me. I felt so free describing the situation without inhibition, speaking English for a change, communicating with a kindred spirit. Sarah said that she really wanted to have a place on the southern coast of Turkey and I asked, "Oh, do you think it's safe?" and we started laughing again.

Maybe years from now, (when my bathtub is still in excellent condition) I'll be slowly walking in this alley with a white cane and a chihuahua seeing-eye dog and people will whisper, "There's that stupid American who wouldn't pay for water."

THE WOMAN FROM FRANCE

I sliced open more boxes but it seemed futile as there was no place to put what I unpacked. At least my desk was in order and I'd found sheets and towels. One morning a young French woman stopped at my door. Her little dog sniffed and we talked. I'd been looking through a box and we'd chatted through the bars. Monique spoke English and was writing a screenplay. We agreed to go out for a drink and met again in the late afternoon.

Her favorite place was a short walk away; high stools were set out in an alley. Half French and half American, I guessed she was late twenties, early thirties. She said it had been an awful day as her scooter was stolen. I commiserated.

She told me she wanted to write, has been in Palermo for a few months; I told her I'd come from New York on one of the first flights allowed after the worst of COVID.

"COVID! I faint once in awhile, it's not serious," she said with a little hand gesture. She pulled her little dog closer to our table. "I was in Paris last year and fainted and hit my head. Someone took me to a hospital just to be sure I was okay. Right away they wanted me to take the test and I refused to take the test."

I asked, "Why?"

"It ees my right," she said in her heavy French accent. "I told them I felt fine." She took a sip of wine and continued. "They tied me to a bed and put a diaper on me for three days."

I did not say one word. Later she said something about how bad-tempered and rude the nurses were!

I thought of how New Yorkers beat pots and pans on their balconies and applauded out their windows cheering the exhausted nurses and doctors after their shifts. "They worked so hard. The doctors and nurses. It was terrible in New York City."

"Do you believe it?" she asked.

"Believe what?"

"In COVID. The fake news. The fake statistics. All those people dying of other things . . ."

I stared at her in shock. This well-spoken young woman. I described the huge trucks parked on New York City streets with the generators humming day and night to keep the corpses cold because the funeral homes were overwhelmed. The gravediggers were overwhelmed. It was like talking to a four-year old. "I didn't know anything about that," she twittered. "I was living outside Paris."

Outside Paris but not on the moon. I took a deep breath and said, "So, yes. I believe in COVID. My cousin died of it." I couldn't tell if she believed me or not.

But it was her *right* to refuse a test and to go out and possibly infect people. I didn't pursue it but I felt a sense of outrage. We did talk about writing and her work. She teaches "marketing by the hour" on Zoom for private clients. I encouraged her to write and she kept thanking me. She wants to do a screenplay on Peggy Guggenheim which is a super idea and I told her to *do* it. Monique said she loves Palermo because it's so "authentic."

Yeah, try living in Alley of the Gardenia. You'll get authentic. Her French-accented "It ees my right," rings in my ears. I won't see her again.

LIFE IN THE ALLEY

In days to come I'd see men watching my doorway when I came out and then they'd punch in a number and say a word or two on their cell all the while staring at me. Sometimes it was a Pizzeria Triplet but there were others, too. Of course, Trump of the Alley had pals. They were exactly like the spotters, the lookouts, on Canal Street when I was doing undercover work to catch counterfeiters. I told myself not to be paranoid but wondered what these Palermo spotters might be scheming.

Today I left La Tana at about one after waiting since eight—that's five hours—for the fabbro/blacksmith. He did not come and didn't answer his phone. I had told him I would pay him 200 euros for changing the glass he had told me he was not charging me for. I hated the idea. He told Gianni the same untrue story. I had to pay as maybe he was the only blacksmith in Palermo or even on the entire island. I remembered my days at the Joli trying to find one. Walking all over town to addresses with locked doors, calling phone numbers that never answered or were no longer in service. I hoped bars on the little bathroom windows and on the one kitchen window would be the final thing I ever needed from a fabbro.

I was in my old neighborhood near the Joli when my phone rang and a woman said she was la postina and she had a package for me. I was wondering how she had gotten my number and was she at La Tana and was it normal to do this?

I wanted to tell her to push it through the bars but didn't know the word for bars. I must look that up for the fabbro, I thought. La postina said that my neighbor at number two named Fatima would take it.

Later I went across the alley to the door which was usually only a piece of hanging cloth and called for Fatima. She put her laundry in the alley to dry so I knew she had children. Petite, her hair was covered and she usually wore a long dress. Handing me two small packages, she smiled but kept speaking Arabic on the phone. I could see one room with a bare electric bulb hanging from the ceiling. Like my place, like all the others, it was without side windows. I walked the twenty feet to La Tana with the hair bands I'd ordered from Hong Kong. I got a little crazy online in London.

Fatima and I progressed from the smile to the nod to the ciao. Later, she told me she was from Morocco, has been in Palermo twelve years. I would later dub her husband Casablanca. Motioning towards the motorcycle shop about twenty feet away I understood that he works there with the tall, slender man I call Nigeria and with Paolo, who owns the shop. Paolo rarely said buongiorno. I thought of him as bad-tempered and knew he could get mad in three languages: Italian, French and Arabic. He drove a grey Peugeot which I found amusing. It was so *French*.

I read somewhere that we don't make architecture –that it makes us. The alleys are lined with sand-colored buildings, three and four stories tall; colorful laundry hangs like flags overhead. Often a basket on a rope is pulled up with a few groceries. Long conversations are conducted from those same balconies with friends in the street, people chat in doorways. The Palermitani never stop talking.

Motorcycles, bicycles, women in black with faces covered, strollers with babies, the African women in their brightly colored print dresses and turbans making them over six feet tall, the delicate, small-boned Bangladeshi women in saris of such beauty, the men in pillbox hats all parade past me as I sit at my desk.

The alleys are alive.

I never worried about the cats. In the boarded-up doorway of an empty building there was an official-looking, printed sign which warned that it was illegal to leave food there but the two bearded drug-dealer brothers did. Directly below this sign was a row of four little saucers for the pretty grey and white kittens who usually sprawled languidly beside a nearby Fiat.

From noon on, the rich scent of cooking was in the air. Kids played futbol in the late afternoon. At about five, one heard the mournful goodbye blast of a horn that signaled a ship leaving port. The cobalt sea was right there, you could smell it on the wind. Men played cards, drank beer and gossiped at a red table in the next alley. In the evenings there was often music.

• • •

The days here gave meaning to the word perfection. Bright sun, clear skies, a temperature in the mid-seventies Fahrenheit and a cool breeze most of the time. I still couldn't wear a dress because my legs were so banged up but I kicked off my boots for high-heeled sandals.

I was on the via Roma bus two round trips today. After four minutes of waiting for the bus, anyone standing there shrugs in annoyance, patience wearing thin. The Palermitani would be marching on

City Hall with torches if they ever had to wait for a bus in Manhattan.

When the bus comes into view, everyone masks up. No exceptions, no complaints. The Sicilians do things differently. The back doors have the arrows for entering and the middle doors say 'non entrada' but the back doors often don't open so everyone gets on the ones that are meant as exits. Today I was the only person at the back door and had to run to the middle one—everyone else *knows* the situation.

This bus was crowded and a well-upholstered woman in black with a shopping cart was last to get on. She was very plump and having trouble. One man yelled something and grabbed her cart. It was lifted onto the bus. Then about 10 arms reached out to pull her aboard. She grabbed hands and hands grabbed her and she was hoisted up and in. I felt we'd just landed a tarpon. Someone yelled at the driver to go, the doors snapped shut and the bus belched forward on via Roma.

People I found so well-mannered: offering seats, standing up, scusa scusa scusa. A young skinny African in a white pillbox, masked, offered his seat to a tiny white-haired, masked Sicilian woman and she reached up to put her hand on his shoulder and told him what a very nice person he was but she was getting off at the next stop. All three of us were smiling behind our masks.

I don't think we Anglo Saxons would ever touch a stranger in that way. I was lucky to witness that little scene.

If I sit next to a woman and like her earrings and I tell her then before I know it she has her phone out and I am shown photos and hear about every single member of her family at the big Easter lunch. If I ask—in what I think is a quiet voice—about a stop or a street, not only will that person tell me but the person next to them will tell me and people will turn in their seats and give me their opinion of the location. At least five fellow passengers would become involved. Then someone may get off the bus with me and walk me to the corner and explain about crossing the street. I am foreign and everyone is determined to take care of me.

Another moment yesterday: a pretty girl with black hair and tight jeans leaning over the side mirror of a parked motorcycle checking her lipstick. I've done that. This is a town of motorcycles. Twenty of them line the curb in front of Lidl's. The storage rooms across the alley are filled with them. Sometimes I see a motorcycle driven by a man with a woman behind him and three kids behind her. Holding on, packed in a row, on their way like an entire family of possums crossing a country road in Mississippi.

THE BLACKSMITH'S HEAD

The jockey-sized blacksmith arrived at last after days of not showing up and insisted I needed two bars and not one on each window. There were two bathroom windows and one kitchen window. I said one bar was okay because the space was so small. So we discussed whether or not our heads were a typical size. The space was 45 centimeters across and one center bar would mean 23 centimeters for a thief's head to fit through. Then you turn, said the tiny blacksmith, and you can get your shoulders through. I surrendered, thinking of a child being hoisted up and inside to unlock a door. Okay, we will have two vertical bars on each window not one. He gave me a price of half of what he quoted a few months ago for one bar. It seems it's all according to the mood of the moment here. Or maybe phases of the moon?

ANOTHER MEETING WITH THE HAWK

Late one afternoon I met with the Hawk again. We sat at the same corner table watching the front door of the little caffè. The tea wasn't up to her standards so she ordered prosecco like me. "How was your exile?" she asked and then added, "I don't know if you can call it exile, actually. Exile is being sent from your own country."

I countered immediately. "But now this is my country. Everything I own came over on that boat and I have no other address."

She blinked. "You are a very brave person."

The flutes were put before us. "Exile was insane. I was all set to catch the 2:30 a.m. ferry to Tunis on Monday night which was day 90 of my time in the Schengen but I met this Anglican nun on Sunday afternoon who offered me her house in Cambridge except it wasn't in Cambridge but in the middle of nowhere and I arrived and the men living there told me it wasn't even her house and she had cheated everyone for miles around and sometimes the sheriff came looking for her and so then I realized she was a con artist and also a lesbian possibly attracted to me and I ended up in London."

Hawk burst out laughing. "A lesbian, con artist, Anglican nun?"

I nodded. "Exactly. A friend offered me a room in a house in Golders Green and I escaped The House in the Middle of Nowhere before the electricity was turned off."

Hawk shook her head, smiling. "I was thinking the other day of how much the Sparrows are missing by not giving you a chance."

"And I was thinking of the women you described, your friends, and how you all came here decades ago and ran households, raised children . . ." I sighed. "I admire that."

"The only person I might like is Diana. She seems reasonable."

"Not a Sparrow," nodded Hawk.

"I had prosecco with Thomas the evening before last. It kills me not to be able to tell him he has an ally as I could tell he is having a tough time." Hawk started to protest but I stopped her. "Don't worry. I won't tell him."

Hawk took a sip of prosecco. "Thomas is dealing with old problems and new ones. The tax man is interested in the church. My understanding is that the taxes weren't paid for years." She sighed. "Several years. There should be money to pay the taxes as the church owns various properties and should be getting quite a good income from these but there seems to be no money. Things like rent have been casually decided ages back and no one can find anything in writing." She continued. "When money is involved, it all seems murky but lots of things are simply stupid. For instance," she frowned. "A man in the church said he would renovate one of the apartments if he could live in it while the work was being done. Well, the work has not been done and he is living rent-free." I listened as she went on. "The organist is, well, not to put too fine a point on it, he is terrible and he doesn't even use the pedals. He is paid nearly twice the fee every Sunday that a professional musician would get but 'he's family' so they want to keep overpaying him. Almost the entire collection every Sunday goes to him. The gardener was the same. Father Thomas did eliminate him over cries of protest."

"A gardener? To take care of those potted shrubs and the few trees in the back?"

Hawk nodded her head. "Ridiculous. With all us English women gardeners!" She went on. "And then there is the council. Thomas told us, when we finally did meet, that the term is to be for three years. One member has been on the council for twenty-three!"

I rolled my eyes as she continued. "Father Thomas requested the minutes of the last year's council meetings." She took a sip of prosecco as if it might give her strength to continue. "They don't exist. No one wrote anything down!"

"What can we do? My first idea is to find allies. You're undercover, of course, but others. The handful of Italians are always nice to me. I think they like Thomas."

"They do. And that's a good idea. But we must wait until the next election which is months away."

I made a face. "If Thomas could stick it out . . ."

Hawk said grimly, "If Thomas could stick it out for five years half of the Sparrows would have fallen off their perches."

I laughed then was serious. "I went to the lunch for the Lutheran minister from Sweden last Saturday and I did not see one English person there. I felt terrible for Thomas because he invited her to come, they went to Lampedusa to see the situation there with the refugees and I know he wanted a good turnout. I noticed the same thing at church the next day, Sunday."

Hawk nodded. "I wanted to go to support him. The Sparrows all decided not to go. I couldn't without being seen as on the other side." She sipped prosecco and said, "But you don't know the background. Thomas said the least we could do was pay her plane fare to come and he put it on his credit card. But the money to reimburse him was—" She frowned. "It was in cash at home with someone. They don't even have a bank account in Palermo for the church."

"You are kidding!"

"There is a safe but this woman took the money home—she is big on control—and then there was a discussion about the fare." I was breathless as she continued. "This same Sparrow said, oh, alright, I guess we will pay for the plane fare but that means there will only be 34 euros left."

I sank back in my chair. "I had no idea it was this bad. He is the vicar, the capo! Why does he have to ask someone for the money! This is all crazy. Does she keep it under her mattress?" I gulped for air. "I know he has the apartment but he told me his salary and, really, it's pitiful."

"And," said Hawk, "It's given to him every month in cash in a white envelope!"

I shook my head. "Italians treat avoiding taxes as a national sport but these women are *English*."

Hawk said. "This church in Palermo has gone rogue."

"In the business world, this is corporate malfeasance. Cash in an envelope?" I stopped. "But isn't he paid by London?"

"No, this parish supports itself. No money from anywhere else." She paused. "Actually, a surviving member of the Whitaker family gives ten thousand euros every year. They built the church in 1875."

I thought, that's not a lot of money to maintain the building, pay Thomas, whatever.

We ended our talk with the idea of seeking out possible allies for Thomas and then persuading them to consider being on the council. "The way it's been going for years and years is that they nominate each another and then they all vote for each other."

We were standing now, leaving money on the table. I waited as we always left separately. In the doorway, Hawk turned to me and said, "Things have to change."

I walked home thinking of Hawk and the church. There were about 35 members but not all of them came on Sundays and some said they'd never come as long as Thomas was vicar. There were only about a hundred Anglicans on the entire island. I turned into my alley where Fatima called to me and waved an envelope. I smiled, thanked her and then I sighed. The postino or postina (often different ones) has never put anything in my mailbox and I have a very good-looking mailbox.

PROSECCO WITH THOMAS AND THE VIGILI DEL FUOCO

Thomas texted about meeting at Spinnato's for prosecco. I needed these debriefings and I think he needed them, too. We met at half past six and sat at a little table outside. As usual we ordered a bottle which arrived with nuts, tiny ham sandwiches and potato chips. "How are you?" I demanded as we leaned back in our chairs and took our first sips. Thomas shook his head. "I can't talk about the church. I can't."

Poor Thomas. He had no idea I was so au courant. "Well," I said. "I have had a bit of drama in my life."

"More drama?" he grinned.

"It is horribly embarrassing but I'll tell you if you never tell another soul. Actually, dozens of people witnessed this so I guess it doesn't matter who else knows."

"Now you have to tell me!"

I sighed. "Yesterday morning I got up and thank God I got dressed and walked to my front door which was jammed with flattened cardboard boxes for the recycling place. They were between the iron door and the glass door. There was a loud CLICK behind me. The glass door had swung closed and I was now locked in between it and the door with the iron bars."

Thomas started laughing.

"I couldn't believe it. The outside iron door was locked, of course, from the night before and the key was inside. I had no phone and –"

Thomas interrupted. "But that space between the doors is what? About a foot?"

"About that," I nodded. "And it was packed full of dozens of flattened cardboard boxes. I stood there, it was standing room only, hands clutching the bars like a forlorn little monkey."

Thomas was smiling. "What time was this?"

"Seven o'clock." I sipped prosecco. "I saw Paolo, the Moroccan, getting into his car about eight meters away and called him over and he told me in Italian that a locksmith opened at half past eight and said he was late and just left me there."

Thomas was laughing.

"Anyway, there was barely enough room to sit down on a piece of cardboard with my knees under my chin and I told myself everything was fine. But then I thought, I can't reach the fabbro because I don't even know his last name and he doesn't use email so probably isn't listed online anyway. I was helpless without a phone and even if I borrowed one I didn't know anybody's number. Remember when we used to?"

"How long were you like that?" insisted Thomas, grinning.

"I saw several women in long robes go past clutching the hands of children. School. Women facing straight ahead and kids turning to stare at me. Time was passing. Luca Iwanttomarryhim and Gianni had promised to come even though they promised yesterday and didn't come and I was thinking, IF they come, it won't be until after 11. The two Giuseppes finished their work long ago so they weren't coming. The Norman would have the fabbro's number but he probably won't come even though he is meant to. Then I realized today was the day for appointment #3 for the internet man coming at 8:30 and if I were locked in here, he would just go away and I would have to make another appointment a week from now. I stood up, clutching the bars feeling pretty tense."

"Is this the embarrassing part?" chortled Thomas.

"No," I said. "It's coming. I told myself that the locksmith would come and free me and to look on the bright side. First, I was not naked. I've been sleeping naked because I've been unable to find even one nightgown but they'll turn up. I was dressed. Second, nothing was on the stove as every time I got to Lidl's I forget the olive oil until I'm in the middle of a very long line at the checkout. So I haven't made popcorn even once."

"A triumph of sorts," said Thomas. "Not naked, not hungry." He refilled our flutes.

"Awhile later when I was sitting down again with my knees under my chin, I saw this skinny man with a sleeveless red T-shirt, tiny beard, glasses, and arms full of tattoos walk past lighting a cigarette. I called out to him and he turned and came over. Ugo found the situation interesting. I told him about the Moroccan and the locksmith. He punched in a number and kept repeating, in Italian, one thing I understood which was 'She is a prisoner. She is a prisoner.' He hung up. He'd called the police and the police were sending the fire department!"

Thomas was laughing, I was cringing at the memory.

"This man—Ugo—was somebody from the next alley. We chatted. I had no choice. He came down to my level, squatting on his haunches, smoking and talking. At one point, he left and came back and handed me coffee through the bars. I said, no thanks, so he drank it. I worried about the time and he said they would come but it was not urgente. Not to him. Ugo showed me a photo of his twenty-year old daughter who was movie-star gorgeous then we went through all the family photos on his phone. Birthday parties, graduations, weddings, and at least the past four Christmases with me oohing and ahhing and saying 'bella' about 79 times."

Thomas was enjoying this.

"I was panicky about the internet appointment. A man in a navy blue polo shirt and a clipboard arrived. Internet man! On time, unbelievable! He looked at me and laughed. Ugo told him the fire department was coming. At that moment, a huge red fire truck roared to a stop at the end of the alley. Too big to get in. Mortified I watched at least ten men in full regalia—slickers, boots, big hats, hatchets—dramatically leap from the truck. Ugo started yelling, "Solamente un uomo! Un uomo!" Only one man! One man!

Thomas had his head thrown back, laughing. I could see all his perfect teeth.

"Suddenly I was facing all these Palermo firemen announcing that they were the vigili del fuoco. There I was—standing up, clutching the bars, peering out. One asked if he could bring me a panino and they all chuckled. I explained how it had happened. I felt so stupid but they all said oh, no, you're not stupid. Staring through the bars at those faces, I was the human equivalent of a cat stuck in a tree. I told them the fabbro was coming on Friday and I was going to tell him that this door was too dangerous to lock automatically."

Thomas was still laughing.

"I pictured fire and red-hot ashes as they blasted away my locks and wondered if they'd give me some protective gear to wear against the sparks. An asbestos suit or something like you have at the dentist office when you have x-rays. A muscular arm reached through the bars with a thin black piece of plastic about 20 inches by 10. He put it between the door frame and the door and tried to pull it down, the way people do in the movies when they open doors with credit cards. Again and again. One asked if he could touch me and positioned my sandalled foot to push against the door. A few of the firemen were starting to take the iron door off the hinges but I told them that was not important because opening the glass inner door meant I could get the key to the iron door. The plastic sheet was not quite working so one of the firemen climbed up the iron door over the head of the man using the sheet and reached in with a file. He pried open the top as the plastic sheet suddenly moved the lock and my door sprang open! At this point there were at least a dozen people in the alley behind the firemen and everyone "ahhhed" as one. I ran in for the keys and unlocked the iron door."

"They actually opened it with that plastic sheet?" asked Thomas.

"Yes! They were magnificent!"

"Did you have to pay them for this rescue?"

"No, they wrote down my name and took a photo of my passport. I wanted to call them my heroes but I didn't know the word. They left. I felt so lucky. No charge, no damage to the doors and I was liberated."

Thomas and I toasted the fire department of Palermo. "They were so sweet. Kept telling me I wasn't stupid." I leaned back in my chair and looked at the bright blue sky. "The internet guy watched the whole thing. Then he started work and took forever. On a ladder. Wires across the alley. Holes drilled over my front door. I expected Trump of the Alley to appear and demand 800 euros for the internet. Done. I have internet!"

"Finally," sighed Thomas.

I sipped prosecco. "It was just ten o'clock in the morning and I was exhausted. The tension, the firemen, the—"

Thomas said, "I'm finding everyone exhausting." His handsome face looked tired. He was my best friend in Palermo. On the entire island. He was staring off into space. I couldn't betray the Hawk but longed for him to realize that he had an ally.

I broke the silence. "How can I help?"

"You can keep coming on Sundays and you can entertain me with stories about the Palermo fire department."

"Happily," I said.

He looked at me. "This is my first church. I've assisted in Paris, in Rome, all over but nothing prepared me for Palermo."

"That church is so lucky to have you." He didn't say anything. A woman's laughter rang out from a nearby table.

As one, we changed the subject to U.S. politics, both of us looking forward to the January 6 hearings. Of the same mind, politically, we could talk for hours and we did. The prosecco vanished as did the appetizers. Later, walking towards via Roma, I said, "We are both so new here. It's another world."

He responded. "Alien. Populated by aliens we Anglo-Saxons struggle to understand."

I nodded. "But look at that sky. And the air. Sometimes it's so perfect it reminds me of Beverly Hills. Except I hated it." I shook my head. "The year I was there the men were having calf implants and everyone talked incessantly about their cholesterol."

"Cholesterol? Mine is high!"

I said, "I have no idea what mine is."

"And I was told it's linked to drinking."

"No, it can't be!"

"Yes, it is," said Thomas. "And this is a problem as we like to drink." We ambled down via Roma in the spring twilight discussing cholesterol.

KINDNESS AND CORRUPTION

I had a terrible time finding the salon to have my legs waxed yesterday as the correct street number was a wrecked building shrouded in dusty sheets of plastic. A man with TIM (the phone company) written on his shirt took mercy on me and actually called the salon, got directions and delivered me to the front door as if I were a lost child. Such kindness. I am always amazed at how much *time* people will take to help me. As if they have no appointments, no watches, no reason to do anything but deal with this pathetic foreigner. The people of Palermo take care of me.

The two women at the salon were tittering, giggling. I was told later that when I thought I said I was embarrassed by all the mosquito bites on my legs I had actually told them that gypsies were biting me every night. The words for gypsy and mosquito are very similar.

I had a few words that I hesitated over. Cane means dog, carne means meat. I speak to all the dogs I see and when I want to ask what kind of dog it is I am afraid I often say what kind of meat. The owner smiles and tells me and I walk away thinking, oh, no! Did I screw that up again? And, of course, there is ice which is ghiaccio. Sometimes late in the afternoon, after waiting all day for workers who never came, I'd walk over to via Maqueda and sit in a lovely courtyard on a lime green divan and order a Coke Zero. The waiter would smile and ask if I wanted ghiaccio. The first time I had no idea what that was but nodded and said, per favore. I thought, yes, a handsome South American cowboy in a big hat is just what I need right now.

It's not only speaking, it's being careful with spelling. I sent out Happy New Year greetings by writing 'Felice Nuovo Ano' which actually means 'happy new anus.' Year has a double n. I was close.

My favorite word is piano. It means the floor as in piano secondo. It means the instrument and it means slowly or softly. I said piano piano every day, all the time. Best of all, it means plan. When I have a piano, I'm okay. My other favorite word is dappertutto which is adorable and means everywhere. I worked this into conversations whenever I possibly could.

The closets were to come today. I ordered them in January and this is the third appointment. But the armadio men cancelled half an hour before they were due to arrive. Something about traffic. They are coming tomorrow. They promised yet again. Seven o'clock. I hope. I wish. I wonder.

Gianni wrote in WhatsApp: "Your neighbor keeps calling me and asking for the 250 euros."

Trump of the Alley? "How did he get your number?" I wrote back.

Gianni wrote that he told that man to contact him if he had "any problems with Clarissa."

What? Because Gianni speaks English and could convince me?

I wrote back on WA that it didn't involve him and to hang up the phone. He wrote and asked if I had ordered an independent water line because "they will turn off the water sooner or later." I wrote that it didn't concern him and he answered with, "They will surely come tomorrow when my father is there."

I was up and dressed by six and the armadio men arrived at 06:45 with huge pieces of lumber. Mount New York had to be rearranged to allow them to set up equipment but they were very careful moving things and very cheerful. The Norman had said he'd come at 10 and I hoped the armadio men would be finished. The Norman didn't come, Luca and Gianni didn't come and the armadio men soldiered on.

At noon, with my iron doors wide open and the mirrored ones, too, there stood Trump of the Alley with trousers pulled up to his armpits. If he didn't have arms that belt would be a necklace. A Sicilian Mickey Rooney. He shouted and I ignored him until Gabriele, one of the armadio men, told me someone was calling me. I stood in the doorway as he demanded money or he would cut the water off. I said I'd talked to the water company who said non paga/don't pay. I had talked to my avocat/lawyer who said non paga. He was interrupting me, shouting that they didn't matter. He said he paid for the pipe, owned the water. Behind him stood Gabriele with raised eyebrows as if to say 'don't pay him.' I said I wanted to look at his fattura/bill and he shouted there wasn't one and to give him 250 euros.

He ranted on. I was very pleased with my Italian and said we should go to the water company together and talk to them. No! He wanted his money or I would have no water. He left in a snit. Matteo was listening, holding a hammer in one hand, as Gabriele filled him in. I had to act out the car keys threat and they were mutually horrified. They said they'd be gone for one hour for lunch and to close and lock the door. I did.

The armadio men were terribly nice, cleaned up at about four o'clock and promised to come tomorrow to finish. I was delighted. In twenty-four hours I could hang up my clothes!

After they left, I was talking to Victor, my friend in Boston, on Skype when one of the Pizzeria Triplets called to me from the front door so I said I had to hang up. Unfortunately, a son of Trump of the Alley, The Enforcer, lives upstairs. He and the two other look-alikes whose names I did not know comprise the Pizzeria Triplets. They'd been so friendly and had introduced themselves that first day and then The Enforcer had come back wanting to buy La Tana. On the other side of the iron bars, The Enforcer was not shouting this time. He seemed to be on my side, wanted to be my friend. Finally, I understood: I was not to give any money to his father. I was to give him the money instead.

I didn't understand some of what The Enforcer was saying and called Victor who speaks fluent Italian back. I held my laptop up to face level and he listened in Boston as The Enforcer, in the alley peering through the bars, ranted on. Occasionally he would suddenly stop and say, "Hai capito?" and my friend was understanding very well. The Enforcer left me, commanding in a loud voice, tomorrow you pay! You tell me yes or no!

Of course, I was going to the police. I told Victor I'd already written and translated my esposto (a statement of events, a complaint) with Michael's additions and was ready to hop the 101 on via Roma and go to the stationery store and have it printed. Then I would go to the police.

HOW DO YOU SAY 'GOUGE' IN ITALIAN?

The next day the armadio men arrived at half past seven as promised. I liked Matteo and Gabriele and told them to call me if they had to, for any reason, but I'd be out for an hour. At the cartoleria/stationery store, I petted the little dog, Rosy printed out my document and then I walked to the police station at 194 via Roma.

All the way there I thought, am I doing the right thing? There are plenty of ways to make my life miserable if everyone thinks I am wrong. For instance, a few days ago water was dripping from the terrace above mine onto my cortile with a great splashing noise. I went out and a woman who must be The Enforcer's wife peered over her railing down at me. I said "Acqua!" and she said something. Maybe she was watering plants. Today it happened again except this time it came down on books and a chair covered in plastic. On purpose?

La polizia. Huge doors surrounded by stained glass of many colors. I was buzzed in. A sentry box for a guard or concierge was well-lit but with no person. A poster of a man and woman kissing covered the back wall of the phone-booth sized structure. Pictures of Jesus were taped up and there were plastic flowers and a plump, colorfully patterned seat cushion. Just no person. Did not look very police-stationy at all. A man came in behind me and said it was the second floor. Did I look like a person here to see the police? I took the elevator and then walked into a waiting room with about eight people sitting there. One man had a black eye. It felt like a doctor's waiting room but without a coffee table or magazines. A woman at a desk behind glass gestured to me. I told her I wanted to make an esposto and she nodded. Wanted to know what it was about. I started to tell her about the water but when I got to the minaccia/threat I forgot the word for gouge so I turned and asked if anyone spoke English. An African said, "A little" but he didn't know the word for gouge either so I acted it out which entirely horrified everyone. A ruffle of distress swept the waiting room. The woman asked to see the document for my house and when I didn't have it said to come tomorrow.

Back at La Tana, the armadio men had carefully rearranged boxes of Mount New York; I apologized for the confusion. At one point, Gabriele asked where I was from and I mentioned NYC and his voice went soft. It is my dream, he said. I said I liked Palermo very much and we went into a sort of back and forth describing people here as warm-hearted and generous. I said New York City was quite liberal in many ways. Then he said, yes, the people here have open hearts, he grinned, but closed minds.

SO MANY SECRETS

As I moved papers and files in the chaos that was my desk, I wondered if I were doing the right thing to rat out Trump of the Alley and The Enforcer. I had to find the deed to La Tana first. I didn't want the Pizzeria Triplets or anyone as enemies but were they really 'friends' if they extorted me for money? They will ask again, Victor in Boston and I agreed. Next time it will be more and it will never stop. How many men would split the money? How many men were watching me? This is the dirty underbelly of the Alley of the Gardenia.

At least twice a day I saw Luciano or someone opening the padlock on the church door and going in then coming out. Luciano lives in a four-story building on the other side of the church on my side of the alley. It's a short alley and his building and La Tana are the only ones not counting the church. On the opposite side of the alley which is about fourteen feet wide are three storage rooms full of motorcycles. I stood in the church doorway, peered into the gloom and saw three motorcycles parked right in front of the altar as though the Christ figure were looking down and blessing them. Felliniesque. Yesterday the door was open and Luciano was pushing a wheelbarrow full of lumber and bricks in. That church is a thousand years old and one would imagine it to be a place of serenity but it's not. I am unsure what goes on in there but it sees a lot of action. The church has secrets. The alley has secrets.

SMILING, LYING.

The fabbro/blacksmith finally came and put the arched iron band above my front door. I handed him the star I'd painted green and he centered it. Then he changed the door so it would never lock automatically again. I'd paid for everything but that adjustment and he said," No charge." Just like that, in English. I repeated, "No charge." It was exactly the same scene as January about the glass. We looked at each other, shook hands and then he laughed and I managed a tight, humorless smile. He had said no charge for the glass in the cortile door then lied about it and he knew that I knew it.

A PEACH ON A BEACH and MORE LIES

I was on the bus at quarter of seven and in the water at seven-fifteen. Another glorious morning eating a peach on a beach. All else disappeared for me. That moment, that strip of silvery-blue, those ships like toys sitting on the straight string of a horizon—I want to recreate and repeat that moment again and again in my mind. I wish I could bottle it and take a sip when dealing with those men.

Lying in the sun, I couldn't help thinking of Gianni. I had trusted him so much to do the right thing. That first time he and his girlfriend had come to the Joli to deal with the account for electricity I gave him 200 euros as he had guided me through the sale with no compensation. I appreciated his help very much and asked if he worked for his father as liaison because he spoke English and he said 'yes.' I did not want to feel I was asking for favors. He understood but weeks later told me I owed him a percentage of The Norman's fee. I was very surprised and told him so. He claimed he told me that in the beginning but he had not. I looked him in the face and said that, as a journalist, I took notes all the time. He hesitated and then confessed he hadn't told me, he said he had forgotten. I paid him but emphasized if he wanted American clients then this must be in writing on day one. Weeks before, at his request, I had written a letter that he could send to realtors offering to help English-speaking foreigners navigate buying and renovating property in Sicily. Happily, he reported that within a day he had two clients because of my letter. But now? I was sorry I'd written it.

I wrote Gianni an email though we usually did WhatsApp and said that I wanted an invoice for the E 400 he had asked for on such and such a date as a percentage of The Norman's fee. I also wanted an invoice on letterhead stationery from the architectural firm I'd paid and also the work product, blueprints, whatever.

His response was to call me and angrily shout, "Are you accusing me of stealing the money?"

I said, "I am not accusing you of anything. I am a client asking for invoices." He hung up then wrote back that he didn't have them, he had nothing to do with the architect as she is the sister of Giovanni. He is the man I call The Norman. Then he called and yelled at me, asking if I were accusing his father of cheating me. And then, "I know you are taking legal action!" All on WhatsApp.

Gianni refused to give me an invoice for the money I paid him. I told him to label the reason 'expenses.' Of course, he did not charge IVA so it must be an invoice for E 320 plus IVA which is a tax. At one point he wrote that I had gotten material "black."

His invoice never came.

This had happened before. Gianni had asked me to pay half of his father's fee and I had sent it. He kept saying it had not come. I checked and it had been taken from my bank account. On the fourth day, Gianni wrote me "Blackmail will not work!" I picked up the phone and told him that was ridiculous and that he was very rude. I had sent it to his father's account and it was there for days as I had not been instructed to send it to his son's account for tax purposes.

The trip from Sambuca to me is 40 minutes and Gianni told me his father was "tired" of coming to Palermo. I said, "Well, tired or not, he must finish the job." As a client, I behaved well. Gianni knew that every single time I was asked for payment for work or for material the money had been paid within 24 hours. As for The Norman's constant pleas for money I told Gianni that I had sent him yet another 500 euros just six days before. He hadn't known and this seemed to cow him a bit.

Gianni changed so much in a few months. I was well aware his father was difficult but I continued to insist on an invoice from him. He yelled at me that this was the worst job he'd ever had and he wanted nothing more to do with it! I knew I'd never get an invoice from him and said, "I wish it were over, too. Buona giornata," and hung up the phone.

I could not have done all this without him in the beginning but he was compensated generously for being with me at the sale and then helping me during the last half of November and first week of December. My calls after that were to ask if his father were coming that day because his father never answered his phone. In a matter of months, he had become a different person.

There was also the strange matter of his becoming a sort of liaison between Trump of the Alley and me. Why would Trump call him? Was he in that position because he could speak English to me or was it more than that? I suspected it was more.

I sat up and stared out at the Tyrrhenian Sea.

Unfortunately there were still things to be done. The most durable kitchen counter is lava from a volcano. I had no idea what it looked like but asked for black. Wouldn't lava *be* black anyway? The counter must be cut and is not ready, the part for the leaky bidet was in the truck, the AC/heating unit is also in the truck. I have a list of what Luca must do and what The Norman must do. Those two men were still fighting over who should hang the bathroom door.

I sighed then got up and marched towards the clear, blue water.

LONGING FOR THE PAST

Last night I had this sudden homesick pang and thought I know what I want. I miss being a private detective in New York City. I want to be back on Lexington Avenue in my apartment watching a *Law & Order* rerun in the afternoon. On the top floor in my walk-up, the Crow's Nest, with Marvin across the hall and Stefan, the Frenchman, on the third floor and Hayko, the Armenian, and his weavers on the second floor.

Then I want Mickey, my p.i. pal, who called me Charlie, to call and say, "Got a crayon? Take this down. Address is blah blah blah. Come into the office tomorrow morning and I'll wire you up. Client antsy, wants it done right away." Then he might add, "There's another case. It's one of those things I hate and you like. All my instincts were screaming to turn it down. But now I'm stuck with it. It's a fuckin' cluster-fuck, Charlie. But I know you and you'll love it."

I would have missed the first two minutes of *Law & Order* but it would be worth it. Mickey would laugh if he knew where I was now. He always said, "Charlie, if you don't stop taking chances, you're gonna end up in an alley."

• • •

I can waft myself back in time—quite vividly. I recall the feeling with great detail, the shadows, the colors, even the scent of the place and for a moment or as long as I want—I am there. If I were ever in prison or stranded alone on an island this would serve me well. I guess it comes with the curse of near-constant daydreaming. I feel at ease with slipping away from the present reality. Like a row boat untethered from a pier. The only time I am not daydreaming is when I'm lasered in on a case. Maybe it's why I love being a detective so much. It's a change from the perpetually adrift me.

A POLICE STATION IN PALERMO

Same old story of hoping Luca Iwanttomarryhim would make a visitation. His final one. The Imperial Luca of Sambuca. A whale in a fish bowl. Plumber to a star—Lorraine Bracco. The Norman arrived but had to wait for Luca to do his thing and Luca was AWOL. The Norman went away. Back in an hour. No word from Luca or Gianni. I refuse to call and then I do. Gianni is not answering. His phone is grafted onto his left hand so I know he knows I've called. Texts unanswered. It is typical and infuriating. All I wanted to know is if his father were coming today.

Hours later Luca strode in, as far as anyone can stride along the obstacle course of my boxes. His assistant followed carrying a huge box containing the AC/heater unit. My cortile was fast being eaten alive with stuff. The fabbro left. The Norman and Luca conferred. I have no kitchen door and my requests for this were dismissed but their dispute over the bathroom door continued. The Norman will put tiles in my kitchen, build a loft but will not install a door. He says Luca must do it and Luca says he must do it. Gianni said to get a falegname/carpenter to do it. Meanwhile I kept asking about the kitchen pocket door and no one answers me. It has not been purchased.

My iron doors were open and I saw that Trump of the Alley had stopped his car and was staring in. He was in the driver's seat less than two feet from my door. I turned away, ignoring him. He shouted, I ignored him. As Luca passed me, I said, "Non parla con lui" which is don't talk to him but he went out anyway. He came in and I said I am not going to pay him. We blah blah blah and he said they are bad people and used the word Mafia. I said again that paying him is stupid and I won't pay. I don't give my money away to a stranger who asks for it. Luca won't argue, he will have Gianni call me. I knew the routine now. Sure enough, my phone rang about three minutes later and it was Gianni insisting that I don't understand and I have to pay! I told him I won't discuss it with him and hung up.

I saw that Luca will be busy with the flood from the bidet and installing the AC unit and I won't have to make decisions about chandelier height for several hours.

I decided to go to the polizia at two thinking that everyone would be back from lunch. I buzzed outside the big ornately carved wooden door and this male voice came through asking what I wanted. I said I wanted to make an esposto. He said come back and I thought he said in a little half hour.

At a nearby café, I ate an arancina which is rice and ham and butter is the shape and size of an orange, hence the name. I rang the bell again at 2:30 and the same male voice told me to come back at three.

I went back to Luca and his assistant and saw that they were involved in installing the AC/heater and there were no decisions to be made. I was back at the big front door on via Roma at three then followed an African inside and up to the 2nd floor. We were told to sit down and wait thirty minutes as it was not open yet!

This is one police station. Are they all taking lunch for two and a half hours? Is that the best time to rob a bank or kill somebody? If you committed a crime at one, you'd have a great head start to go on the lam.

At 3:20 I was sitting in the waiting room with the African when a man motioned me to follow him across the hall to an office with two desks, one computer and doors opening onto a balcony overlooking via Roma. There were green leaves outside and from my chair I could see the Italian flag flutter listlessly as if exhausted by the heat.

Two men entered. One looked like a young Marlon Brando and the other was older with glasses and grey hair. Both wore jeans and polo shirts. I noticed the older one with a nice brown leather watch band and later I saw that he was wearing exquisite brown leather shoes with tassels. The cut, the gleam of the leather—excellent taste. I said my Italian is very bad but the older man boomed cheerfully," It's fine! We speaka da English here!"

Well, that was not entirely true.

They read my esposto huddled together even though I offered a second copy. At times there were three men all staring at the computer. I saw three heads and the back of the computer and I often spent long periods staring out at the flag, thinking I preferred the firemen's efficiency. For about five minutes they worked at finding my alley on a map. I despaired. All this activity was punctuated by bursts of Italian as they stared at the screen. I tried to speak and whenever I did this, the older one would admonish me, saying carefully, "We are-a working for you-a."

I explained about this man saying he owned the wall of the building and telling me to dig up the street to have my own private contadino or meter. I said that I had a contract with AMAP and thought I already had my own private contadino. At least I thought that's what I was saying. The first time I said it, the older one asked Brando what I was saying and there was a low murmured response.

At one point, they turned the computer screen so I could see and there was the son's life-size face and I said, "That's him!" and the three men whooped in triumph. The Enforcer is 42. Later I was shown a photo of a man with greyish hair who may have been the father, Trump of the Alley. The name is common and I have no faith at all in victims recognizing perps. I learned that they reverse names here and his first name is Luca not Di Lauro. I had seen him several times but the photo showed a younger, thinner face. I thought about how I wouldn't trust a woman identifying my client as the person who attacked her in the dark wearing a hoodie. I would not say 'yes' to the image on the screen. When facing him I am usually feeling stress and besides, now he is fat and wears glasses. Born in 1942 so he must be 80.

The polizia knew both father and son and told me they are Mafia and pericolosi/dangerous.

I did manage to tell them that since that esposto was written, the father and then the son had come back to threaten me and that just today an hour ago the father had come back. They were aghast.

"Oggi? Oggi?" they cried. Today? This upsets them.

They asked how long I have lived there and I say only about a week and before that I was in a hotel. They want to know how much my hotel room cost. Then the two of them got very, very interested in this. Three months in a hotel! They must know how much per night. I tell them it was 42 euros a night with breakfast incluso. "Tre mille euros!" The only excitement was my hotel bill and the idea that I had been threatened a second, a third time and more. I don't know Italian data bases but I could have found The Enforcer in about one minute if he'd lived in the States and I knew his address. My confidence in them was greatly diminished by how long it took and by the euphoria it aroused.

Brando directed someone else to print this or that. I signed papers. I asked what next. My esposto is okay because they say they understand it but it must be rewritten for a magistrate. Google translate is not legal language. I'll ask Michael. This will be submitted to a court in five or six weeks. What should I do now? They advised not to pay and if they threaten me again, I am to come and report it. Luckily, it's a six-minute walk. They kept saying, he threatened you. All this was communicated with the older man typing on his phone and then a robot voice would say whatever in English. That phone was extended to me time after time and there'd be a siren outside or a horn honking and I'd barely hear, dimly understand.

The gist of all this is: every time they ask for money I must come to the police station. It was a little odd but they cannot go to the thug and son. They must wait for the magistrate and only then can they interrogate and do whatever they do.

I was there in that room with the breeze coming in the open doors, staring at Marlon Brando from 3:20 until 5 o'clock. It would have been longer but I explained that an idraulico/plumber was at my place and I must go before he left.

I felt my Italian was worse than ever and as I stood up to take my leave, Brando spoke to me in broken English and told me that the word I was using for water meter was really not a meter but a person. The older man chimed in, in English. "Is a man who works in a forest."

I was very embarrassed, blushed hotly and thanked them. How nice of them not to snort with laughter when I kept emphasizing over and over again that maybe I should get my own private man who worked in a forest.

• • •

Another box, sliced open, flaps folded back. Sorting letters, documents and unfinished novels, rereading . . . it's like looking through a kaleidoscope. The assumptions and memories are shifting. Confirmations and revelations. If we live long enough, do we get all the answers? Do we finally figure everything out?

* * *

I go to Flower Ferramenta/hardware store at least twice a day, sometimes three times a day and Antonio always grins and calls my name when I walk in. He will make phone calls all over town when he doesn't have what I need and he explains things clearly. I told him he was Five Star/Cinque Stelle and today he introduced me to his mother and told her that he wants to be Six Stars.

I may have to wait ten minutes for him to finish with another customer but it is all so polite, so good-humored, so warm an exchange. I'm watching and listening and thinking it is so *kind*. Palermo has taught me patience.

I bought a three-meter tall, eleven-step ladder from Antonio. My loft is really high and my cute wooden ladder doesn't reach. I was disappointed that I can't have the new ladder until Thursday or Friday so Antonio said I could take the store's ladder until mine was delivered. It's always these generous little touches that surprise and delight me. I don't think a hardware store in NYC would offer to lend me their store ladder.

Two days later my new ladder arrived and Antonio and I discussed it being lightweight and I got the gendered word ending wrong so we joked about the ladder being a woman ladder. La scala. Like the opera house. We carried the ladder outside—it's maybe 12 feet long—and I said, "Sono felice" –I am happy—and he beamed. As I turned into my alley a plump woman in black with her shopping cart wanted to know all about my ladder, held strong opinions about the size, thought it should fold up, etc. Every little thing seems to be *interesting to people*. It's enormous and I can imagine it being used to rescue small children from a burning building.

It was not only Antonio. So many men, so many women, too, are very nice to me. When I drop something I cannot even look down at it on the ground before it is being handed to me by a male of any age: older than me, middle-aged or teenaged boy. With a smile. Everyone says my life would be easier with the renovation if I were a man yet there are advantages to being a woman here.

When Nigeria who works at the motorcycle shop sees me, even from a great distance, he shouts, "Am Er I Ca!" He often asks, "How was your night?" and I want to say, 'Loaded with sex and passion and this morning I am exhausted' but, of course, I say, "Fine. How was yours?" It was nice to speak English. I asked if he were from Lagos and he was surprised I even knew Lagos. I told him I'd been all over Africa but couldn't get a visa for his country. It was right after Biafra and they did not want foreigners to see how bad it was. He was probably not even born then. Now he insists he will take me there. I told him to be careful because I might really go with him.

At six or seven in the evening, I often go down the street to put out my garbage and am usually greeted by a very stout man, T-shirt stretched over large torso, who booms, "Good morning!" It never fails to make me laugh. He has a dog that looks to be part pit bull maybe part boxer who greets me with wagging tail. A few days ago, I pointed to my watch and explained it was "good evening" but I think he likes the sound of good morning better.

• • •

There he was. The Enforcer of Trump of the Alley, in the alley: one of the Pizzeria Triplets who had turned on me. He was looking down at his phone then greeted me with "Caldo oggi, si?" Hot today, isn't it? This was the man shouting at me to pay him the money or he'd cut off my water and that tomorrow, again and again, was the deadline and to tell him "si" or "no!"

I don't understand these people.

• • •

Today I went to the caffè to see Miss Blue Glasses and tell her my falegname/carpenter, was coming and we both screamed about the bathroom door. She shouted, "Privacy! Privacy!" in English which surprised me. "Finalmente!" Finally.

A BLONDE, BLUE-EYED CARPENTER

The falegname/carpenter, Ferdinando, who was friends with Francesco who laid the marble floor, arrived the next morning at 0830 to install my doors. Finally, I could pronounce 'falegname' with confidence. Carpenter. At long last I would have a bathroom door and a pocket door for the kitchen!

Ferdinando was smiling, blond and blue-eyed, with a shaved head and these stunning arms and shoulders. I wondered if his waist were smaller than mine.

Nice man. I realized he was shining with sweat so I turned the AC on and surrendered the standing fan to him deciding he needed it more than I did.

Madly curious about why I came to Palermo. Why not Milano, Venezia? What would I do here? Did I know people? I told him I was writing a list of men I trusted and Francesco was the first on the list and he would be the second. A very short list.

He showed me dozens of photos of his work on his phone. A staircase of jaw-dropping beauty, a bureau of teal blue. He'd been to New York. He said a Sicilian there sent for Sicilian workmen to do his townhouse in Manhattan. All the material—even the concrete—was put on a container ship which sailed from here. He wanted only Sicilian material and Sicilian workers. Very rich. A chain of super mercati/supermarkets. I guessed D'Agostino but he said no and that he could not remember the name or maybe he didn't want to. The D'Agostino supermarkets are all over New York City. Then he told me that D›Agostino had to leave Sicily because of the Mafia and Ferdinando extended his arms with crossed wrists. So fleeing jail, he went to the US and made a fortune and a new life. Again, I see that everybody knows everybody.

The four worst words in Italian: Signora, c'e un problema! Signora, there is a problem.

Luca didn't cut the door property and it's too big and must be cut again. Under Ferdinando's questioning I told him about Luca and how he and Gianni took me to the store in Sambuca where I was told, every single time I asked the price, not to worry and buy it all here and we will add it up and give you a big discount.

In Italian, of course, but it was clear. Toilet, bathtub, vanity, bidet, all the marble for the bathroom wall, for the floor, the baseboards, sink, the counter top of lava, all the fixtures. The bill was thousands and the discount? E 120! Ferdinando was horrified. I told him I felt stupid and I argued about it to no avail but I trusted Luca because my conversation partner in Genoa had recommended him.

He said don't feel stupid. The firemen told me that, too, but I do. All these Sicilians comforting me.

I tried to call Gianni who didn't pick up and then I texted him and his father that the door measurement was incorrect. Ferdinando told me the store was responsible for cutting it and Luca should take care of that. How well I remembered insisting on knowing the price and being told it was E 200. "Wood is more expensive than marble here," said Gianni in explanation. I was appalled but stood there thinking, I need a door. Ferdinando said it should have cost fifty euros. Of course, Luca and Gianni received a kickback for bringing me to the store. I don't resent that but I do resent the promised discount.

Who needs the Mafia when every single person has their own little angle to play?

I still had not received the certificates for the plumbing and electrical work. I texted Gianni. He wrote back that he would get his father to sign them. Of course, he had told me at least four times that they had been mailed. And now they were not mailed and not signed. I am tired of these men.

Ferdinando told me to not deal with Luca again and that he would find a cutting machine and bring it and install the bathroom door!

I thanked him profusely and wrote Gianni to forget about the door. He wrote back a nasty note claiming he had nothing to do with the door. I knew the pattern. When something was wrong Gianni would first deny having anything to do with it and next pretend to have no idea what I was referring to.

That evening he wrote: "Thank you Clarissa, and sorry I am truly sorry for everything. you are always very nice to me. good night."

DRINKING ACTUALLY HELPS

The Norman came today but Luca had not installed the kitchen counter so what about the backsplash? The tiles were *fatto a mano*. Last week I told The Norman that they were made by hand and a bit irregular in size. I explained to him the meaning of "wiggle room" and we understood each other. I even reminded him with a drawing yesterday morning but he still has not told Luca the counter was to be 99 cm high instead of 100. So all the drama was over one centimeter. It was finally decided that one centimeter should be chopped off the tiles so they would fit between the bottom of the cabinets and the counter. I left, feeling exhausted with all the passionate discussions. Everything is life or death. *One* centimeter is one-third of one inch.

I walked to Piazza Rivoluzione wondering if I were an emotional eater or emotional drinker. Did I want chocolate or alcohol? I ordered prosecco at a table under an umbrella and the usual scruffy blonde brought the little bottle. Two euros which is $2.14 at today's rate.

Having had prosecco for lunch and then again, I was feeling quite calm. I talked to Bob, a good friend in Paris, who made me laugh and I told him I was now *sedated*. I could face anything. World War Three, multiple homicides or one centimeter—I mean, who cares?

KEYS AND SURPRISING KINDNESS

At our last meeting Marlon Brando said it might come down to a 'he said, she said" situation. I knew how that plays out all too well so even though I have that signed receipt I wanted something rock-solid and bulletproof. Luca Iwanttomarryhim, Trump of the Alley and The Enforcer were three against one and could say I didn't speak Italian, had misunderstood. For the last week I'd been wondering how to get The Enforcer to threaten me on tape. I saw him four times a day and, as directed by the polizia, did not speak. He became invisible to me even when passing within two feet.

On Saturday, I went to the cartoleria/stationery store one minute away across via Roma and bought a box for my cassettes then went back to exchange it for two larger boxes. I walked through the alley and Nigeria called "Am-er-i-ca!" from the doorway of the motorcycle shop and I called back, "Ni-ger-i-a!" and he shouted, "Do you love me?" and I shouted back, "Of course!" He was grinning. At my front door, I had no keys. Emptied my bag on the ground. No keys. Slowly, I retraced my steps. The store clerk looked for me. No keys. I crossed via Roma imagining calling the fabbro/blacksmith on a Saturday. I entered the alley staring at the ground and suddenly in front of me was The Enforcer holding my keys out. I swallowed and said weakly, "Dov'e?" Where? He said in the alley. "Grazie mille," I said and took them.

This is the man who shouted at me my water would be cut if I didn't pay him. This is the man Marlon Brando says is dangerous and I am not to speak to. He could have kept all my keys and watched the fabbro/blacksmith come and change the locks. Now this!

I don't understand these people.

• • •

Today was a bit tough. The Norman came to me at my desk and asked me to look at the kitchen tile backsplash. I said, "Bella" but added that the green and white tiles go a few tiles farther on either side towards the side walls and not just over the sink. I pointed to the remaining tiles in the box. Maybe 14, not a great number. He looked at me as if I'd asked him to swim the Straits of Messina in the middle of the night wearing handcuffs. He started to work but kept breaking tiles (I don't think on purpose) and after I'd made three trips to Matteo's shop I said to just finish it even though the design suffered. I told his assistant if anybody asked I'd say we drank too much wine. He laughed. I thought, It's fine. *I don't care.*

• • •

I could not wait until this was over. I told myself this isn't so bad. It's not getting hit on my bike and breaking both arms and both legs. It's not getting a divorce. It's not having your container with all you own fall off the ship into the Atlantic. There *are* things worse than renovating a Tunisian nightclub in Palermo. I kept trying to think of examples.

• • •

Maybe the good and the bad all shake out in the end. The postino rang my doorbell which sounds like someone stifling a cough at a funeral and shouted, "Clarissa!" as he called my phone. I answered the phone and laughed then I went to the door and he handed me a letter through the bars. Grinning, cap pushed back over black hair above a round, pink face, he asked how I was, said Clarissa was a beautiful name and told me to have a good day.

• • •

On Sunday Francesco did several things that needed to be done, was finished and paid and about to get on his motorcycle. He hadn't left because he wanted to hear the story of the fire department. I was standing at my front door and nearing the end when The Enforcer came over and started telling him I owed him money for the water. He kept using the word condo and said he was mad that I wasn't paying.

I heard 500 euros several times and felt like chiming in, hey, what about the 800 your father wanted? You didn't get it, did you? Then you wanted 500 and you aren't getting that either. I want my 250 back, you rotten ladro/thief. I did not say anything but I wanted to. He didn't even look at me, directed all at Francesco. Either my Italian is too bad or he knows I will say 'no' so he only says 'ciao' and 'buongiorno' to me these days. He ranted on and on. I just stood there, staring at him, thinking I'd go and see Marlon Brando tomorrow. The Enforcer had Francesco follow him around a parked car to stare at my little metal door with the padlock. Minutes passed. Then Francesco came back alone and motioned me inside, came in after me, closed the two sets of doors and spoke very quietly. The gist of it is: He is a bad guy and I am to be very careful. He is dangerous and I am alone. He also said that he is going to cut off my water.

I said, hey, it's been a month and I still have water and I still have eyes. I told him not to worry because I was getting two chihuahuas for security but he didn't think that was funny and kept telling me to pay attention and to be very careful and that he was dangerous. Francesco is tall, well-built and appeared afraid.

At about half past eight, I rode my bike to the Rouge et Noir theatre to see the Elvis movie and Francesco was so worried about me that he texted to make sure I was okay. Of course! I was with Elvis!

La Tana was coming together and a visit and a minaccia/threat from the alley thug was not bothering me. Marlon Brando will have a fit about it. He couldn't believe they had threatened that 2nd and 3rd day and so many times and now, yet another minaccia.

This was all okay. A slightly larger vocabulary. Minaccia.

A CONFUSING TIME WITH MARLON BRANDO

It was the Fourth of July and picnics flashed into my mind but Palermo was here and now and I went to see the polizia this morning at nine. I was told to come back at two and I did. I was the first person of five to sit in a plastic chair and wait. No air conditioning or fans but the doors in the waiting room were open to a tiny balcony and I was comfortable, reading a trashy novel.

I kept reminding myself that it is minaccia/threat and not minutiae. A few times, I thought, am I *really* in a police station in Palermo? Waiting to complain about extortion in my alley? Really? It was three o'clock when Marlon Brando wheeled his bike in. He must carry it up three flights of stairs as the elevator is the size of a phone booth. A black bike. Perfect. Very sexy.

Five minutes later a woman mysteriously wearing a white lab coat called, "Signora" and waved me to come. I knew where his office was.

Handsome as ever, he remembered me but I gave him a copy of the esposto anyway and said, "Ho avuto un altra minaccia. Molte." which is Italian for I have had another threat. Many. First he held his finger to his lips but later it was at the side of his nose but mostly it was his index finger under his right eye. He spoke Italian and I didn't understand one word. Not a one.

He was pointing at the ceiling and talking in just above a whisper. A cool breeze was blowing in from the open balcony doors; he was at his desk behind the big computer and I was in the same chair as last time. It seems that the investigation has begun but I am to tell no one. Have I told anyone? No, I said, which is, of course, not true as so many people have been on the scene. Francesco and the armadio men know. Victor in Boston talked to The Enforcer on Skype. Pietro knows because I told Maria and, of course, I have talked to Thomas. So I lied to Marlon Brando.

Marlon Brando's face was pink and his forelock was hanging over his forehead sort of like Elvis's last night in the movie. Everyone was red-faced and sweating and I was not feeling the heat. Not yet, anyway. The first thing Marlon Brando said was that I was to call 112 if I felt any danger. Anything at my door, anything. Police cars were around the neighborhood and they would come right away. I asked if they knew the situation and they do! They know about me. That was a surprise. They will come immediately and write a report.

I didn't mention Francesco and that The Enforcer had talked to him; I just said I had been threatened again. He was speaking terrible English and I was listening, leaning forward in my chair as if proximity would help. I was speaking terrible Italian, helpfully translating his bad English into bad Italian for him. Marlon Brando was not doing the investigation but pointed upstairs. Other people are. It had begun. There were cameras, they were watching me. This was muddled. I didn't think there were any cameras in my alley. If anyone were watching me they must be bored into a coma. My life was wretchedly dull. I go to Lidl's or out to lunch and make regular forays to Antonio's hardware store. Sometimes I go to the electric store. I have been rescued by the vigili del fuoco. I hoped that humiliation was not recorded anywhere.

Marlon Brando said the police would believe me because of my reports. He tapped the esposto on his desk and I nodded. Then he put his finger under his eye again and I stared at him frowning in concentration.

I am not to speak to The Enforcer when he says buongiorno and not to give him money. I told Marlon Brando that this happened five times a week, almost every day. Calling 112 was mentioned three times. He was firm about it. I am not to tell anyone of the investigation. This was said with his finger to the side of his nose again. I think this means it's a secret.

Most of the time he held his right index finger under his right eye. I am to pay attention, to be careful, just as Francesco told me. I had the feeling that Marlon Brando knows more than I do about this father and son or he wouldn't have mentioned calling for help so many times. I asked if they were dangerous and he said yes. I wanted it confirmed yet again.

I will be called—he pointed with one arm up—to come to the station and be interviewed within two weeks. The big thing is the investigation has begun.

I thanked Marlon Brando and stood up to leave. But with this finger-under-the-eye thing, side-of-the-nose thing, pointing up at the ceiling and the adorably atrocious attempt at English in a voice just above a whisper I was not entirely sure what had happened.

RIGHT UP BY THE ALTAR

It has been a marvelous day because what I wanted to happen weeks ago, has happened.

I have two Parsons tables that I really like. One is so attractive even the international movers complimented me as they packed it in New York but the other is my favorite. I couldn't stand the idea of giving them away or selling them. I may live somewhere else and want them in a few years. They were taking up so much room near the front door that I had to slither past them several times a day. At last, I dragged one out to the cortile but knew it shouldn't be exposed to the elements.

Two weeks ago I followed Luciano into the church next door. It's a magnificent ruin with rotting roof and crumbling walls. Nonetheless there are tremendous marble columns, an altar, statues of angels, Jesus on the cross and windows thirty feet up letting in shafts of sunlight. Luciano has high cheekbones, a square jaw. Black hair, olive skin. His defined biceps were shining with sweat in the gloom. He wears this black sleeveless top all the time and has acres of tattoos. He said no, I couldn't put my tables in there because he was not the owner. I asked where the owner was and could I talk to him. "Fuori. No." Away and no. I asked if he would talk to the owner for me. The answer was a shrug.

I stepped over piles of metal and various tools and went out into the alley, thinking I'd ask him again. Last week I saw him and asked him if he would help me with something heavy. He came in and lifted the huge French framed poster into place on the wall as if it were paper then hurried out looking neither right nor left.

Today I saw him in the alley and again followed him into the dark church. No, he hadn't talked to the proprietor and I said, okay and left. He came out into the alley after me and asked to see the table. I showed him as he stood in my doorway and I said there were two, the same size. He nodded and started to pick it up. I told him to give me five minutes. I swept all the workers' water bottles and general debris off it and then hurried out to the cortile. Superhuman strength poured through me as I knew he was waiting and I somehow got the really heavy table in from outside and moved it the length of La Tana and halfway out the front door. One of the Alley Men was passing by and offered to help and so both tables were out in the alley by the time Luciano finished his phone call conducted on the hood of his black Mini Cooper. The alley is his office. We got the tables into the church and carried them right up to the altar, pushed them side by side against the wall and then we put my blue tarp over them and Luciano put a board on top. I thanked him profusely.

So my tables now live a few feet from the altar with the ghosts of all the monks for the past thousand years. The dormitory for the monks was off to the left but now it's only the idea of a staircase leading to a very blue sky. I kept thinking the church was 800 years old but something built in 1200 is a thousand years old. This was too much for me to comprehend at first. I had to get used to it.

• • •

Today I marched in a manifestazione to mark the death of a courageous judge, Paolo Borsellino, who was murdered July 19th, 1992, in Palermo by the Mafia. He grew up in Kalsa, my neighborhood, and his family still lives here. It is now 2022, thirty years since the murder and Marlon Brando said I was dealing with the Mafia, that they were dangerous. For some reason I am not afraid, I am angry. It felt good to be in a crowd, all of us of the same mind.

FOREVER IS NOT VERY LONG FOR ME

One aspect of unpacking is pulling away a scrunched-up NY Times page dated November something, 2011, and remembering that I was in Philadelphia dismantling my house, preparing to put it on the market. Everything went into the warehouse and I went to Paris. I was going to be there forever.

Slicing open my cartons of books and lifting them out has given me such pleasure; I've missed them. I remember my Aldous Huxley glut one teenaged summer in Mississippi. No one had ever heard of him and wondered why I was interested. My books on Egypt. Everything by Oscar Wilde. Opening a box filled with books on the Mafia and thinking, oh, wow, I'm here and it is, too. I had forgotten how much I like Jim Thompson. I shipped over all my Faulkners and everything by Tennessee Williams and Graham Greene. *THE COMEDIANS* set in Haiti strikes such a chord in me. In one of the boxes I came across a letter professing love, written by Aubelin Jolicoeur who was Greene's Petit Pierre. I am so thrilled to hold these books in my hands and have them here with me. They are like my paintings and prints. I feel they belong with me or maybe I belong with them.

The biggest surprise was unpacking eight silver goblets, monogrammed with Mother's initials and quite black with tarnish. These were a wedding present in 1933 and had only been used for our family Thanksgiving and Christmas lunches. Filled with water, of course, in those days. Doing the math, I calculated that our last Christmas was in 1965, before the 1966 divorce, so these had languished for 57 years. It took an entire weekend but I worked diligently on cleaning them and the silver began to show. Mother would love the idea that her goblets were now in Palermo and that they were usually filled with prosecco.

The plastic bins were all in the cortile and could be brought in one by one and unpacked but it was clear I had too much for the space inside. One morning I put a beach towel down at my front door and arranged what I would not keep. I put three little carry-on suitcases with wheels and two sweaters and some kitchen duplicates (salad tongs, serving spools, etc.) out in the alley with price tags. Heard a whoop and went to the door to see Nigeria putting on a thick goldish bracelet that Gema gave me. It closes with a magnet and he kept saying, "I love it. I love it" and trying to get it to close. I helped but I don't think it will stay on him. It wouldn't stay on me either. Gave it to him and he was pleased so I'm really sad he won't be able to wear it.

Later a young African in a threadbare T-shirt stopped and picked up the computer speakers. They were marked E 25 but I was prepared to let them go for far less. He apologized and put them down again and said, in English, "I thought they were free." I said to take them. A gift. Don't pay anything. His face lit up. He saw the little carry-on suitcases and I said, take one. He chose the orange one and pointed to the broken down canvas shopping cart at his side. I said, Take anything you want. He was delighted and took several yards of green and white plaid cotton fabric I had no use for. The money would never have made me feel so good. His name is Alex, he is from Ghana and lives around the corner.

No one bought a thing! At about 2 p.m. I called at Fatima's doorway and she came out holding her youngest, a curly-haired little cherub who smiles constantly. She was worried about paying until I could make her understand that she was a neighbor and everything was free. She took a blue canvas suitcase with wheels. Very curious about what I've done to this place and told me when the workers go that she will come to clean. I asked how much she charged and she grinned and shook her head. Don't worry, don't worry! In Italian. She said I can always come to her door and I said, yes, the same for you.

The last person was a heavy-set African woman who wanted the olive-green suitcase and took some kitchen things. From Nigeria, her name is Gorgeous and she lives at the edge of the alley.

Every woman was too large for my sweaters. I put out a sign saying "Prendi! Take!" and that all was free. After dark, I will put whatever is left out beside the garbage pile at the end of the street. Having those people smile and thank me was a hundred times better than taking their money.

MARCELLA

At half past six I was at Spinnato's at a little table under lovely trees, waiting for Marcella, my insurance agent. We immediately threw our arms around each other. What a terrific person! She has long, light brown hair and an open, pretty face, is in her forties but looks younger. We traded compliments for three minutes and then we talked for *three* hours. I'd promised Champagne for her big favor to me but she wanted prosecco so I ordered a bottle and something to eat.

Her immediate opening, in English, was, "I want to know why someone like you, someone from New York—why would you want to live in Palermo?" I said I wanted to know all about her life.

She said there are five different types of high schools in Palermo and she went to the one with the classic studies. She was a very good student but her father made her stop school at age 18 to work in his insurance office. Marcella said she kept on, read Homer, read everything, still reads everything. When I mentioned her husband, she said, "He isn't. I'm not married. We have a son and a daughter together and have been together for 23 years but I don't want to be married. We go day by day."

I must have looked surprised for she laughed and said, "I'm not a typical Sicilian woman." We talked about expectations. I was expected to get married, have two children. Then and now expectations. She asked lots of questions about where I'd lived, being a writer, being a detective and finally, I said, "Enough! I don't want to talk about myself!" and she said, "Oh, don't stop! It's like a movie!" The time flew and she had a family at home. We embraced goodbye and I felt I had made a friend.

WE ARE ALL IMMIGRANTS

I was stopped by a woman in the alley who, with her multitude of massive curves, reminded me of a female Michelin tire man. Nigerian, a nearly-shaved head with orange tufts, bright T-shirt, bejewelled sandals, I realized it was Gorgeous from the other day. She started talking as I was unchaining my bike preparing to do errands. Suddenly she was complaining in English about her nearly 600 euro electric bill. I said it couldn't be true. How big was her place? Two rooms. I saw the bill on her phone. 592 euros. I was shocked. I told her to fight it, that someone was tapping in. We discussed what to do.

I thought of the Tunisian woman with the beautiful headscarf who asked me at the bus stop what to do about the bill she was to pay at the post office. I thought of Gema who called me yesterday from the laundromat in Astoria and asked me if Paul should change his name from her name, Hernandez, to his Haitian father's name which is French. Gema is worried about the prejudice against Latinos in the U.S.

I heard about a Sri Lankan who was paying the Mafia a huge sum every month. The reason: he was foreign, didn't speak the language and they didn't think he would ever go to the police.

I know how this story ends. He will be unable to buy stock for his store. It won't matter if they beat him or threaten his family because he will have nothing on the shelves to sell and no money. Then they will offer to buy his store for nothing and he will have no choice but to give it to them.

Yesterday the Nigerian woman named Sapphire stopped me in the alley and talked and talked. She didn't speak Italian so she couldn't get a job and when she wanted to go to school it meant she missed work and she needed work to have money to live. I told her there was an immigrants' Italian class starting in September for free and I was going and she should come, too.

Every time I agreed with her, she said, "Thank you." It was as if she were grateful for my confirming her every thought. I said, "Italian is difficult," and she said, "Thank you."

"But we have to learn it to survive here," I said.

Sapphire said, "Thank you. I will come again and greet you." She and Gorgeous are of the next alley.

I told Thomas, "We are all immigrants," and to my amazement, he used that line in the next Sunday's sermon.

PIZZO

I never imagined myself sitting in the Palermo police station with a cross-section of humanity waiting to see an ispettore/inspector. Just the way I never thought I'd be putting my laundry out in an alley to dry. Fatima gets the sun before I do. It hits my side of the alley around two in the afternoon for about an hour.

Several of my American friends have infuriated me by insisting I should just forget about the 250 euros, pay the other 250 euros and move on. My reaction to that is to please, spare me that garbage about good neighbors. I am doing the right thing and have never doubted it.

This was serious. The polizia were treating it as a crime and it only escalates, it won't go away. They will demand more money. It is against the law for them to ask for money and against the law for me to give them money. It's called pizzo. They see me as weak and frightened when I refuse to be. I am arrabbiata. Angry.

As for neighbors, good or otherwise, I wondered if I were the only person in the alley asked to pay these thugs or the only one to refuse. Maybe Luciano pays them every month. I don't know but I do know that everyone knows that I paid that first day and would not pay any more.

THE TEMPTATION OF RE-INVENTION

I was very thankful for Thomas. When I move to another country I often become friends with someone I would not have been friends with in the States. Not so with him. I think we would have been friends in New York, anywhere. It begins with language. If they speak English, it's an easy start and deceptively comfortable. We are both in a new venue and we need a dentist, a hairdresser, the post office. Reticence can evaporate. I'm aware of this and am wary.

Many succumb to the temptation of re-invention. An idyllic childhood with servants and horses? An unhappy marriage to a count? A celebrity relative? A modelling career in London? In Rome, in the 80s, no one bothered to check and what were the odds that someone from your flyspeck home town in Oklahoma would arrive and blow your cover? The internet has changed things but the spirit of re-invention among expatriates lives on.

THE LOFT

Four men constructed the loft which is beautifully done and would probably support a Mini Cooper. The ceiling there in the front part of La Tana is about 15 feet high so the 3 1/2 feet comprising the loft is easily absorbed. I don't think it will be that conspicuous.

There was a great deal of expended effort with the youngest worker, wearing a baseball cap that said CORLEONE on it, running from the front, dodging the debris of Mount New York to the bathroom where Emanuele was operating a chainsaw. The man on the ladder would shout "Ottanta cinque!" and The Norman would shout, "Ottanta cinque!" and Corleone would shout "Ottanta cinque!" as he ran past all the boxes, leaping over cables, dodging anything in the aisle to get to Emanuele who would cut the piece that size. Then Corleone would grab the piece of wood and run back. It would be passed to The Norman and then up to the man on the ladder with the hammer. Then I'd hear banging, silence and "Ottanta sei!" and the exercise would be repeated. There were at least twenty pieces of wood put in place between the two huge beams. Corleone was in top physical form.

It will be painted on Monday, I was told. Well, maybe . . .

The Norman and I were very, very nice to each other. His phone rang constantly where it sat on a box. Emanuele would look at it and call out the caller's name and The Norman would grunt and shake his head. It would stop ringing then start again. He was busy, he had loads of work, I must be careful. I would have done the loft five inches differently but decided to let it go. It was fine and it was not a discussion I wanted to have. The color white was not the color white for the walls I would have picked. I would have matched the marble floor and gone for whitest white. Never let a contractor pick your white paint or *any* color paint. I wish I'd been two people doing this. I did my best but communicating in Italian, making drawings, trying to concentrate on meters and centimeters—I just wasn't quick enough. Details slipped past me.

The loft was in place at 2:30 with no break for lunch and I realized they'd all been working on empty stomachs. They hurriedly packed equipment and were out the door in about four minutes. On Monday, the painter would come, Emanuele will finish the baseboard. I'll be here at eight to let them in. I wished everyone a good weekend.

Then the orange truck started to extricate itself from the alley. The rearview mirrors were flipped closed and the men stood around waving arms and directing as The Norman in his orange T-shirt struggled at the wheel. I ran out with a levelling tool and someone's black bag left behind and was thanked profusely. At last, the truck was out of the alley and all the men leapt aboard and it sped away.

NIGERIA

As I passed the motorcycle shop there was this really loud shout: "AM ER I CA!" and I shouted "NI GER I A!" Sometimes we did this a few times a day. It was difficult to exchange more than a few words as he had work to do but this evening when he was closing up and on his own, we talked. He told me that he and his wife had made their way from Nigeria and crossed the Mediterranean. "That is so dangerous," I said. "When was that?" It was six years ago. His wife was five months pregnant and she drowned. He held his phone towards me to show me the photo of her grave. "In Lampedusa," he said in a whisper. I felt my eyes fill and swallowed tears. I thought of Nigeria, a good man, risking so much for a new life with his wife and looking forward to a new baby and how he had arrived alone in Italy. "I'm so sorry. So sorry." I walked the few yards to La Tana, holding my breath so he couldn't hear me cry then went inside before he could see my tears.

• • •

I try to give the Bangladeshis my business at their little store instead of Lidl's when I can. They are nice men and the store has the coldest Coke Zeros and the right size. They put everything in my bag for me and we comment on the weather. Now every time I go in there, I have to resist buying Nutella.

Last week I bought a small jar. The store is so hot that it was like chocolate sauce and I made the mistake of dipping a breadstick in it. One bite and I felt faint with pleasure. Hooked. I went through the whole jar in two days. In my defense, it was rather a small jar. I congratulate myself every single time I escape the Bangladeshis without Nutella.

THE HUSBAND AND WIFE CARPENTERS

At about 10, on Monday as he had promised, Ferdinando's car pulled up and out of the front seat came a woman with pink hair, a ponytail and the sides all shaved. Very punk. Ferdinando introduced her as his wife, Alessandra. Both came inside with loads of equipment. That other time he'd promised to bring a machine to cut the bathroom door to size and now he had.

"Signora, c'e un problema." There is a problem. The door was like paper. I had resisted the 200 euros price but that huge discount had been waved in front of me. Another lie. Anyway, Ferdinando was showing me how bad it was but said he could fix it. At one point I was thinking I could live without a bathroom door and maybe I'd put up a row of hanging colored beads. At this point, who cares?

Evidently the door was cut wrong two different times. I remembered Luca delivering it and then literally running out to his truck. Ferdinando said he didn't want you to see it. He and his wife, Alessandra, said they could fix the problem. They went to work and they did.

Things take a long time here because everyone wants to show you their family photos and they want to know about me. All on their phone. I've seen photos of first communions sitting next to someone on the 101 bus. Today I saw the son and the daughter.

Alessandra said that everyone sees the kitchens in movies and wants American kitchens. I said mine was a Manhattan kitchen and they were surprised. Thought all American kitchens were huge. She showed me her kitchen which was "shobby chic" and Architectural Digest gorgeous. Cabinets, the island, a pale blue and white. Tiles done by an artist friend as a backsplash. Excellent taste.

She works with Ferdinando and I asked how it was but I could see they are perfectly in sync with measuring, handing each other tools. Married 23 years, are never apart. Ferdinando said she is my best friend. She said he is my best friend. She was nodding speaking a little bit of English. They were born eleven days apart and met and married when they were twenty-three. Ferdinando looked at me and asked how old I was. Francesco knows because he and Giuseppe Due were here on my birthday and I told them and they are good friends, live in the same village. I winced. He said maybe sixty, held up fingers. I shook my head and said seventy-five. Settanta cinque. They shook their heads. This enormous number was confirmed with fingers and they seemed surprised which was nice. "Complimenti, complimenti!" they erupted. I winced again.

Then it was about the pictures. I said my mother was an artist. A family of artists, they said. I said, not really. What did my father do? Then they taught me to say surgeon in Italian which is difficult. Salaries are big in the U.S., yes? Yes, but expenses are high, too. Salaries are low here, they said, and no one wants to pay. Alessandra said people are shocked that she is a woman carpenter. Would that be okay in the

United States? We talked, woman to woman, about things as Ferdinando worked on the frame for the door.

Suddenly I had a bathroom door!

I had towel racks and a dish towel rack plus a knife rack in the kitchen. The board was up so that I could hang pictures on the wall that houses the pocket door which was finally ordered with help from Francesco and delivered. And all the time, one or the other was sweeping, putting out garbage. I thanked them, paid them and we embraced. So much smiling, so much. goodwill that it took half an hour to say goodbye.

* * *

On Sunday, Francesco came and now the broken wall by my front door with the grey pipe showing is closed and I painted it white. It was hacked open on the first day of The Water War to frighten me. Trump of the Alley will have nothing to point at now. I think The Enforcer and his watchdogs have gone to the beach today. Maybe they'll be eaten by sharks.

* * *

Last night I went to bed and set my alarm for 2 a.m. so I could see the January 6th Committee Hearings. My eyes snapped open and I pointed the flashlight at the clock which said exactly two o'clock. The alarm never went off. I watched until five, both fascinated and horrified, then went to bed and slept until seven. I told myself I'd need all my strength to deal with ENEL.

Dreaded going to ENEL, the electric company, which was located on a small street named after a prince. As I tied up my bike, I rehearsed how to tell them to send my bill to me and not to Gianni. I knew I'd fumble it on the phone. Had my passport, wondered if I needed the deed to La Tana and I had a letter addressed to me. Packages had come but my only letters were from Kenny Kimes, a murderer who was in the slammer sentenced to 127 years plus life. I was prepared for problems at ENEL but it was a snap. No letter and no passport examined. I just told the woman what I wanted and she wrote my email down in a notebook with a ballpoint pen. I never showed ID of any sort. This is for electricity and gas. I asked about the water bill and she said she thought it only comes once or twice a year. I was terrified. Paying for 182 or 365 bubble baths at one time! I'll have to sell my body in the alley. Or maybe I could sell it for parts. Get more money that way. A kidney first.

I AM A FISH

La Tana was nearly finished. I wish I could say that it ended on a happy note and invitations to a house-warming but it did not. The cheating started before I even bought the place with Alberto, Agata's "wonderful realtor," charging me that 4880 euros which is more than eight times the legal fee. I will take them to court.

I exploded only once during the renovation and that was when Serafino was taking four days to paint the bathroom. Using a tiny brush for nail polish? When I saw him in the alley, staring into space with the omnipresent cigarette I laid into him. Perhaps my rage was cumulative. All the wasted time, all the broken promises. I was seething. Painting the bathroom was his only job. Quattro giorni! Four days! He faced me, smiled, shrugged, stubbed out the cigarette with one dirty running shoe and went back inside. The next morning, he greeted me as if nothing had happened and I followed his lead.

The Norman complained nearly every week of needing money to pay his workers and nearly every week I transferred hundreds into his account. I wondered if he had a gambling problem. Maybe he was being blackmailed. I had been told initially that his price was thousands above what was correct but I'd been promised all would be done before Christmas.

It was now June. I felt bad about changing the position of the loft when he had already bought the wood so gave him money for that. A contractor should have noticed the damp wall I shared with the church and prepared it before painting. I gave him extra for that extra work. If anything, I overpaid him. When Gianni called for the second time and said The Norman was upset and couldn't pay his workers and would quit unless he were paid the balance, I relented. The loft was built and there were only a few things to be done so I paid. He was to power-wash and paint the cortile in a few weeks when I'd removed the plastic bins I was sorting.

Then I was told that I owed money for 'extras' which were never described. These would cost over 2.000 euros. I sent him a copy of my hotel bill for January before London and then the days in May before I'd been able to move in to La Tana. I asked him to pay half reminding him of his promised finish date which was before Christmas. I never saw The Norman or his orange truck again.

In Sicily, I learned that a person who pays before a job is finished is a particular kind of fish. Check me for fins.

I paid for an architect because Gianni told me this was necessary and I finally received a receipt from her office. I never met her and no architect ever came to La Tana. With an Italian dictionary, measuring carefully and drawing what I wanted on notebook paper, this place came together.

There were jokes, occasional laughter. Often I fetched coffee for the men who arrived in the morning. Everyone wanted to know how old I was and why I had chosen Palermo. A few of them admired my art. Several saw my framed family photographs and asked who everyone was. What did my father do? Lots of questions about me, why I was here, what I would do here and where was my family. The men were patient with my Italian. I grew fond of Giuseppe Uno and Due though they were probably the least educated, the fattest and –poor things—missing the most teeth.

Luca Iwanttomarryhim was still meant to install the Venetian chandelier, a kitchen light, take care of an internet socket, seal up a huge hole he had drilled in the wall for a light I did not want and cover all the electric sockets but—fish that I was—I was prevailed upon to go ahead and pay him as all that could be done in a few hours. He took his money and he was gone for good.

Fine with me. I asked Pietro, the owner of the Joli, if he knew an electrician and was very surprised when he arrived with tools and put up my kitchen light himself! We had no ladder tall enough for chandelier hanging so I found an electrician named Signor Uccello with one. It means bird so that's what I call him to myself. If he were one, he'd be a crane as he is splendidly tall and thin with long arms and legs. Uccello is also slang for the male organ. I don't understand that at all. I'll pay Mr. Bird to finish what Luca should have done.

Later I realized Luca hadn't installed the washing machine properly and it bucked like a rodeo horse. I had to turn it off at a certain point and pull out my twisted wet clothes. The kitchen counter was cut wrong which meant I could never close the stove top. The chandelier from Philadelphia blinked with the defective dimmer. The bathroom door he pressed me to buy was garbage, according to Ferdinando. Gianni did understand that because his father did not show up day after day that last week in January, I had no bathroom and no kitchen when I returned from London. Half of my hotel bill for those two weeks in May was deducted.

The worst thing Luca probably did was to tell Silvia that I was a horrible client but I could say nothing about him and didn't dare contact her until after the investigation was over. She had recommended him as the best thing since peanut butter but the polizia were certain that Luca Iwanttomarryhim and Gianni were in on the extortion with Trump of the Alley and The Enforcer. Silvia and I were good friends and I missed her.

Luca did a lousy job with the dimmer on the one chandelier he hung but Mr. Bird will get the right dimmers then come again. He was smiling behind his mask when he changed the plug on Mother's desk lamp. The off/on switch you never see anymore, he said. It delighted him. He turned it off and on like a happy child. I thought of our house in Mississippi. I almost left that lamp behind but I remember Mother sitting at her desk so late at night in the otherwise dark living room doing all the bookkeeping for Daddy's office. I asked why she had to do it. "Because your father doesn't want anyone to know how much money he has." So the little blue and crème porcelain lamp had come all the way from Mother's desk in the Old Canton Road house to my desk at La Tana on an island in the Mediterranean.

I kept careful track of what had been agreed upon, what still had to be done. I remembered that cold, rain-soaked night in November of 2021, when I met The Norman for the first time with Luca Iwanttomarryhim at La Tana. Me in my sopping wet ballet slippers. I couldn't see my hand in front of my face. The men pointed their cell phones here and there for light as The Norman decided what was required and how much he would charge. Nobody wanted to put anything in writing. A wave of misgivings swept over me but I told myself to listen carefully and to keep requesting, "Piano, piano, per favore." As we all shook hands in the dark, I thought, okay, this is Sicily.

The diminutive fabbro/blacksmith did an excellent job with the front doors and the back ones, both iron and glass, but Gianni and I both caught him in lies. There was the "no charge" situation and then the demand for 200 euros. Not nice. There *is* more than one blacksmith in Sicily and I hired a new one to install a gutter over the cortile. He disappeared when I asked him to come back to make an adjustment so the only two blacksmiths I've ever known were both a disappointment.

Actually, pretty much everyone behaved badly when it came to money. Francesco did a beautiful job laying the black and white marble floor and was a great help. He put together all the Ikea bookcases and kitchen cabinets, did some painting and corrected my Italian. Francesco's youngest son can speak some English so I asked if he could read English and gave him books. Francesco wanted them autographed and stood over me as I signed five different titles. I thought he was a cut above all the others but he overcharged me outrageously one day which became his last day. I paid him and then sent a list of what I had paid for other work and pressed him to explain the sudden huge fee. No answer for months and at last he texted that The Norman owed him money! Is that the thinking? If someone is unfair to me then I will cheat the next person to make up for it? Francesco was my favorite of the original team but I won't hire him again.

Ferdinando, the falegname/carpenter and Alessandra, his wife, were terrific. Their work together was a crisp duet. A bathroom door in place was so astonishing to behold that I kept forgetting to close it. The armadio men, when they finally arrived, were a delight. Unlike The Norman or Gianni or Luca Iwanttomarryhim, they were exceptionally apologetic, sincerely sorry for all the delays and I instantly told them it was nothing and how happy I was they had come.

Mr. Bird, the electrician I hired to do what Luca had not finished, was perpetually hours late but excellent. I was worried about his footing on the ladder as he hung the Venetian chandelier but he laughed and told me he was an electrician at Teatro Massimo and the ceiling there was nearly 40 meters high!

We talked about the church next door. The cortile was still filled with plastic bins but it was his idea to hang my new three-meter ladder on the wall. At a few centimeters too tall to go in a kitchen corner, this was the perfect solution. He thought the outdoor space had possibilities when I'd almost surrendered to using it for storage. Affable as he sipped his water, tall in khaki shorts and very tan, Mr. Bird is always more than an hour late, but he makes my list of good men.

I was much calmer these days when the men didn't call, didn't arrive. I lived here, I was sorting, clearing, cleaning. It was okay.

If I were Mafia I'd put a hit on The Norman, Luca Iwanttomarryhim, Gianni and The Enforcer, too. No quick and easy shot to the back of the head. A slow death. Make them wait for it as I have waited so many hours, days, weeks for them. The lies, the carelessness, the arrogance. All this time, I felt I'd been holding my own, trying to be tough and careful. Linda Ronstadt sang, "I've been cheated, been mistreated . . ."

Well, that's me.

THE ARGENTINE AT THE POST OFFICE

Michael, the visa lawyer in Rome, wanted a document printed out and signed saying that I was having him as my representative in court. I was to mail it raccomandata/registered mail at the post office.

The Fascist architecture is bold; the building looms over my bus stop with the bottom step right there. Fat, solid, unadorned columns stand at the top of those steps. The place was nearly empty at lunchtime but it was still necessary to go to a machine and get a ticket. Open doors, marble floors, wooden benches. A young woman and I, getting tickets at the same time, started talking. I waved my envelope and said I was dealing with a lawyer for a visa. Floodgates opened. Adriana was Argentine, had arrived from Berlin the day before, found out she was pregnant last night, said her partner was in Denmark and she wanted to live in Palermo.

We were summoned to separate windows but she waited for me outside at the top of the steps. Happy about the baby which is good. A big surprise. Her ancestry is Italian and she was told it would take six or seven months for a permesso di soggiorno but "Now I am in a hurry." I introduced myself and asked her about going home. "Oh, no, I won't go back to Argentina!" She wondered if we could keep in touch. I'd told her that if my lawyer was good, I would recommend him. I gave her my card and took a good look at her. That wonderful olive skin and pale grey eyes and rich black hair. In her twenties, I guessed. She asked where and how to find TIM, the phone company, for an Italian phone number and I told her. Then I added, "Get in touch for any reason at all. For anything." Adriana said she was so happy to meet me. She was reading my card as I asked, "What can I do right now to help you?"

She took a deep breath and said, "Give me a hug."

I did.

We separated at the top of the steps. As I watched her descend, I made a wish for her. A tiny prayer.

The Mafia Works on Saturday

I must look honest. One summer day in Mondello a woman approached me as I read a book in my little beach chair and, in bad Italian, asked me to watch her bag while she swam. Later, out of the water, information poured out of her: Turkish, she left Istanbul, lived in Vancouver, lived in Germany, was a project manager, is lactose-intolerant so no pizza, no pasta, is looking for a house in Mondello, can pay 300.000 euros and will I help her, can we have coffee? Her name is Defne and she lives in Palermo right off via Liberta on the street with Hermes on the corner. I knew it and she knew Lidl's. Not as swanky a landmark as Hermes but better. You can't eat a purse.

What was I doing here? Where was I from? Where did I live? I told her I'd bought a deserted nightclub and renovated it and her mouth dropped open. This was about the only time she stopped talking. "But how could you—I mean—how did you do that? You don't speak Italian and how did you find people and know what to do and . . ." I felt a bit offended because I really do speak enough these days. People here are very New Yorky with their questions about real estate and she wanted to know how big and how much. Yes, 75 square meters was very good for one person. Very good. I told Defne they wanted 39 thousand but I paid 30. It is the only time she did not speak for a full five seconds. Whenever anyone is astounded at the price, I think: I did good. I explained it had been on the market for years and no one saw the possibilities. She wanted to make sure I was not *on* via Roma because of the noise then said, yes, yes, it's near Piazza Rivoluzione.

Then another woman came over and asked me, in Italian, to watch her things. I really should set up a little kiosk and charge.

The next day, a Saturday, Defne texted me that she was at Lidl's with her bike so I met her there under a palm tree with mine. I was elated to retrieve it from the morass that was my cortile; I'd bought a new padlock and chain and was all set except for flat tires.

We walked to her bike shop as her bike had a problem and my tires needed air. It was the hottest day in Palermo I could remember. Blazing sun, burning-my-skin heat.

When a Turk or an Italian tells you something is very near it isn't near to an American. We finally arrived and I was introduced to Stefano who was young, bearded and busy in a small room festooned with hanging bike tires. Stefano immediately put my bike on a sort of platform to begin checking the gears. He replaced a cable or two, was quite thorough. Meanwhile Defne kept up a constant monologue in bad Italian and when he wasn't answering but was intent on his work, she went into an adjoining room and talked to a dog the size of a Shetland pony. This poor animal was trying to take a nap and here was this woman bending over him talking talking talking. Stefano's mother came and I was introduced. I stood outside but I could hear Defne telling her that I paid 30,000 euros for my house and that it was 75 square meters. Then I was summoned as they wanted to know how much I paid for renovation. I said I hadn't really added it up yet which is true. They were insistent so I gave a guess. The woman asked the precise location and nodded in approval. Well, at least no one has asked me how old I am in an entire week.

The fee for the work on my bike was five euros. I had Stefano write his address down for me.

Defne left her bike there for repair so again we were walking. But this time through the Saturday crowds to the shoemaker. He sat at a table piled high with shoes in a room about four feet wide. The strap on my pocketbook needed sewing but he didn't have the right machine so he recommended another shoemaker. No name, no address, no street number, no sign—these are the secrets of Palermo. I was to go to via Torino, keep walking to via Maqueda and then find an arch and go through it for 20 meters and somewhere in the immediate area I would see the tiny shop. When I did leave off my shoes or my computer or anything to be fixed there'd be no stub, no ticket; I would be remembered.

We left off her shoes then Defne wanted to show me another "very close" place but I decided to go home. I had things to do. Delighted to be able to ride my bike for the first time since last September I went whizzing down deserted alleys with the wind in my face.

A little knot of people were crowded in via Padua at the start of my alley and I went past and was at my front door when Trump of the Alley materialized. The thug was right at my elbow as I fumbled in my bag for my bike lock. I grabbed my phone from my market basket, said 'scusa' to him and held it to my face saying "pronto, pronto" and then I shrugged as I pushed the RECORD button. Seven minutes of threats. I got him to say his name, that I had paid him 250 euros, that I owed him more.

   I pretended to be meek and said, no, I didn't have the money, I didn't speak well, blah blah. I wanted to talk to a friend who spoke Italian better, blah blah. He kept asking, when will you have the money? When will you talk to your friend? We have done enough talking! I don't want to wait! I was glad he could not point to the broken wall with the exposed pipe again.

Only two weeks ago, I went to the police with the photos and asked if I could seal that off or was it necessary to leave it that way for the investigation. Marlon Brando wasn't there and I was with an older heavy-set ispettore with a fleshy face who kept repeating 'Clarissa' as if he liked my name and offered me coffee even though there were ten people in the waiting room. I told him I never drank coffee so he offered me water and asked me what I would do if he came to my house. Did I offer him water? I listened carefully not entirely sure if this imaginary scenario would keep him from coming to La Tana. He did not read the esposto carefully and asked me questions that were answered in the esposto. He said if I had 'before' photos then to go ahead and have it sealed.

As I fumbled with my brand-new bike lock which wasn't cooperating, Trump of the Alley stood way too close to me demanding the money. He had two fingers out and made jabbing motions towards my eyes. I could smell him. Finally, the lock clicked into place and I could go inside. He lumbered away. He has this huge belly and looks exactly like the old photos of any Mafia capo. I thought it was better to put my bike inside but then I wheeled it out again and went to the polizia. I was told to come back at two-thirty. It was half past twelve. I rode home and there sitting on the steps of a door on via Padua was Trump just watching me. Absolutely wet with sweat, I went inside and thought I'll have a quick bath and change my clothes.

NO WATER.

I called the number for the police and there was no answer! That toad was sitting right in the alley waiting for me to run out and be upset. To run out with the money? I sat down at my desk and realized most people I know here I don't trust. Certainly not Luca Iwanttomarryhim or Gianni or The Norman. Thomas is at the farm with Marcello for his summer vacation and being American he is just as new to the mysteries of Palermo as I am. I didn't want to reach out to my authority on the Mafia but called him anyway. I had met him the first week I was here via a journalist friend in Rome but he'd only wanted to sleep with me. No answer. Called Pietro at the Joli on his cell. No answer. My Mafia authority called me back and told me to go to the polizia at 1430 and to demand they do something about the water. I think he was a bit impressed that I had the recording. Wanted me to call him afterwards. He's in Corleone so not in Palermo. At 1400, I was out my door then decided to take a quick photo of what had been the wall with the exposed pipe. Didn't want to stand there and examine it but wondered if something, somewhere were actually cut. Was it something in the armadio at the corner of the building? When I turned around there was a man on a motorcycle watching me. The Enforcer, Trump's son? Wearing a helmet so I couldn't tell. I got on my bike and rode out of the alley.

Of course, Marlon Brando wasn't there and I was led into a room with last week's older inspector (or maybe he doesn't have that rank) who had stared at the esposto as if it were in Chinese and kept repeating my name. He pointed with an index finger to the 500 euros on the page and said I'd only paid 250 euros. He decided that I had not paid my workers and they had shut off my water and that I should pay the second 250. I wanted to scream. He had me turn off the recording, didn't want to listen. I could see I wasn't getting through to him. I said, "Grazie," through clenched teeth and left. I found out that Marlon Brando would be there on Monday afternoon.

At Lidl's I bought three huge bottles of fizzy water and put them in my L.L. Bean canvas bag out of sight. It was the hottest day of this summer so far and everyone was complaining. Back at my desk, I found the emergency phone number for the water company but it is only answered Monday to Friday so I can't do anything until 8 a.m. Monday. I called the Joli and luckily Maria with her excited blonde curls answered the phone and screamed how much she missed me. I told her I had no water, that the awful man had cut it off; she couldn't believe it. No room at the Joli but she could put me in a room with no windows. She said she would take care of me. I told her I would come in a few hours.

Then I thought, okay, think! I washed my face and hands with Ferrarelle, turned the fan on, felt better. I poured myself a glass of prosecco because prosecco is the answer. I decided I needed a calm person. Called Thomas. No answer. Called my Mafia authority. No answer. Then called Liz, my English friend from New York who moved to the south of France. She is resourceful, relentless, discreet. She possesses every quality I have ever listed on a business card. Any English woman friend I've ever had has cut away the jagged edges, all the superfluous and announced, "Okay, here we are. This is the situation and this is what we do." She is like that. As I listened to her, I thought, I don't need a hotel room. I am staying here and I will go in and out of the alley looking calm and normal. I will let them think they screwed up and that I still have water.

So, with a plan, I was fine because I had a piano. Maybe the second flute of prosecco helped, too.

Then Thomas called and he said, "Well, being very American I would try to find the panel where he turned the water off." I didn't think that was possible. We chatted about other things. Marcello is leaving the house at 4:30 in the morning and coming home at 8 at night. Working. Crops. We joked, said we missed each other. He is planning a trip to the beach, the Adriatic, if Marcello can break away from the peaches.

Then my Mafia authority called from Corleone. He was angry that the police had treated me that way. I am still very bad on the phone in Italian so he said he would email me. The email was very clear. He advised that I go to the water company on Monday morning and ask that a worker come to my house to turn on the water and that a municipal police officer come "to distrust the man who threatens you and turned off the water. You have to solve this problem forever! Keep me informed."

I don't know what Google translate means with the word 'distrust.' So that is that.

I can't go to bed dirty. Not ever. I took baths north of the Arctic Circle in the Mackenzie River every night. I actually dipped myself in the Arctic Ocean, washed my hair. It felt like my scalp was on fire but I was clean.

I can wash my hair with one bottle of water. I can deal with the rest of me with another bottle of water. Fizzy water stings! But I am clean. I fell into bed and read for awhile. It was a lovely interlude and I was happy to be here in La Tana and not in a windowless hotel room even though the Joli is like home.

This is easy. Thirty-six hours till I see Claudia Cardinale who will be horrified that this has happened. And now I know—the Mafia works on Saturdays.

THE WATER COMPANY OF PALERMO

August 1, 2022

Avoid going to the water company, known as AMAP, at all costs. On Monday morning I went to the main office on my bike and was told Dottoressa Spera aka Claudia Cardinale, was not there nor was her assistant. No idea if she were ever coming again. I was directed down the street to a wrought iron gate where about six people waited for it to be 8 o'clock. A plump woman asked my name and then addressed the crowd announcing that I was a foreigner. Nods and smiles all round. She was taking names on a tablet but we would be given tickets inside. I had to spell mine Milano, Como, Napoli, Ancona, Ischia, Roma. I wondered why this scene seemed so familiar and then remembered being in the bitter cold and dark at 5 a.m. with Shirley and Andrea, the courtroom artists, taking down names in front of the courthouse in New York so we didn't have to stand in line for the Harvey Weinstein trial.

It also had the feeling of being an extra. Waiting with a group of people early in the morning to be herded from one location to the next and told what to do.

A tall young man in shorts with a backpack came forward, announced he spoke English. This was Marco and I couldn't have survived without him. Having forgotten the lock for my bike, I wasn't going to leave it anywhere so he hefted it up all the steps and I wheeled it into the office with the group. A small guard in a navy blue uniform with a gun on his hip in a black leather holster would call a name and another man would hand that person a ticket. He skipped my name! I went up to him and said, yes, McNair, and pointed at it. It obviously made no sense to him so he just ignored it. I was number 10 instead of number 6 but this actually worked in my favor as he felt sorry and helped me.

The place was air conditioned but the door was open. There were three clerks but the first people, 1, 2, and 3, were not finished in 40 minutes. There'd be a ping and the next number would go up quite uselessly on a screen the size of a small TV. Marco asked me where I was from and when I said I was born in Mississippi but had lived in New York, he interrupted. "Jackson?" He had driven from Florida to California and remembered Jackson. He loves the U.S. and loves Americans. He was my great good luck that day. He hates Rome. "Rome is hell," he stated. Many Sicilians *hate* Rome.

Marco has come to this office three times since May to change the name on the water bill because his mother died and he lives in her house now. "And I am still in mourning, doing this." I said I'd done this at the electric company and it was easy. I gave him my card and said, "You have been so nice, if you ever need anything." He took it then smiled. "You are a novelist! Congratulations!"

The guard wanted to know why I was there. I told him. Sick of being quiet. The minaccia—one after another—and no water since Saturday morning. He went behind the glass partition and I could see him talking to a man behind a computer. This man, Signor De Santis, would talk to me and to Marco and then go back to his desk and stare at his computer. It seems I have no water meter. I told Marco I've never gotten a water bill and the electric person told me they came twice a year. Marco looked mystified. I described the tiny armadio/closet of steel, said it had a padlock, the AMAP man had come, here were the contracts. Why didn't Dottoressa Spera notice I had no meter? Or the man who came from the water company?

At one point, Marco told De Santis that I was a writer and the small man looked up at me and nodded. Would this news be important at the Palermo water company?

Dottoressa Spera/Claudia Cardinale will come to her office tomorrow and I can come back. Marco then became very heated as he and I agreed that *I must* have water today. He was shouting through the glass at De Santis. Shouting. It was wonderful. Someday I will be able to shout in Italian and actually make people do what I want. Signor De Santis who is bald and sunburned and comes up to my breasts went back to his desk and picked up the phone. Marco said, "He is calling the technical department." Time passed. De Santis came out again to report to Marco. The technical department was not answering the phone so he was going there. A long time passed. Someone called Marco on his phone and said his wife had made lots of pesto and could he drop some of it off at his house? No, Marco was not home. Marco and I moaned. We decided we were starving.

I told Marco I understood if he had to go home. We had both been there for hours, standing in this crowded room. No, we are almost finished, he said.

De Santis was back. Long, long explanation. They think that the pipe has been cut. If it is cut between this and that point then it is the problem of AMAP and they fix it but if it is cut outside that section then it is my problem and I must fix it but no matter what—it is illegal to cut the pipe! So a man from AMAP will come today and see the situation and I might have to call my plumber and get him to fix it and pay for it. I said, "I can't call my plumber, he is in on this." Marco said, "Find another one."

I never would have understood this without Marco. These were quite long monologues by De Santis. Marco parsed it all down for me. He thinks that maybe this time they have changed the name on his bill. We left together, he lifted my bike down all the steps and we went our separate ways. I went home to wait for the AMAP man.

The phone rang. A woman speaking very bad English but trying so hard that it was endearing told me to come to the police station at 9:30 on Wednesday. I am to go to the second floor –I always go there, could find it in my sleep—and I will meet a man named San Felice Massimo and then we will go to the fifth floor. I now know that often the last name is put first so it was Massimo San Felice. Finally, my interview. I told her I'd had another minaccia/threat on Saturday and the water had been cut but I had a nastro. I know nastro from Radio Vaticana. "A tape?" she said. "Certo!" I cried. I am to bring everything on Wednesday.

At nine o'clock that evening I realized that the AMAP man was not coming. I could not believe I must go back tomorrow. At least Claudia Cardinale had a real office and I could sit in a chair and gaze at her soulful portrait of Jesus.

August 2, 2022

At eight o'clock the next morning I was with Dottoressa Spera/Claudia Cardinale. She was wearing a loose black linen dress and before even saying buongiorno, said, "Sono incinta." I'm pregnant. This was spoken in the defeated tone of "I broke my leg." We went to her office and I told her my story. She heard me out, got on the phone, and a woman arrived whose English was entirely terrible but evidently better than my Italian. Actually, I doubt that. I decided that when a Sicilian speaks any English at all this is greatly admired by other Sicilians and assumed to be excellent English.

It was my understanding that a man would come to me in two or three hours to check the pipe situation. Same story with the place of the cut.

Claudia Cardinale asked me if I would teach her daughter English. I guessed she was about twelve. Of course, love to. The baby is due in February. I tried to cheer her up by saying it would be Aquarius which was me and the absolute best thing to be. She was smiling at that. Poor thing. Six months to go and it was very hot weather and she looked awfully big.

On my bike racing down via Cavour, my phone rang, I pulled over to stand beside a parked car and it was AMAP saying they were at my house. Could they please wait 10 minutes? I sped home and was there in seven. Two men stood beside a white AMAP truck parked in front of my door. One of the Alley Men was standing, staring. When I said this to Thomas, he said, "Clarissa! That is what they DO!" I pulled out my key to the padlock of the little steel door and it didn't fit. The man tried it. No. He handed it back to me, shaking his head. The padlock had been changed. The AMAP man got it open and reached inside and turned a lever. I rushed inside and had water. Out again. The padlock had been clicked closed but I asked them to stay for 10 minutes while I went to the ferramenta to buy a new one. They wouldn't. One of them was around the corner talking to The Enforcer who was leaning off his balcony talking loudly. I jumped on my bike, pedaled like mad, ran into the ferramenta and tried to act out a padlock. Antonio was mystified. Finally, I bought two sizes, told Antonio I would explain later, jumped on my bike and raced back. Truck gone. Raced inside, checked for water again and then out to click my padlock on top of the other one.

A minute later I put a racing stripe of nail polish on it. Pink to match my pedicure. Then I took a picture.

I'd already been to the stationers and had huge color photos printed of the men hacking away at my wall beside the front door on May 18th. I had before and after photos. I had water. I felt so powerful. I had a cool bubble bath. Every time I get into that tub I feel like I'm stepping into a canoe on a lake somewhere in Vermont. I turned on the dishwasher. Running low on flutes.

Then Trump of the Alley was reaching through the bars and banging on my mirrored doors. He pressed his fat, doughy face against the bars, shouting, "Signora! Signora!" Horrid man. I don't care how much real estate he owns, he smells. Then it was The Enforcer ringing my doorbell again and again angrily. Striding back and forth in his tight blue jean shorts, tight T-shirt showing all his muscles, mirrored sun glasses and running shoes. Angry. A tiny triumph for me is seeing them and being invisible.

I could hear hammering and drilling from next door. Were they finally going to get the pizza parlor operating? Were they going to say they had to turn off my water for construction?

Then I saw The Enforcer drop my new padlock at my front door and I raced to the kitchen and had no water!

Marlon Brando had said to call if I felt any tension at all. He'd written a number under his name on one page but it wasn't his number but the police station number. A man said he was not available until five and "Va bene?" and I said, "No. Non va bene," and hung up, feeling miserable. Honestly! No one calls the police because everything is alright! I called 112 and was on hold for a long time then told to call this number and that one. At one point I'd been transferred, as promised, to someone who spoke English. I told her the situation and she told me she had nothing to do with the police and to call 112! Was she someone's girlfriend? When I had given up entirely the phone rang and the police had called me. A man listened, took down the information.

I wrote an email to my Mafia authority I n Italian as I don't think he has ever said as much as OK in English. Then I wrote Claudia Cardinale and she wrote back, in Italian, of course, You did the right thing to call the police!

Twenty minutes later two men arrived. Tight little navy blue uniforms. My god, the police wear such tight clothes here. I let the police in and told them about the esposto and no water since Saturday, about AMAP giving me water and then the banging on the door, the cut padlock and no water again. They photographed my passport. Were terribly nice really. Listened, asked questions. I wondered if in any of these immersion classes there is an exercise in dealing with the police? Much more interesting than asking for the train station.

I told them that maybe it was better to do nothing as I had the appuntamento tomorrow. But I had no water! They knew Marlon Brando. I thanked them and thought, hey, I have Alamo-ed it out this long, had a bath, have clean dishes . . . it's fine. I had a little break and I'm okay for the next round.

They went out, trim, muscular, tan, black-haired, brown-eyed. Told me to lock the iron door. I did. Then, of course, I saw that they were in the alley, deep in conversation with both father and son extortionists. Maybe it lasted for half an hour. Nobody is succinct here. Nobody condenses anything. A person at the post office window can take 15 minutes buying one stamp.

I told myself not to get involved but I knew the Di Lauros were lying. I was here at my desk knowing all this conversation was going on, hating myself for not speaking better. I looked out through the bars again and they were, all four, in front of the little steel door. One officer motioned me to join them. Trump was waving his arms around saying it was his water, etcetera and I said softly, "No. AMAP mi ha detto questo è mio." No. AMAP told me it was mine. Trump went on and on as The Enforcer, muscular and menacing in his tight shorts and sunglasses, looked on as backup. I went inside then the officers were at my door again. I let them in and they told me that my contatore (meter) was inside that box and that Trump says he owns the box. I said no, AMAP mi ha detto è la mia scatola. No, AMAP told me it is my box.

One officer said that he would move the meter. You need a muratore (someone who works with walls or plaster) and you put it right here and that's that. Don't give him any money. Pay for this to be done. The officers were calm and reasonable and I thought maybe this whole mess is solved but I would still like these cretini/cretins to be punished for the threats and for making me live without water for the four hottest days all summer. The police turned the lever and gave me water again.

I had the lead man write his name and rank down so that I could tell the investigators.

The plan was to wear my white linen dress tomorrow to look pristine and believable. As pristine as possible in this heat. Silver jewelry but subdued and my leopard-print high-heeled sandals which I wear every day anyway. My everyday straw hat. I wished I were seeing Marlon Brando. I wondered if it would be a panel of ispettori or men of higher rank. I wondered if there would be stacks of epaulets on the broad shoulders of beautifully-tailored uniforms. Will anyone speak inglese? I used Google translate and have written everything that happened from Saturday to now. I am a bit tired and it's not even time for lunch. Everything here is so emotional.

THE INTERVIEW

August 3, 2022

"Thanks, without presumption we are people who put our heart into our work, thanks and good evening."

This was the translated response from the Ispettore Massimo San Felice to my texted thank you note.

He and the woman did put their hearts into their work. They understood the situation, all was written down, I signed, and now we let the Sicilian system of justice take over.

That morning I changed from the white dress to a black one and was glad I did. I looked too dressed up in white and black was appropriate. Putting out the garbage today and, of course, there was The Enforcer but I didn't look at him. I didn't ride my bike because I didn't want anyone to see it tied to that tree outside the station right on via Roma.

I was escorted from the usual waiting room by an officer who held open the elevator door, got in after me and pushed five. This was the exalted place Marlon Brando had mentioned in a whisper with one index finger pointing up. I wondered if men would be in uniform, if I'd face a panel behind one long dais or what. Instead it was a woman with greyish-blonde hair in a print blouse and a man with a closely-trimmed white beard, glasses and a very handsome face wearing a polo shirt and jeans like every other male in the building. Ispettore San Felice. I positioned myself so I could see them both and wasn't behind a giant black computer.

I was prepared. I had headed a page 'Palermo and Sambuca' and then listed the two fathers with their two sons. I had the large color photos of the men chopping away at the wall to expose my pipe. There was Luca Iwanttomarryhim and Trump of the Alley and The Enforcer, son of Trump, and several bystanders. Dated May 18, 2022. I had photos of the wall and my front door before and after and today. The photos were invaluable and Ispettore San Felice referred to them constantly. Who at the water company? I handed over one page with Dottoressa Germana Spesa written in caps with her phone number and email.

We covered May 18th and the threats and the urging of Luca Iwanttomarryhim to pay Luca Di Lauro whom I called Trump of the Alley. I told how Gianni on the phone from Sambuca told me I had to pay. Then the next day how Luca told me I should pay because Luca Di Lauro was Mafia and dangerous. I remembered things I had not said before. San Felice was good and even though there was the struggle with the language, I could flesh out the situation as I had not done with Marlon Brando. San Felice typed it all into the computer with two index fingers.

Once in awhile another officer would come in and listen to me and San Felice.

Sometimes he would ask something in a very long monologue and I had trouble following exactly what he was asking and the woman who spoke some English would step in and help. I had listed how many times I had seen and talked and emailed Dottoressa Spera at the water company. The dates. How many times had I been threatened. They were both amused when I told them how the son came after a few days and said, Don't pay my father. Give me the money!

I handed over the receipt for E 250 that Luca Di Lauro signed. They were smiling and laughing. What an idiot! The extortionist signed a receipt! San Felice said, in Italian, "He signed it because he never thought you would be brave enough to go to the police."

Brave enough? This isn't brave, I thought. This is normal.

We proceeded to last Saturday. I had written all that had happened from Saturday to the time of the new padlock. Then I showed them the broken padlock with the nail polish. San Felice examined it. Another officer came in and it was passed to him and he examined it, then he put it down on a piece of white paper and photographed it. The little padlock with the bright pink stripe was treated with the same importance accorded a bloody knife.

I told them I had recorded the threat on Saturday and was told to play it. San Felice looked at me with what I interpreted as a bit of admiration. They listened. The woman said that I sounded frightened. I was just off my bike and bending down fumbling with the brand-new lock and it wasn't cooperating. I started to explain this but it seemed important for it to be written that I was afraid. So I said yes. The woman was very sympathetic as she listened to me on the tape answering this shouting man. They asked if either father or son had touched me and I said no. Then I did tell them how they pounded on my glass door yesterday and shouted at me on the other side. Also how they get too close. This is intimidation, this is threatening behavior, they agreed and San Felice kept typing.

At one point, he broke into a grin. It was when Trump of the Alley was telling me how many buildings he owned and how powerful he was. "Il padrino di Palermo!" The godfather of Palermo!

But 99 percent of the time it was dead serious. Yes, it was pizzo I was being asked to pay. I think San Felice was surprised I knew the word.

Pizzo. Illegal to demand it, against the law to pay it!

The word 'estorsione' was used again and again. Extortion.

Ispettore Massimo San Felice said we take this very, very seriously. You must not think of yourself as stupid. These men are stupid. You are not a victim because you are here. You are doing the right thing to report it. This was repeated more than once. I was actually thanked for reporting it.

The men could be prosecuted for several counts: extortion, fraud, threat of bodily harm and could each receive up to five years in prison. These men are Mafia and they are dangerous.

The system is not good, said the woman, when we were alone and I asked her to explain what would happen next. In summation, the magistrate controls the police and tells the police what to do. They must wait for that. When would the magistrate decide? The woman said, "It's not like the United States and . . ." She sighed, looked uncomfortable. Her embarrassment and reluctance to answer communicated that everything was far into the future.

It was nice in that room with the balcony doors open, a breeze wafting in and being with two people who really wanted to understand, wanted the report to be correct. Things I had not recalled came back to me. I described how the Pizzeria Triplets were so friendly and then how The Enforcer came alone and offered to buy my place, how he showed me through the brand-new kitchen of his pizzeria the next day. Even how he said he wanted to knock the wall down and use my space for an indoor restaurant. I said to the woman but why now? It's been empty for ten years which is why I got a good price. Empty! He could have bought it five years ago, last year. Then she and I realized at the same time: the kitchen next door looked brand-new. The pizzeria was probably a brand-new idea and suddenly the space was bought by me.

Because of that pizzeria, this may be only the beginning.

I have to be tough until they are arrested. It might be months. I told San Felice that Di Lauro now has the key to his padlock on my meter closet. He has control over my water. When I go home will I have water? He said officers were going today to warn him that he was breaking the law. I was told to be careful. These men are dangerous. Call 112 if I feel any small fear. Well, no, not a great idea as I remembered calling it before and getting someone's girlfriend who spoke English.

I signed the pages and was alone with the woman who told me her name was Fiorella. I told her I was so grateful to have her speaking English and to call me if she ever needed anything. I gave her my card with my address and my little square writer business card. San Felice had gone and a young man entered the room to escort me down the hall and to the elevator. The fifth floor is not casual.

I stepped out onto via Roma and looked at my watch. Only a few hours had passed. From May 18 to today, the characters, conversations, threats and motives had all been discussed intensely and carefully.

Thomas wrote me today for an update. I wrote a few sentences and he wrote back. "What a drama. But I must say I am kind of giddy that an American is sticking it to this mobster mentality that dwells in Palermo."

I fell asleep thinking of San Felice thanking me for coming to the polizia. No one is driving me out of La Tana. I am not going anywhere. The Sicilians won't win.

August 4, 2022

At 6:30 this morning I WhatsApped Ispettore San Felice and said I had forgotten to ask for a copy of my two handwritten pages and could I stop by the 2nd floor and pick them up? Certo was the instant response so I knew he was awake.

I was on the first of the two buses to Mondello at quarter of seven. It was packed. I saw the balloon men, the umbrella men, the water toys men rush past my door every morning carrying big bags on their shoulders and this time I was with them on the same bus. The water was serene, looked like a massive lake.

I've noticed we single women seem to find spots next to each other. With just a smile and a tilt of the head as we stand up to head for the water, we know we will watch each other's bags.

I was restless and left at nine to get back to my desk. Thought of all these things I should have said yesterday. Gianni talked to me so much—in English—about paying and yesterday we scarcely mentioned him. He also shouted that I was not to call the police. "Do you want to get my father in trouble!?" When I asked him to explain he talked again about how many thousands of euros it would cost to dig up the street for a new pipeline and wasn't paying 250 euros better?

I wrote this, used Google translate, jumped on my bike and had the stationery store print out the pages. I put it in a big white envelope, wrote San Felice's name in green on the front and leapt on my bike for the police station.

I went to the 2nd floor and said I had something for Ispettore

San Felice and had he left something for me? The woman picked up the phone then said someone would come for me. I hadn't counted on going up there and I hadn't counted on Marlon Brando suddenly standing before me, grinning and joking with another ispettore. Both tan and good-looking in jeans and polo shirts.

"Tutto a posto?" he asked. Everything okay? I started to say no, it's not but he stopped me and said he knew everything and it would all be taken care of, one step at a time. I was amazed. You know everything? Yes, he said, I read all the reports. I know all of it. I said I met yesterday for the intervista/interview. Brando knew all about it. He pointed at the name on my envelope. Said he was number one. The top man.

The other one in a red shirt nodded. Yes, the most important. A man with grey hair from yesterday arrived to escort me upstairs and they said, He's number two.

I asked Marlon Brando what number he was and he laughed then said he didn't know. These two men were joking around like teenagers. I see this all the time. Yesterday two men probably in their sixties were having lunch and laughing uproariously and then I could see they were going back to an office. Why didn't I notice that in New York City? Life seems lighter here. It's not just my neighborhood with people calling down from balconies, it seems to be all over Palermo. People are having a pretty good time.

For some reason all three men jammed into the tiny phone booth of an elevator with me and on the 5th floor, Brando and the other one called "ciao" and raced each other down the stairs. Laughing.

As we walked down the hall, all I could think was: I am bothering this man. The number one, the most important. He was in the same room, behind another desk and he rose, smiling, took the envelope, opened it, read it as I sat watching. Then he passed it to number two man who went to another desk and read it. Then I was shown the form that appeared to be an arrest warrant and there in clear printing were the names of the two Lucas. Iwanttomarryhim and Trump of the

Alley. I asked about the sons and was told they would be next.

I have never felt so miserable as today about not speaking, not comprehending Italian. Ispettore San Felice was giving me information and I was understanding nothing. He may as well have been talking to a dog. Then he said, I understand you are an important writer. I laughed and said, "Solamente una scrittrice ma non importante." Only a writer but not important one. I handed him my postcard with all the book jackets pictured and he said, "Gialli?" and I said yes. That's crime. I pointed to the ones that were. Then *he* walked me to the elevator himself. We stopped in the hall to talk or rather he talked. I can't even say I listened, I just stood there like a tree stump but I understood him to say that it was a pity I did not speak Italian.

At the elevator, I asked him if my situation were typical and he answered. He could have been explaining birth control in Romania. I have no idea what he was so excitedly, eyes alight, telling me.

* * *

Last night, Ruth called from London and kept saying, "Think what you've done. Think where you were a year ago. Your chandeliers are up! Think what you've done!" She's right. A year ago I was in Astoria getting estimates from shipping companies.

* * *

Am having a call from the United States tonight at nine. A new case IF they hire me. A billionairess has disappeared in Paris after an ominous phone call. Her embassy won't help, French police won't help, the law firm who handles her business affairs won't help and Zachary, my producer friend in Paris, recommended me. Of course, I have ideas but it will be a tough one. The more difficult it is the more I like it. It's adrenaline, I guess, because I refuse to fail.

IF I am hired, this will be my second missing person case in Paris. That Russian prince.

I hope I can find this woman. I hope she is alive.

Hawk went on a trip to England. We text about twice a week. She works behind the scenes and keeps me au courant. We will meet again when she is back in Palermo.

On Sunday morning, I grabbed the L.L. Bean canvas bag with the cookies Thomas asked me to bring for after church and wheeled my bike out into the alley. I had trouble opening the metal fold-out side basket and was laboring over it when a huge motorcycle roared to a stop and a young and handsome man took off his helmet and asked if I needed help. He easily pulled the metal clip open and grinned. I thanked him. He asked if I were on vacation, the usual questions. He lives around here, on via Abramo Lincoln.

We introduced ourselves and he offered to drive me anywhere, to do any work in my house, wanted to give me his phone number. I had a green pen, nothing else so he wrote it on my arm. He kissed me on both cheeks and told me to call him, put on his helmet and roared away. At lunch, Thomas was excited. "Why don't handsome young men ever roar up on motorcycles and give me their phone number?"

PAOLA, WIFE OF THE ENFORCER

Monday was a good day. First off, Angelo came; he was a small, nice-looking man, recommended by Ferdinando the carpenter. Poor thing. I showed him the cortile that The Norman had promised to power-wash but, of course, he had disappeared instead. Angelo looked forlorn in the doorway but bravely began to clean.

He worked right through the lunch hour until three o'clock. I have his number if I need a ride to the airport, a ride anywhere. I am to call him for anything. He said he and Ferdinando were—he put his index fingers together.

I really appreciated having another person to deal with the cortile.

The big plastic bins stack up but look terrible. I'd consolidated down to twelve. Angelo stacked them on the side then said no, let's stack them at the end. So he did. He wouldn't let me help. I bought a forest green tarp to put over the mass and it looked like a dying green elephant.

Then we placed the wrought iron table that Mother had made from the garden gate at the Old Canton Road house in the middle. The marble top had broken in transit but I found an extra rectangular piece of marble initially meant for the bathroom wall. It was larger than the wrought iron frame but it worked. It's snow white and pretty. I paid Angelo and he left.

Unsatisfied, I went to the Chinese department store on via Abramo Lincoln—which always has the right thing—and bought a bundle of fake green ivy leaves that unrolled to four meters and was a meter high. I could put that over the green tarp. That was the plan. The piano.

I moved all the boxes from the back of the cortile to the side and it was sweaty work. That was good because it covered the gas cannister which looks like a two-foot tall bomb and means I have hot water and can use the stove. Then I decided the cortile was too narrow to lose two feet so I was moving all the stuff to the back again when I realized a woman was leaning over the railing on the terrazzo above me. This had to be the wife of The Enforcer. She said her name was Paola but with the sun behind her, I could only see a silhouette of wild dark hair. I introduced myself using only my first name as McNair makes no sense to any Italian speaker. When she hesitated over 'Clarissa' I impetuously said that my diminutive/nickname was Cici and she decided to call me that.

Paola was opinionated and told me my plan wouldn't work, that I needed this and that and I didn't understand what she was saying and she kept laughing. I sense she is a very rough woman. She will be fifty on October fifth and wanted to know how old I am. I told her I had a bad time with numbers and was confused but that I am January, Aquarius. I am not going to let the entire alley know how old I am.

She watched as I pushed the heavy bins around then wanted to know what was in them. I told her books, too many books. Then I told her they were my books and she had the same little gasp of respect when I held one up and said that I'd written it. Tell your beastly male relatives, I thought. I moved boxes back and forth, sweating, as she told me that wouldn't work and it wouldn't work that way either and the ivy would come down in the wind, etcetera. I sweated, she supervised. But it was very nice thinking how annoying for The Enforcer if his wife decided I was okay.

Ispettore San Felice said he would call me when he was going to interview Luca Iwanttomarryhim and Luca Di Lauro/Trump of the Alley. The sons, The Enforcer and Gianni, I was told would be next. I would like to know how things are going but I dread the call as I will be my typical idiotic self on the phone. Maybe he thinks I am not entirely pathetic since I can write a book.

I wonder if Paola knows how her husband and father-in-law threatened me?

Deciding to go back to the Chinese department store for more ivy, once again I noticed the man in the yellow jersey staring at me as I locked my iron front door. Then he made a call; I sensed he was reporting to somebody.

Riviera Man, my longtime client, called at around seven and talked forever. His fourth ex-wife is giving him problems again. Or still. He is very coy and won't tell me what she is holding over him. An unethical business deal? Unpaid taxes in one of the seven countries he does business in? I await specifics and a retainer and then, like a leopard, will leap into action.

It was difficult to hear every word from Riviera Man as Paola was screaming in rage at The Enforcer. It was early for the evening rant.

* * *

I saw Claudia today at the frame shop who, it turns out, is not Claudia at all but Margarita, the mother of Claudia. No one wanted to correct me. I guess when they hear me speak there are so many things to correct that a wrong name is nothing. We decided to have Roberto who is married to Claudia come here to deal with the giant mirror that might go over the bathtub but I envision this nightmare scenario of being killed by this massive falling mirror while taking a bubble bath. It came from a hotel in Philadelphia and must weigh seventy pounds. I hope Roberto can lift it as he is so small, maybe he weighs seventy pounds and looks exactly like the hero in that film, *It's a Beautiful Life*. Maybe it *is* him. Some people say when you win an Oscar your film career goes downhill so maybe he now works in a frame shop in Palermo.

I was working this afternoon at my desk with the mirrored door half open and a man was outside calling my name. Nice looking, in his 30s but how on earth did he know me? He said he had to come by and say hello and he had something for me. A package was handed through the bars—pastry. He wanted to see me again but who was he? Had I met him before? Too many new faces. No idea.

On my list of things to do was to pay TIM 30 euros for my internet and cable so I went to the tabaccheria/tobacco shop and waited my turn to deal with the African clerk at the window. A woman with dyed shoe-polish black hair and the face of a prison warden stared at me. Some women here do that. I smiled and told her I really liked her t-shirt with the sequins on the shoulders. That hard face melted as she turned to face me, exposing GOD SAVES in huge gold letters. I tried to hold back a very wide smile. All these Sicilians run around with slogans in English that mean nothing to them. The garbage man often wears a Harvard sweatshirt. The God Saves woman started telling me I looked exactly like the ballerina named Kessler. Turning to other women who'd been staring at me, she asked them and they all agreed. I was highly complimented I told all five of them.

Meanwhile I'd pushed the TIM bill through with my credit card. Only cash, he shouted at me. So I had a 50 euro bill and pushed that through. The women were still talking about this resemblance to the ballerina. Then the African shouted something through the window and I said, "Piano piano!" and he shouted again. I had already paid the bill! All the women laughed and I said my life was chaos but I was going to learn Italian. Everyone seemed to get great enjoyment out of the whole thing as I made my way out through the cluster of short, plump, grinning women.

PROSECCO WITH THOMAS

This evening Thomas was at a table way on the far edge of Spinnato territory. Often one caffè's real estate bled into another. I felt all was in order: my bike was within arm's reach like a dog, next to the bottle lolling in a frosty ice bucket on its little stand. The air was filled with the background hum of conversation and thankfully, was cooling off at this hour. When I met Thomas for these debriefings and can speak English, it's as if I have put down a heavy suitcase.

I told him I'd invited a Sicilian woman for drinks. She seemed delighted by the invitation, picked the day and the time. Six o'clock on Tuesday. At seven, I texted and at eight I called her. No response, no answer. The table in the cortile had candles, little appetizers, the prosecco was chilled. "Dammit, I even bought flowers." I took a deep breath. "At two minutes of nine she texted that a friend had arrived from Naples and wished me a nice evening!" Thomas shook his head. "The Sicilians do what they want, when they want."

"The next day I wrote her and she texted back, in English, 'I don't think it's such a great guilt.'" I gulped a bit of prosecco. "I would never do that to another person. Just not show up!"

Thomas said, "They don't care."

I said, "I keep my promises, I meet deadlines, I'm on time."

He nodded. "Time is different here and if something comes along they'd rather do then they do it. Forget the plan."

I stated firmly, "Well, I am not learning the future tense." Thomas threw back his head, laughing.

I still have a long way to being cool in Palermo. Yes, I am okay at walking right into traffic on the zebra lines of via Roma and imagine I am Moses parting the Red Sea. Very different from Rome where they say the zebra lines are a target. When cars stop, I mouth 'grazie,' nod at the driver and hurry across. The Palermitani, blasé to the core, wander across like cattle if cows spent time staring down at cell phones.

Palermo is full of tourists—I blame *White Lotus*—who don't know how to cross via Roma and look hot, tired and anxious. When I see a cluster of them immobile and staring out at the traffic, I signal them to follow me and deliver them to the other side.

CONSULTING WITH THE F.B.I.

I called my FBI contact and was delighted to hear his voice. Jim always had excellent advice and he's never steered me wrong. I always felt so happy—and safe—knowing he was in my corner.

I told him about my conversation with the referral from the Beast of Barcelona. He was dodgy; I could smell it on the phone. In a deep, Spanish accent, he was holding back on me which is not good in a client.

Jim and I played around with the possibilities and where this might be headed and I decided not to take the case. "He wanted to know if I had a man on the ground in Paraguay." We both laughed.

International world headquarters is La Tana in this alley in Palermo and I do have excellent contacts but I had to tell him the truth. "No. I don't have a man on the ground in Paraguay—not this week."

But it's nice to be asked.

A TRIUMPH

It was time to celebrate La Tana. First, Mount New York was gone, whittled down to nothing which meant I no longer had a narrow path from the front door to the bathroom and a second narrow path from front door to cortile. The open space took on the look and feel of a loft.

The chandeliers were hung, all three of them, and my paintings were up and clothes were put away in the new closets. Francesco had painted the raw wood white and they were nearly invisible which is what I envisioned. When I told Thomas I was painting the walls of the cortile with bright green stripes he bemoaned the fact that he was away with Marcello and pleaded with me to wait until he could come back. "I want to paint stripes! We'll drink prosecco to inspire us and then afterwards to celebrate!" We joked about the outcome of this project paired with alcohol.

However, anxious to begin, I bought tape, brushes and green paint to match the star over the front door then stood on a stool and measured. I began painting. When I'd done the back wall, I pulled away the tape and thought, well, no one comes out here until it's almost dark anyway and if they do notice that these stripes are a bit wavy they'll think it's because they've been drinking. The next morning, I called a painter who understood what I wanted and we agreed on a price. He obviously subcontracted and two quite elderly men arrived a few hours later with a ladder and tarps. One, poor thing, suffered an asthma attack so work was suspended for awhile but they soldiered on until six o'clock. They finished the next day and had done a superb job for 100 euros. My swaying stripes had been replaced with straight, bold, emerald green bands.

The black and white marble floor looked sensational. Mother's large Haitian painting hung over Moby Dick and dominated the room. The glass-topped coffee table I'd found on the street in Philadelphia was two-tiered. Painted high-gloss white, it held an Egyptian backgammon board and my magnifying glass collection on the lower level and on the glass top I put candles and flowers from the Bangladeshi's post on via Roma.

I was so happy every morning waking up to my pictures and my books. Sometimes I fell asleep thinking: I did it.

THE CHARM OF PALERMO

No matter what was happening to me, waiting for workmen or fighting for water, I was not immune to the charm of Palermo. I must always wait for the light on via Cavour and it's a very long light before we can cross. Giuseppe always leaps out of his very chic men's shop and today he held my handlebars so I missed the first green signal. I was laughing as he talked, told me he lived in the country, pointed to his bike that he rides to where his car is parked. He is tan, always looks perfect, big smile. This was our longest conversation. It is so nice to be told I am elegante as I wait for the light to change. I feel very feminine here.

As I walk through these alleys, I look up at the household laundry hanging down and at the men, shirtless and smoking, with elbows on railings, leaning over surveying the street scene or calling down, talking to someone looking up. I like the mornings here. Before seven o'clock, Vincenzo, formerly known as Alley Man, is at his post. He stands behind a steel barricade that is exactly what is used to control crowds in New York City. There are a few of these around and each one usually has a man leaning on it, staring or smoking or chatting. Vincenzo always says my name so it's 'buongiorno, Cici' and 'tutto a posto?' Later it's 'ciao, Cici,' at various times as we pass later in the day. Maybe five times. Luciano, with his wonderful wolf face, wheels his red motorcycle out of the church every morning. A man I call The Refrigerator comes over and kisses him on each cheek. Luciano grins and greets me. Always 'buongiorno' which is more formal than 'Ciao.'

Pipo, the portiere of the via Padua building, always says, "Buongiorno, Clarissa." That would change and I would become 'Cici.'

SPARROWS BEHAVING BADLY

This morning I filled a suitcase with huge coffee-table books on art and sailing and interior design and got myself on the 101 bus to the church. Thomas said the book sale was next Wednesday but the church would be open this morning so to bring what I had. It was hot and the suitcase was heavy. I walked in to the sanctuary where three women stood in the center aisle chatting. I smiled and said, "I've brought books," and they stared at me. The tallest one with three huge moles on the side of her face like chocolate chips, said, "We don't want any books."

I ploughed on, saying, "Thomas told me to bring them here today. For the book sale." She looked at me long and hard and I stared right back. Then, in a tone of 'oh, all right,' she said, "Are you going to leave the suitcase? No? Well, take them out," she ordered.

I walked over to a table against the wall and unzipped my suitcase as they watched me in silence. I felt unwelcome, even unclean. Before I left I asked what time the sale started on Wednesday and the big, tall one with the white hair and the moles said it was 10:30 to 12:30 and four to six. I said, "Sounds good," took my suitcase and left. No one said goodbye or thank you. I felt they had spit on me and was proud of myself for resisting the 'thank you' that comes so naturally. Those hideous Sparrows!

SONO UNA PALERMITANA

In the hardware store, a man heard me talking to Antonio and said, "Oh, you're American." I responded, "Io sono Palermitana," and he laughed as Antonio chimed in, "Clarissa e Palermitana." Clarissa is a person of Palermo.

I looked back at my 2021 date book and it was June 21 that I first saw this place and said, "Oh, no. It's impossible." That was a Monday. On Wednesday evening I saw it again and on Thursday afternoon, I made the offer. On Friday morning I took the train to Roma and my offer was accepted on Monday. In September, three months later, I became the owner of a Tunisian nightclub in the Arab section of Palermo and here I am—a newly-minted Palermitana.

PROSECCO WITH THOMAS

A splendid evening with a clear sky; two of Mother's silver goblets and a bottle of prosecco sat on the marble table between us. Our debriefings were often now held in my cortile and lasted hours as we sat with lit candles, surrounded by green stripes. The conversation veered into gun control and the United States. "Australia did it," I said.

Thomas and I talked about Congress, the NRA, public opinion. He is a talker and it's relaxing to just listen.

I felt pretty good. I still had the dizzy spells but not while I'm up on a ladder so that's okay. I did something to my little finger and it's swollen which is actually a good thing as I can now wear a ring that was always in danger of falling off.

"The book sale was a modest success," said Thomas. "Between that and the Christmas bazaar it's a few thousand euros."

"I left off lots of books. Actually, I made three trips but my first drop-off was the most memorable." I told him how the women had behaved.

Thomas shook his head. "I apologize for my flock," he said.

"Oh, no! Don't apologize. I am only sorry you must deal with women like that."

He frowned. "Well, they *are* my flock."

"Baaaaaaa!" I said and we both laughed then changed the subject.

MY ALLEY HAS A BAD REPUTATION

You would think that a thousand-year-old deserted church in an alley in Palermo would be enjoying a serene, ecclesiastical slumber. A rotting wooden staircase leads nowhere and the monks' quarters are now open to the sky. The sanctuary was the setting for christenings, weddings, funerals for hundreds of years and that church should now sit in dignified though ruined, silent splendor. But no—a few days ago, two hard-faced men went in. Came out. Luciano wasn't with them. They knew the padlock combination. Luciano goes in many times a day. Sometimes with a motorcycle, sometimes bringing one out. His is red and polished like the sun. If I squint it looks like a giant candied apple on wheels. The other day he was putting a white one in. Two days ago, two men were lifting enormous flat-screen televisions about the size of a single bed out of a truck and carrying them in. Movie night at the church? Probably not.

I met an English woman named Eleanor who overflowed with information about my alley. She said that the pizzeria had been talked about forever. This was not a new idea, they had years to buy the nightclub which had been empty for at least ten years. "I'm surprised you were able to buy it. You acted quickly because if they had known they would have threatened the realtor and told him not to sell to you." Not only had La Tana been a Tunisian nightclub but, for awhile it had been a Romanian nightclub. I sighed at this news. I didn't know how much more exotic I could take.

Eleanor put her head in her hands when I said Luciano was my friend. "He is bad and dangerous!" I shook my head. "I don't think so. He's awfully nice to me, my tables are stored in the church up by the altar and I went to his daughter's first communion." She gasped. "And that church next door to you—you've been in that church?" I couldn't tell if this frightened or intrigued her. She said it was full of drugs and that's why there's so much traffic all day long. "Stay away from Luciano!"

I won't stay away from Luciano. I like him.

Trump of the Alley is a different story. Evidently, he owns thirty buildings and is very powerful. Someone else told me that most of the Nigerian women were prostitutes. Sapphire and Gorgeous? Ruby? No!

The world passes in my alley. Lobo, the black dachshund trots by, always cheerful about the new day. That dachshund-Mini Cooper-chihuahua-sweet feeling sweeps over me when I see him. My heart aches a little bit.

I'm used to Luciano who always greets me in the morning. Vincenzo calls "Ciao, Cici!" whenever he passes my front door. Even when it's closed. Nigeria shouts, "Am Er I Ca!" when I'm in range. Sometimes he follows that with "I love you!" and I laugh and "Ni Ger I A!" him back.

I like my alley.

THE CHINESE DEPARTMENT STORE

At the Chinese department store, where one can buy anything from an egg beater to eye shadow, I bought a wooden screen to cover the gas canister in the cortile. Too heavy for me, one of the Chinese men put it on a trolley and wheeled it back here. I traipsed beside him walking my bike as we chattered the whole six minutes. He is tall and jovial and when he smiles his eyes disappear and are replaced by two little black lines. At my door I tried to give him a few euros but he waved his arms and exclaimed, "No, no, no!" I said, oh, please, for a cappuccino! But he would not take it. I told him he was molto gentile and molto bravo and he left with the trolley clanking over the paving stones, grinning, with his two little slits for eyes. An African watched the scene and said that the Chinese were very nice. Why are the ones on Canal Street in New York always in a bad mood? The Chinese here are so different.

I rode my bike to see Antonio and buy the smeralda/emerald green paint. An older man was there and insisted on talking to me. Antonio knew I wasn't understanding and advised, "Piano, piano." The man looked a bit confused but dropped his voice to a whisper. Antonio and I doubled over laughing as Antonio told him he meant piano, piano as slowly! Not softer! Then we all laughed.

I realize that I laugh so much more here than I did in New York. Every transaction is personal.

I painted the screen green and it will exactly cover the air conditioner and the gas cannister in one corner of the cortile. The next time

I went to the Chinese department store I showed them the photo.

AN ISLAND

In Manhattan, I never feel I'm on an island but here, in Palermo, I never forget it. It's not just a cool breeze from the water. What a kick to see a tremendous white ship docked at the end of the street. And to hear that deep, bass blast of the horn late in the afternoon as it leaves port. Off to sea, maybe to Africa, maybe to Greece or Spain—one would have to be made of stone to not feel a little spritz of excitement.

GUESTS IN THE CORTILE

A guest from New York. I met Joan standing in line at the Harvey Weinstein trial in February of 2020 and we'd kept in touch; she, in turn, wrote me that a friend of hers was in Palermo so, of course, I invited the friend to come for prosecco. I bought zinnias, baby's breath and large shiny green leaves from the Bangladeshi flower man and put them in a brass vase I bought at the thrift shop in London. I couldn't open the big jar of olives so went down to the motorcycle shop to ask a man to do it. Nigeria and I went through our affectionate shouting routine and a few people smiled, looking mystified. He opened the jar of olives, I told him to take one and he handed it back.

Joan's friend was Brazilian. I liked her and conversation was lively. We sat in the cortile and talked for three hours.

There would be many guests to follow. Friends came and sent me their friends: writers, two lawyers from St. Louis, someone in film from L.A., sisters from Mississippi and a producer from the south of France. A Palermitana in the opera world who now lives in Paris. The great-great-granddaughter of Garibaldi and her British husband came for drinks. The cortile was always lit by candles and alive with conversation.

• • •

Tearing down via Roma on my bike with the breeze in my face was exhilarating. I must stop passing the 101 bus then racing it to the next stop but it's irresistible. Sunday evening, I left here at about seven and found narrow, beige, winding alleys leading to one piazza after another I'd never seen before. In the light of a golden sunset there would sit yet another massive church. All of them the color of sand. One outdoor caffè after another with tables filled. The hum of conversation. I stopped at one and saw that there were several Americans sprinkled around, all finishing dinner at the early hour and most of them with Coke cans in front of them. The couple nearest me were probably in their early 30s and never spoke one word to each other. Both eating with one hand and staring at their phones held in the other. I asked if the food were good and the man looked up and said it was wonderful. "We found this place on Google."

HOW MANY YEARS DO YOU HAVE?

I was in vicolo del Forno and had just passed the little red table with the men drinking beer when a young man walking behind me, asked me to wait. We exchanged 'ciaos.' The next words out of his mouth were, "Quanti anni hai?" How many years do you have? I was stunned and asked why he wanted to know. Just curious was the answer. Then he held up six fingers. "Sessanta," he said. I shrugged. Okay. Today I'll be sixty. "Complimenti!" he grinned. I nodded and walked away but then turned back and asked him how old he was. Twenty. I said, "Complimenti!" and proceeded on to Piazza Rivoluzione. At the caffè, at Lidl's, at school, buying my trees, my workmen. Why do all these people want to know how old I am?

AN INTERESTING FRIDAY in AUGUST

I put the AMAP padlock on over the Di Lauro padlock yesterday and now it is gone! A big new padlock is in its place. I guess I go back to Claudia Cardinale and tell her. This missing one was definite water company property as it had AMAP in big letters on it.

Claudia Cardinale had assuaged my worry about access to the meter. She said the Di Lauros could not change the numbers so that I'd have this outrageous bill but I should come for another padlock. The falegname/carpenter was coming at 09:30 to adjust the kitchen door and I thought I could be back at La Tana in time.

I went to the main entrance of the water company as usual and tied up my bike. The guard with curly grey hair recognized me. I told him Dottoressa Spera had asked me to come but this elicited no reaction at all. Had he not heard me or was he simply irritated to see me yet again? Then the guard from the other day arrived, greeted me effusively, waved me into the building and motioned for me to wait. He disappeared as I stood in the hall then returned with a tiny box. I thanked him and went outside. As I was leaving, he and another guard came out the front door and waved their arms that I was to keep walking beside the building. I didn't understand. Was I to go in another door?

Then there was shouting and I looked up and Claudia Cardinale/Dottoressa Spera was hanging out her window from the waist up, shutters open and motioning for me to come back. Then the guards were waving at me so I went back to the front door and was taken to her office. A skinny teenage girl was sitting at the second desk and Claudia Cardinale was on the phone. The girl had long dark hair and a veritable cyclone fence of braces across her front teeth.

Claudia Cardinale broke off her conversation to introduce her daughter, Aurora, and we chatted a bit while her mother was on the phone. She was entirely in awe of me and said, in Italian, "You are a beautiful woman." I was stunned. Then her mother hung up and joined our conversation. It was a social visit as we waited for the document I was to sign. They asked why I had chosen Palermo. I spoke in careful Italian. I said I had never liked Florence and they both nodded in agreement. Then I said I knew Rome and had worked at Radio Vaticana and knew what it would be like to be there again and wanted a change. Un cambiamento. I said I thought about Venice but there was that water problem. Then I said, So I am here in Palermo with a water problem! We were all laughing. It was fun. Maybe they were laughing *at* my Italian but I didn't care. I talked anyway. I said, "Questi uomini!" And Claudia Cardinale, hugely pregnant and plainly suffering from the heat, said not *these* men! All men!

Of course, Claudia Cardinale knew about Luca Di Lauro and filled in her daughter. I said he was an ugly animal. More laughing. The phone rang again.

Aurora was openly staring at me. A sweet girl. I don't think I looked odd but just different with my tight red jeans from Paris, a striped jersey, high-heeled sandals and my Panama hat which probably should be called a Mexico. I sat down in front of Aurora's desk and we spoke alone while her mother was busy. She was tear-y when she said she was having a very difficult time with English. I told her I was very slow at learning a language and we were just alike. I told her not to worry because there were lots of different ways to learn and we would find a way. She has plainly suffered and I know the feeling. My stomach hurt and I wanted to cry during every 90- minute session with the French tutor. It is a particular kind of pain to not understand words directed at close range and to realize the situation is not getting better.

I gave her my postcard with the books on it and my photo and email on the back. I told her to call or write me when she was ready. She burst out in English, "Oh, you are so beautiful!"

Her mother, off the phone, was obviously pleased that we were getting along. I said that coming today and meeting Aurora was serendipitous and I guess there is nothing that sounds like that in Italian. I said fortunato and destino and they smiled and nodded. Then I put my hands together, looked up and said, "Molte grazie, Signor Di Lauro!" and they laughed.

I find not having words means I am more dramatic, more physical than I would ever be in English.

I signed the paper for the new padlock and grabbed my bag to go. I told them both that I had to get home because the falegname/carpenter was coming and he was bello. They erupted in laughter. It was a sort of us-three-girls atmosphere. I must never forget that it was Pietro at the Joli who sent me to Claudia Cardinale.

I went outside to unlock my bike and heard my name called. I turned and this time they were both hanging out the window. I walked back to them and Aurora was holding the postcard and pointing to the little *KISS THE RISK* picture. She said they studied it in school and she knew my name. McNair. I hardly believe that fourteen-year-olds in Sicily are reading a novel about an international call girl ring but she was so excited and so sure of it. Okay, I thought. I won't argue. I will modestly accept being famous in Palermo.

At home, I painted both sides of the new padlock which clearly says AMAP with my pink nail polish. It is just the same size at Di Lauro's and the one I bought from Antonio. I clicked it on top of Di Lauro's and went inside. I was at my desk when The Enforcer started ringing my doorbell. Fast. Again and again. I didn't answer and he stormed away. Then the man in the yellow jersey I'd seen watching me in the alley rang my doorbell and I thought okay. So I went out as he was walking away and he said, You put a padlock on top of the other one. I am going to break it.

I went outside, glanced casually at the little door and because I could see the pink I knew it was there. Went inside. Turned on the water in the kitchen. Then The Enforcer was back ringing my bell over and over again. I grabbed my phone, opened the door and started recording. He was furious. Same story. Pay me the other 250 euros and you will have no problem forever. He said if I need to get in there then I can't because of that new lock. I said call AMAP and he shouted No! That belongs to Luca! Not AMAP! Enraged. He is muscular and in tight T-shirt and shorts and trainers plus the mirror sunglasses, he looked exactly like a character on The Sopranos. New Jersey thug. Mafia enforcer.

I kept saying non capito which further enraged him. He was breathlessly puffing on his cigarette in between shouting at me. It was staccato; it was short, quick barks. I wondered if smoke would come out of his ears. His shouting at me brought back Daddy shouting at me nearly every single night until I was 18 and escaped to college. The Enforcer would shout for a minute and then demand to know if I understood. I would say, Non capisco and he'd be furious. Daddy used to shout at me and then demand, "Do you understand?!" And I would look him in the face and very calmly say, "I understand." My tone of voice, very clear and very calm, was like a red rag to a bull and I knew it. So does *not* understanding with The Enforcer.

The Enforcer left then came back to my front door. Of course, I was recording it all. Doorbell again and again, in anger. Finally, his phone rang and he had to stop his tirade and I closed the glass door and didn't open it again. I fluffed up my hair, swiped on lipstick and rode my bike to the police station. Yellow Shirt, one of the Pizzeria Triplets, watched me from one end of the alley then punched a number into his phone.

At the police station, up on the 2nd floor there in the waiting room was Ispettore San Felice and two other men. Ispettore San Felice told everybody that I was McNair. I told him it was more minacce/threats and banging on my door and ringing my doorbell. They wanted to hear the tapes. I showed them the latest photo of The Enforcer who did look mean and muscular. The waiting room was clear of anyone in trouble on a Friday afternoon so it was just cops. Marlon Brando locked eyes with me as he walked through. Ispettore San Felice said this was urgent and it would only be a few days more. I heard him explain to the two officers who joined us that the Di Lauros wanted my property for their pizzeria.

Once the bad stuff and my instructions were out of the way, I told the men I was getting a dog the size of a horse. Then I was told to get a recording of a huge dog barking and to just push a button when the doorbell rang or when anyone pounded on my door. Ispettore San Felice said to get a pet lion. So we discussed that. He must have a keen sense of humor because the men often laughed after he spoke. Or else they are buttering up the top cop. Number One.

I had to pull out my book to get at my phone and I put *THE HONOURABLE SOCIETY* face down on purpose. Ispettore San Felice reached for it and then looked at me and asked, "Posso?" May I? and I said, "Certo," hoping he didn't find it odd that I'd be reading a book on the Mafia. He looked at the cover of a capo with a huge belly and suspenders and I said, "Signor Di Lauro," and he grinned. We had a sort of conversation about it. I understood nothing. I said I knew more about the American side of the Mafia but Palermo was a different world. Un mondo diverso. Actually, I am not sure it is so different.

Bottom line: these are bad men. If I feel any fear at all, if they keep ringing the doorbell I am to call 112 and say I have an esposto already and will they please come. Otherwise, I ignore them or I can open the door and behind my bars, tape them.

Ispettore San Felice told the others that I had written careful notes. The one who spoke a bit of English told me to write down the time and what happened. Un listino, I said and they all nodded. Si, si, si.

Those men in their jeans, the very air laced with masculine energy, the testosterone in equal doses to oxygen—it all makes me miss those detective days in New York, working with Mickey and John Henry and Bobby and Mas and wearing a wire and being exhilarated all the time and never knowing what next.

So the polizia are aware of me now. Maybe it means a lot to be introduced by Numero Uno.

Well, when you weigh everything on this Friday, I came away with a feeling of happiness. I realized that whether it's with Nigeria, Claudia Cardinale or San Felice joking about a pet lion, I laugh a lot. People are effusive, the mood is gentle and affectionate. It now seems nearly normal for Miss Blue Glasses to call me 'cara' and to call out when I am leaving with my panino, "Ciao! Un bacio! " A kiss. It has been a happy day.

THE PADLOCK WAR

I really must get a chihuahua or maybe a dachshund to talk to in times of emotional emergency.

Friday was a good day but Monday morning at nine o'clock I was back at AMAP. The guard with his curly grey hair didn't even look at me—didn't move his head or his eyes—but said Dottoressa Spera would be in her office tomorrow. He sighed probably thinking, okay it's morning and that idiotic American on a bike wearing the straw hat is here. He is as animated as an old turtle. I asked for her assistant who helped me before. No. Come tomorrow. I walked slowly back to my bike. A man appeared and opened the door of the guard's little booth and leaned in; they kissed each other. I thought, well, somebody likes him. Kissing over, door closed, the man came over to me and my bike.

He wanted to know what it was about. I said some horrible men wanted money from me to have water and they had cut off my water twice and I needed a lucchetto/padlock to put on over their padlock that I'd seen this morning. Mine with the pink stripe was gone. No change of expression, no sign he had heard me, he punched in a number on his phone, said a few words and motioned me to follow. I did. The glass doors opened letting free a cool wave of air conditioning as a young masked man appeared.

I told him the problem and he went to get me another padlock.

I was really sweaty and I don't sweat that much. Wondered what I could mop my face with. The photocopy of my passport? Tear a page out of *THE HONOURED SOCIETY*? I found a piece of Kleenex in the bottom of my bag. but when I looked in the mirror afterwards there were little white pinches of it stuck all over my face. Maybe I should invest in a handkerchief for Palermo. I see people mopping their faces all the time but today was the first time I'd needed to.

I'd told the masked man, piu piccolo, per favore. A smaller padlock, please. I waited for some time. When he came back, I was ready with 6 pages of AMAP documents and my passport. He opened the padlock box and I shook my head, showed him the picture on my phone. It wouldn't fit. The aperture was taken up by Trump of the Alley's newest, biggest padlock.

I needed a smaller one but there was nothing smaller. He put it into my hand, told me to take it anyway. Maybe he didn't want to do the paperwork to return it.

I rode home, put a stripe of nail polish on it and confirmed that it would not fit.

Seven padlocks of various sizes including the cut one from AMAP that had become important police evidence and a tiny one I bought from Antonio that looks to be for a doll's house now reside in a desk drawer.

Tuesday morning, I went back to AMAP and gave back the most recent one that was too big. It was in the box and I guess someone will be surprised to see the shocking pink racing stripe. Very festive.

THE HAPPIEST PLACE

I took the bus today as it looked like rain. I was leaning against the accordian-like connection that links the two parts of the huge bus and it moved and I jumped a little. The man next to me smiled, I smiled, he said something. The woman across from us laughed. Silly, of course. A nothing moment. And yet it wasn't.

I know that people here are like everyone everywhere else: they have sick children, bad marriages, hate their jobs. But people are ready to smile, to be involved. They like to be involved. Ask anyone where a certain stop is and three people will respond and when the stop comes they will all alert you enthusiastically and make sure you actually get off the bus.

I have been happier in other places. Floated over the streets in the throes of a love affair. Been high on adrenaline in those days of undercover. I remember standing on a balcony in Cairo overlooking the Nile and thinking I would never leave. All that was personal. The happiness was *me* because of what I was experiencing.

But here in Palermo, I see a sort of general atmospheric joy. Is it the breeze off the Tyrrhenian Sea? Is it being under the bluest of skies? Don't know, don't care. Oscar said, "To define is to limit."

Palermo is the happiest place I've ever lived.

THE NOISES FROM THE STORAGE ROOM

The two big storage units across from me have padlocks on the big metal shutter and are filled with motorcycles. Last week, the Nigerian was unloading huge brown boxes labelled YAMAHA off a truck and putting them inside the second storage unit just down the alley. The men working for Paolo, who owns the motorcycle shop, come and go, wheeling out motorcycles to display on via Padua and at the end of the day wheel them in again.

On this particular Saturday morning, I was at the dining room table and kept hearing what sounded like a cough from outside. Finally, I got up and realized it was coming from the storage room right across from my front door. The metal shutter was up but the pair of metal doors were closed and locked. I stopped a young woman in the alley and pointed, asked what the noise was. She listened then said it was a large animal. Obviously, an upset animal. I thought a cow but she shook her head, didn't think so.

I asked Luciano. He listened, shrugged, got into his Mini Cooper and drove away. The motorcycle shop was all locked up. On a Saturday morning it was usually buzzing with activity.

A mixture of snorting and crying for help. Some animal was locked in there in the dark. I worried about there being enough air then thought it would be alright but I felt a bit worried. What was in there and why and would the poor thing be locked in all weekend?

The cries became fewer, farther apart and I hoped the animal was calming down, could sleep. When I came back from getting a panino, the big metal shutter was down. No air at all, I thought, or someone took the animal out. I decided the latter.

On Monday I saw Nigeria and asked him what was in there. "Two horses," he said. "My boss, you know he is Muslim. It was a holy day." He drew one finger across his throat. "They killed them."

I blinked in surprise. "Two of them? Where did they kill them? Here?" He shook his head. "Not here."

"In the street?" I demanded. "In someone's house?"

He nodded backwards. "Somewhere that way."

The Nigerian, holding a wrench, said, "I'm not a Muslim." I stood there remembering the pitiful cries. Those horses *knew*.

· · ·

This is a city with more than a dozen shop windows on via Roma displaying evening dresses. Entire stores are devoted to them. Like whipped crème, resplendent confectionary, the colors of sherbet, wedding dresses like clouds of meringue. At least a hundred gowns in each tiny shop. Women wear floor-length sequined dresses to morning weddings, to first communions while their escorts perspire, red-faced in their dark suits. One would imagine the entire population spent every waking moment waltzing under Murano chandeliers in palazzi. But Paolo and Casablanca at the motorcycle shop kill horses.

· · ·

Gianni was to send the original certificates about the electricity and plumbing to me. I have been asking for nearly two months. I have the copies sent via email but he agreed I needed the originals if I ever want to sell La Tana. He does not answer my notes and no certificates have been sent. When I told my Mafia expert about this, he said you must go to the police and make a denuncia. I won't do that as I probably spend more time in that police station than the cops who work there.

* * *

It was my kind of day. Out of here at 06:45, on the bus which was surprisingly empty, hopped on the 2nd bus and in the water at 07:20. There were waves and the tide was coming in with the water reaching the sunbathers. I built a small moat in front of me so my encampment was fine. One long swim later and then I was back here at 09:45.

As I walked into via Padua which is about 20 feet long and becomes vicolo della Gardenia, a roaring motorcycle came within centimeters of hitting me. It stopped and off came a helmet. The Enforcer. I'm used to motorcycles as the shop is right there but they usually slow down, not speed up. A bit of intimidation, I guess. He'd better not hit me. A lot of paperwork.

Just when I felt quite tired something lifts my spirits. This afternoon when I was in the fast-moving via Cavour traffic, tearing along on my bike, I saw Giuseppe out in front of his men's shop. He saw me then raised both arms straight up like an umpire, grinning! I waved and made the turn to via Roma in a pack of roaring motorcycles and growling Fiats.

Lots of activity next door until dark with about five men standing around and lots of equipment in the alley. Drilling noises. Maybe the pizzeria will finally open. I locked up my bike at my front door and walked to Lidl's. When I came back my bike had been pushed over.

For all my 'let's get on with it' nature, I might be under some stress. I woke up at about two this morning and my face was wet with tears. Crying in my sleep. Compartmentalization at its best.

Ferragosto in Palermo

Ferragosto, the pit of August, is the biggest holiday of the year in Italy. In Rome it can begin in the middle of July and extend all the way to September but in Palermo it's much shorter.

This August morning I rode my bike in search of the nearest public library. I turned right onto via Roma and took a left on via Livorno. In minutes I was in a warren of alleys with the stone street signs in Arabic, Hebrew and Italian. African women hairdressers were standing over their clients who perched on stools in the alley and in the street; I had to swerve to not hit them. Men were shouting in Arabic. My favorite sign said PATRICIA'S HAIR SALOON in bright red marker.

I found the library but knew it would be closed. I'll go again in September. I went through the market on the way back and was seduced by the smell of grilled fish. Picking a table outside, I ordered grilled calamari then felt a little sad looking down at him thinking he'd probably had his last swim this morning. My waitress was blonde and blue-eyed and I asked if she were Sicilian. Si. Another Norman, I decided.

I pulled my bike next to my table which is what I do nowadays. It stays with me, within reach. The chaos was waves of noise. Someone was tooting a trumpet in the street, a man was playing an accordion at the next table hoping for money. The jingle of bicycle bells. A song that sounded Neapolitan blasted from somewhere. An African danced with a bottle balanced on his head to drum music. And there were the voices. Loud. Ballarò is one of Palermo's biggest markets.

* * *

I have placed my desk at an angle so that I look out my mirrored doors. People stop and adjust their clothes, their hair and don't know I am just five feet away. Today the man with his broom came and swept the alley; he brings his own dustpan. A few days ago, Casablanca was cooking kebabs on a little grill. Fatima leaves her clothes out drying overnight and no one takes them. This morning two women in long robes floated past with only their eyes showing. I looked up at one point and saw two Africans carrying a double bed with a mattress go past. They were in a hurry. Trotting. About an hour later I saw them again, and again in a hurry, carrying the bed in the opposite direction.

LEARNING THE LANGUAGE

I took the evaluation test for the University of Palermo and had to read every single sentence three times. If it hadn't been multiple choice I would have left everything blank. If it had been spoken to me I would not have understood one word.

I am so frightened of repeating the French situation when I took the immersion classes in Paris. I was stricken mute on the seventh day and had to drop out. I thought I'd had a stroke; the head of the school said my brain couldn't handle so much at once. I must stop telling everyone that I am so excited to be going to school as I may have to drop out again.

I remember when Father Quercetti, my boss, mentor, ally and friend at Radio Vaticana, asked me to meet with a priest for Italian lessons. I had just been hired at Vatican Radio and was so eager to learn Italian, delighted to meet with this very nice Jesuit and thought it went very well. The next day and the next day and the next and Father Q never said a word about it. I was in his office going over something I was writing and asked him. He looked uncomfortable as I urged, "Tell me the truth. Was my Italian really terrible?" As I said this, I was sure it wasn't terrible. I had fun that afternoon, had talked quite a lot. Father Q hesitated and then said, "He said that you think you are speaking Italian but you have made up your own language." It was a body blow. I hurriedly left his office, hurt and miserable. My learning Italian was never mentioned again.

Not speaking Italian was bad enough but being the only non-Catholic at the Vatican was cause for suspicion. It was rumored that I was the mistress of the CIA station chief and that I was a plant. I told Father Q that if I were a plant I would be a geranium. I wanted to say, mistress? CIA? Ridiculous! Why would I come to Rome and sleep with an American?

• • •

"Buongiorno." I was greeted in the most charming way. Where, but in Palermo, would your personal extortionist address you so warmly in between bouts of demanding money, threatening to cut off your water and gouge out your eyes? That's The Enforcer.

The Enforcer's large terrace is above two-thirds of La Tana and last week I climbed my huge fireman's ladder and had a good look at it. A table, chairs and an umbrella, rusting and faded, dating from the days of Mussolini.

Luciano and The Enforcer are working together right now on the pizzeria. I see Luciano going back and forth and I hear hammering.

Luciano is nice to me but how does he really feel? I've seen him kiss The Enforcer on each cheek in the alley and he's worked on the pizza parlor. When I asked Luciano to come inside and lift the big Cheret poster for me, he darted in, put it in place and hurried out again. Did he not want The Enforcer to see him?

Maybe Luciano is secretly pleased I'm standing up to Trump and The Enforcer. I may never know but I know he knows what is happening.

It's definitely Ferragosto as lots of places are closed. A smattering of tourist-y things are open and a few restaurants. I miss Thomas who is away with Marcello most of the summer.

NAKED IN PALERMO

CRASH! I'd been asleep and I actually levitated off my bed. CRASH! CRASH!

I decided that at least three refrigerators had been pushed over. These noises went on for about ten minutes but there were gaps as I pictured The Enforcer up there on his terrace sweating in the dark as he arranged for the next crash. Having a little tantrum. This must be very tiring for him in this heat.

It was hot. Defne said, "I'm running around fully naked and taking cold showers every four hours." A woman from Rome told me she stays home all day, naked, with the curtains closed. I was only naked at night because I couldn't find my nightgowns. La Tana was comfortable. No one believed me when I told them I never turned on the air conditioner but the church kept me cool with its thick stone walls and I also ate a great number of popsicles.

* * *

At six o'clock I rode my bike to Rinascente, an upscale department store, and went up to the roof terrace to meet Defne. Ordering a glass of white wine, I was presented with olives, potato chips and then a plate with prosciutto, cheese and a fork. Six euros. The Sicilians don't think you should drink and not eat.

We talked about Italian classes. She speaks German, English, and of course, Turkish.

Defne and I sat on a couch on the Rinascente terrazzo gazing out at the Church of San Domenico. Below was the piazza and beyond were taupe-colored mountains. To the left, beyond buildings, was a strip of blue water. We sat from 6 o'clock to half past nine talking and I watched the sky change from one shade of blue to another. One blue I had never seen before.

At the next table was a nice-looking man and his teenaged daughter; Defne picked up on their German and we all began chatting in English and German. He was Swiss German and lived in St. Galles. Teasing, jokingly, he asked me to marry him. Something was said about holidays and time off and Defne asked how long until his pension and he said about 20 years so that puts him in his 40s, I guess.

He invited me to fly to Zurich to go to some important parade next week. I said that maybe his wife would not be happy to have me as a houseguest. He is divorced. He asked if I had children and I started to answer and Defne nudged me and grinned. "Do that thing you did with me!" Then she turned to the man and said, "Now, ask her if she has children." He did and I clapped my hand over my mouth and exclaimed, "I forgot! I forgot to have children!"

I rode my bike home on via Roma and the air was cool and fresh on my bare skin.

* * *

No matter what was happening to me here, my two favorite islands in the world are Haiti and Sicily. For excitement and history. World War II. The bandits. How they helped the Allies. The evolution of the Mafia. In 1944, one of the Sicilian political parties wanted Sicily to have a king, another one wanted a republic and yet another party wanted the island to become the 49th American state!

A WEDNESDAY EVENING OF TALK

August 18, 2022

Maybe I will meet someone interesting tonight. Male, female, hermaphrodite—I don't care. The plan was to meet Defne at Rinascente and then I would go alone to an expats' event.

The wine had barely been put before us when Defne began. She had been watching YouTube and, at age sixty-five, had decided that very afternoon that she was asexual. Wincing, I heard about her marriage to a German in far too much detail, wondering how many people on the terrace understood English. "I can tell you've had a lot of sex," she said. "What? Why?" I stammered. "It's just something about you," was her response. I was relieved to be told she was not attracted to women.

Defne was upset about the bags under her eyes, upset that I'm ten years older. She insisted I'd had work done and appeared angry when I said I hadn't. I told her the eye situation was easy to fix and she had the money, to just do it. As she compared our looks and our ages, I saw this flash of temper that seemed borne of a fierce sense of competition. "Look at my hands," I insisted as I put down my wine glass. "I have the hands of a 250-year-old woman. Dr. Kleinberg, my dermatologist in New York, calls them maturity spots." That made her laugh.

The terrace was lovely and I was tempted to just linger with Defne and skip the unknown—the expat thing. She was sure it would be awful with "everyone there just wanting to learn English." But I was curious and I could hear Mother's voice in my head. She would push me to go.

When I arrived at the gathering there were only five of us at a long table outside under white umbrellas: a beautiful African-American woman from California, a woman from Ireland, a Greek man with a cheerful, open face named Sakis and an Italian named Marco. I was surprised but Italians do come to these things. The Irish woman was planning to teach English. Sakis the Greek was here for three weeks taking an immersion course in Italian. I looked at him closely and thought, you are so lucky your brain did not explode the way mine did in Paris. In October, he goes to the University of Bologna to teach sports psychology. It's very prestigious, the oldest university in Europe. He said Palermo is a place you would love or hate and that it reminds him of Athens when he was growing up. Last night he ate dinner and the restaurant didn't take credit cards so he offered to go and get cash but the owner said to just come back tomorrow. Marveling at this, he said it would never happen in Athens. We talked about how affectionate people seem, that there is some joy here that is not in Athens anymore nor in New York. It's been lost. Sakis spent three months in London and talked about the body language and the reluctance to have eye contact and how his mother noticed it when he returned to Greece.

Nearly everyone asked me why I chose Palermo and he was no

exception.

A man who introduced himself as Lucas, sat down across from me. He is an architect from Paris and is here because he loves the architecture. "Norman, Arab. Like no other place in the world just as there is no other place in the world for the architecture of Paris." Most of these people are working remotely. Some are here for a few months or weeks but others live here like me.

Tremendous, glorious platters of food arrived with fried calamari and rice and cold meats, cheeses and several appetizers I could not identify. Generous goblets of an okay wine. All this for ten euros.

Other people arrived, mostly in their 20s and 30s. Next to me was a young Russian with a long dark braid nearly to her waist who was house-sitting in the middle of Palermo, taking care of a cat and plants. Work Away was the program. I thought that was usually young men harvesting crops on a farm or doing construction work for free room and board and she said it often was. A handsome, bearded Spaniard, a woman with butter-yellow hair from Sweden, and four people at the other end of the table too far away for conversation. English was the language; if one is to survive in this world with only one language it should be English.

It was dark, of course, but still hot and everyone, at some point, swabbed at necks.

The group meets every Wednesday at the same restaurant. In the winter there is another restaurant and they sit indoors.

Mother always said if you don't go then you'll never know what you missed and she was absolutely right.

* * *

I'd had enough cold baths and hadn't made popcorn in ages so I called the propane gas people and the man was very cheerful on the phone, laughing when I told him how to find my alley and that my door had a green star on it. In half an hour he arrived on a motorcycle with two big steel, bomb-shaped containers lashed behind him. Hoisted one on his shoulder, installed it and took my orange one away. I told him how happy I was to have a green one because it was il mio colore preferito. My favorite color. I am going to request a green one the next time. He roared away with my ugly orange one. Thirty-two euros for this and not six euros as Gianni had told me. The lies mounted up.

SINGING IN THE TYRRHENIAN SEA

AUGUST 19, 2022

Defne and I planned to go swimming at six in the morning but I opened my door at 5:15 and it was like facing a furnace. The hottest day here—102 Fahrenheit or 38 Celsius. We met the next day at 7 a.m. at the 806 bus stop.

She talks talks talks and does come out with odd statements occasionally as in "People who have a lot of sex have low immune systems." There was no interval to agree or disagree as she just carried on.

We covered a lot of territory on the bus ride. She has her mother's awful family who aren't at all like her and a sister who wanted to send her a video of her mother after her stroke. I was appalled and so was she. I have the awful McNairs and told her how my aunt, my father's sister, picked me up as a little girl and lowered me into Big Momma's coffin to kiss the corpse goodbye. My father's family, her mother's family. We agreed: these people aren't like us.

In Mondello, we picked a spot and immediately Defne was standing over an older couple talking away. The woman spoke Italian very clearly and Defne was doing pretty well. She is not jousting with indirect objects the way I am. I was understanding nearly every word of what was happening and later learned that the woman is a kindergarten teacher.

I got my placement letter from the University of Palermo yesterday even though I will go to the commune school for immigrants. I am A2. The lowest possible is A1 so at least I'm not that. Defne told me she is M2—whatever that means—and that she went to the commune school in Tuscany and loved it. We are both going to the one here in September.

Many of the Sicilians are so olive-skinned that they are really dark when they are tan and I wish I had olive skin. I notice that these people don't wear hats. I looked out and could easily see sixty people on the sand, lying, standing, walking. No hats! Many of them don't wear sunglasses either! The sun is brutal, Defne swims way out between the buoys and does twenty laps which she thinks is about a kilometer. I could see her like a grain of pepper going back and forth.

Defne bemoans the fact that the Sicilians don't swim. They don't. They stand around in the water and talk. In pairs or groups as large as six. Last week and today I spotted several middle-aged men who were standing separately, alone, in waist-deep water all by themselves *singing*. Uninhibited. Appearing quite happy. Singing in the Tyrrhenian Sea.

* * *

I saw Defne crossing via Roma and pulled over my bike to talk. "That Swiss German from the other night keeps texting and inviting me and 'my girlfriend' to Switzerland." We laughed and she said, "Wants me as a chaperone." I saw no sign of jealousy or competition and was glad.

"I probably have nothing in common with him," I said and she agreed. "He is just celebrating his divorce." I laughed and said, "I'm still celebrating mine!"

Defne turned to go one way with her special figs from the Bangladeshis and I began pedaling towards vicolo della Gardenia.

EVERYONE SAYS I NEED A SOUTH AMERICAN COWBOY

I tripped on the fan cord and went WHAM! on the marble floor landing on one wrist and one knee.

Glad I didn't knock my teeth out. I massaged my knee, got up and left the house to do my errands. First, I had to drop off pictures at the frame shop and was a bit out of it with the pain and Margarita said, ghiaccio/ice. Then I went to the farmacia for more magnesium and the farmacista said you need ghiaccio. I rode home on my bike (not using the right-hand brake) fantasizing about a South American cowboy. I went to the fridge and tried to get ice cubes out and couldn't. My left hand might as well be a flipper. I tried and tried. Finally, I just stuck my entire right arm in the freezer and stood there.

Defne called and I continued standing there listening to her talk about everything and nothing and then the cold began to remind me of my Canadian marriage and I told her I had to hang up because I was worried about frost bite. I don't think she even heard me but we did hang up. I took my arm out of the freezer and decided yes, I need a South American cowboy. I found an Ace bandage and rode to meet Melanie, a new friend. I had prosecco and the pain began to ebb a bit. A wonderful evening really. But my left hand is useless and I thought about sleeping in my clothes. I had a tough time brushing my teeth because I had to move my head back and forth.

THE EMBERGENCY ROOM

I tried to ignore the pain for a week but I couldn't sleep. Harold, the retired American psychiatrist, recommended Ospedale Bucchero and I looked it up and it was nine minutes away via bicycle.

As I made the right turn from via Lincoln onto what seemed like a highway, I thought maybe I should have taken a taxi. Traffic was fast. There were three lanes on either side of a median planted with pink flowering trees and palms. Cars whizzed past me on my bike and then I realized I was pedaling along in the shade under olive trees. The sun was bright, the sea was to my left and I could smell the salt water.

I tied up my bike outside a large whitish building and as I approached the emergency entrance a young woman in sky blue scrubs held a door open and motioned me in. I sat down in a chair in a room with one other chair and fumbled for my mask. I had no chance to get it on as a man in scrubs took a nasal swab and my passport. I explained I was American and had no insurance. Didn't matter. He disappeared and before I could get my book out of my bag another man in scrubs appeared and told me to come with him. Everyone was masked. I put mine on as I was escorted to an office with a doctor behind a desk in darker blue scrubs. A blonde nurse in maroon scrubs asked me how I was. The doctor came over to me on the examination table and looked at my wrist and asked what had happened. I told him I'd fallen the week before, that my hand turned black, was very big as I didn't know the word for swollen and he said, It was black? why didn't you come right away? I said, oh, I didn't think it was serious. But the real reason was because I was worried about the cost.

He went behind his desk as the nurse looked on.

I was American which was a cause for excitement.

I was born in Mississippi which was a cause for excitement.

The three of us, all masked, were laughing. They had questions. Why was I in Palermo? I told them because I loved it here and because it was so beautiful. I told them I had bought a Tunisian nightclub which elicited a show of great surprise and enthusiasm. All the while the doctor was typing on his computer. I apologized for my Italian and told them about how wonderful the school for immigrants was. They asked if we had that in the US and I said that I thought NYC had the same classes for immigrants at the main library. The doctor made a remark about the cost of health care. Of course, they then told me I spoke Italian very, very well which was not true.

My passport was given back and I was told to go with the nurse for x-rays. No stairs, no elevators as we walked outside under trees to another building past an ambulance and emergency workers in neon green and black uniforms. 'Radiology' said the sign. A woman doctor placed my hands in position on a table, going back and forth in and out of the room. Eight x-rays were taken of both hands.

Then the nurse and I walked back. I asked if she were born in Palermo and she told me she was from Catania, had married a German and he and her children were in Germany but she preferred Palermo. Did I have children, was I married, family? I said 'no' to everything and she approved. We agreed we were both independente.

The doctor behind his desk told me nothing was broken but he strapped my wrist in place and said to keep it elevated for the next seven days; he would give me a prescription for pain. As he put the bandage on my hand and wrist, I told him I'd gone to a private clinic in Rome with tennis elbow. I described the separation of red and white cells, the injection and the high fee and he and the woman were aghast but I sensed delight, too. I told them nothing had changed in my elbow so far but I had wanted to die when I had to pay 200 euros for the separation process and 350 euros to the medico.

The doctor told the nurse that the process cost 50 euros. Then, of course, they were saying, It's Rome! Rome! Of course, that is the sort of thing that happens in Rome!

The people of Palermo, in general, despise Rome and are certain that terrible things go on there. I've read the history of Sicily and understand it. The Sicilians don't think of themselves as entirely Italian and Rome is the seat of the country's government. Sicilians are proud, fiercely independent, like to do things their way. Rome is regarded as an interference.

The nurse told the doctor that I rode my bike there and they were astonished at that. The entire exchange was a mix of good will and curiosity. Lots of laughing behind masks.

The doctor handed me a typed sheet. I said, "Posso andare?" And he said, of course. You can go. I asked what I should pay and he laughed. Nothing! I walked out, unlocked my bike. The sheet said I was admitted at 09:50 and released at 10:21.

I rode home admiring the pink flowers on the median and smelling the sea then I went to the pharmacy and filled the prescription for pain. Euros 3.90.

Now I have met the firemen of Palermo, I know the police on via

Roma, many at the water company know my story and today I experienced a visit to a Palermo emergency room.

Every day is an adventure.

* * *

The Mafia expert writes for a paper called The New Corleone and today he wrote about a demonstration against the horse-drawn carriages. Barbaric. I suppose it's for the tourists who think it's romantic. Poor animals. So I went to Piazza Verde in front of the Teatro Massimo at noon and there were about a hundred people all yelling at each other. A man with a bullhorn was drowned out, a man blowing a whistle was drowned out. If this was a demonstration then the Sicilians are really bad at it. Lots of police in navy blue stood in a group talking and laughing. Hot sun and everyone in pairs, one on one, pink-faced, perspiring and arguing at the top of their lungs.

I came back here and there was Trump of the Alley standing next to the door to the pizzeria as Luciano painted it. I tied up my bike and said, very sweetly, "Buongiorno, signor" and then pushed RECORD on my phone. I goaded him. He took the bait. Shouting, wild-eyed behind his spectacles but standing way too close to me, he kept jabbing towards my eyes with two fingers which I didn't much like. So now I know that no one suspects I've been taping them. Otherwise, he would have just glared at me.

* * *

I watched Indian Matchmaker last night on Netflix with Italian subtitles and took notes. I learned how to say things like relationship and long-term and family-oriented.

I read somewhere that the average person uses only 100 words a day. If only I could wake up in the morning and know *which* 100 words they were going to be.

Oscar Wilde's Birthday

September is like a new year. I remember how it was in Rome. Everyone came back to town with a tan, looking rested and revived. I wondered if the United States would ever experiment with letting go of commerce and money for the month of August and just exhaling.

PROSECCO WITH THOMAS

Thomas was back from the summer holiday and I had missed him so much. Marcello was in town and we three met for a bottle of prosecco which turned into two and suddenly it was nearly eleven o'clock. We were inside Spinnato's for the faint breath of air conditioning and there were no windows so time passed as if we were in a casino.

Poor Thomas. He came back on Thursday at midnight from his summer with Marcello at the farm and immediately had a Friday morning meeting. After two and a half months of being away, it all started again. One subject is money. There has never been much of it. The council used to move it around to put out fires but there's so little money to move around now.

The air conditioner in the apartment where Thomas lives was broken and the Sparrows accused him of breaking it because he used it too much. Thomas fumed, "They are accusing me of keeping my apartment too cold which broke it while it was never installed property because they bought a cheap one to save money years ago!"

Furthermore, one of the Sparrows saw him and said, "Where did you get that stomach?"

The Sparrows go after him for everything. He told me that when he arrived a year ago the church didn't even have vestments for him to wear for the certain Sundays and Marcello chimed in saying there were holes in the ones that were there. Thomas went on Facebook and his friends gave money for him to buy the ones he needed. Sparrows had a fit "raising money in the name of the church" and Thomas said *my friends gave money to me.*

I could see that Marcello wants him to quit.

I said if there were more money will they pay you more? We couldn't decide.

We need younger people, we all agreed. I suggested we have another bazaar but make it like Porta Portese, Rome's huge flea market, with all kinds of stuff for sale not just books. Thomas wants to get rid of all the books which are on shelves in a corner of the church. He said no one wants old books in English the way they did in the past and they have Amazon. I like old books in English.

"Furthermore," as Thomas said, with a wave of one hand, "There is this thing with the Queen." I burst out laughing. "I told them not to hang the flag at half-mast because the last time it was at half-mast some hooligans stole it." Later, we would walk outside and it was at half-mast.

"This thing with the Queen" means that there must be a guest book and the church must be open from 8:30 to 6 o'clock and the Sparrows thought he should be there all day. I said, "No! Put your foot down! You're too nice!" Thomas said he would not be there. Good. Thomas and Marcello had to buy flowers to put beside the guest book because the church had no money for them. "It's *their* Queen!" I erupted. We toasted Elizabeth then kissed each other goodnight.

I rode home down via Roma under a full moon.

GEOGRAPHICAL CONFUSION

I walked my bike through Principe del Belmonte yesterday around two and the pretty brunette restaurateur called out, "Ciao, bella! La tua casa? E finito?" I said yes, electricity, water, even a bathroom door and we chatted. Then I walked one more block and parked my bike next to a tree at the Belmonte Caffè, went inside and ordered my usual. There was no pollo/chicken so they would give me bresaola/air-dried beef instead. All terribly normal. I sat at a little table out front, flipped my Italian grammar book to the right page and suddenly I felt dizzy, light-headed. I stared out at the trees, someone walking a dog, two women chatting as they strolled with shopping bags. A very blue sky. The entire cityscape was unfamiliar, unknown.

Paris, Rome, Geneva, New York. Like an old-fashioned slide projector my mind went Click! Click! Click! I had no idea where I was. I was in a chair, in a lovely place, dazed. Like someone on a movie set who has forgotten her lines.

This feeling only lasted seconds—it's taken much longer to describe it. I blinked and realized, yes, this place is beautiful and I am in Palermo. Palermo! That very thought surprised me. I leaned back in the chair. Yes. I really *live* in Palermo.

OH, THOSE SICILIANS

They started early today. Quarter of nine. Screaming by the woman, shouting by the man. It comes from above me and it's The Enforcer and Paola. There was silence for four days and I had decided

1. They'd gone somewhere on holiday to fight in a new location.
2. One had killed the other and was quietly hatching a plan to move the body.

Remember Connie Corleone in *The Godfather*, fighting with her husband? It's that kind of rage I hear. Open mouthed, teeth-baring, visceral. Hot.

I hope they have no children and that they have terrific make-up sex.

I grew up with it. I can tune it out though I am concerned when I hear crashes. I am looking forward to the day I can understand what they are fighting about. Lovers or money?

HUMAN TRAFFICKING

Thomas walked into La Tana but waited until we were both out in the cortile before he gave me his news. I knew the back story. He'd let a female American friend stay in the second bedroom of his apartment for two weeks while he was with Marcello during the summer holiday. The Sparrows were incensed.

Hawk had told me that the Sparrows were watching and waiting and they jumped on this situation.

First, the Sparrows insisted that it was church property and the church would have to pay the utilities of someone other than the vicar. Thomas appealed to those at the Church of England in London who confirmed that it was his home and he could have anyone he wanted staying there.

I knew all that. Thomas poured the prosecco and said, "So the Sparrows lost that round but had another idea. Two of them wrote a letter to multiple offices of the diocese accusing me of human trafficking and violating anti-terrorism laws."

I levitated out of my chair. "Human trafficking? Anti-terrorism? What!" then I said, "Thomas, I don't know what multiple offices of the diocese means."

"It means every person who is superior to me in the Church of England. The archdeacon, the bishop, the chief operations officer." He sighed. "That same letter went to DIGOS which is the intelligence branch of Italy's anti-terrorist bureau."

I was aghast.

It was madness.

The Sparrows were vindictive, vicious, insane.

But Thomas had to deal with them at meetings, had to greet them after church with a smile. London was on his side, of course, and called it bullying. That was that! Apologies followed but lacked any semblance of sincerity. My heart ached for Thomas. He soldiered on.

The Enforcer had the gas company man in the alley this morning and they were animatedly discussing some problem. I couldn't open my front door to get out so the white truck was moved with many apologies. Sicilian men are terribly charming when saying they're sorry and I forgive them before they have finished. Last week The Enforcer had a huge machine jackhammering away the concrete so that he could put something in a trench about three meters from my front door at the corner of the building. I'm guessing it is for gas and now there is a problem and I feel like going out and saying, "Oh, you want gas? You owe me 800 euros and then you can have gas. Oh, 800 is too much? Let me lower it to 500 euros. Pay me now and you'll have gas. And if you don't pay me I'll cut the pipe and gouge out your eyes with my car keys."

Except I don't have car keys because I don't have a car. I guess I could threaten him with my housekeys or strangle him with the chain I use to lock up my bike. Somehow that doesn't seem as scary or vivid but it delights me to imagine various methods.

Alley politics are sensitive. I am certain everybody watched the renovation spanning months and knows I live here behind the wrought-iron door under the green star. They certainly know I paid half to Trump of the Alley and they know I have refused to pay any more. Am I the only person in the neighborhood not paying? Am I the only person asked to pay? They know I called the polizia. Am I the only American they've ever dealt with so I'm a wild card and could do anything? Are they waiting for me to leave? Are they making bets on whether I'll Alamo it out?

I've been in this position before. When I worked as a maid in the men's boarding house in London and that first day as a private detective with Vinny Parco. He sent me out to do a surveillance and get photos of an unfaithful, red-headed husband from St. Louis. Everyone in the office bet I'd never come back.

I'm sticking it out. Those Sicilians will not win.

ROME

September 13, 2022

I thought it was time to go to Rome and meet my lawyer after so many phone conversations and emails. As always, the city was splendid, bold, masculine whereas Paris seems feminine. Can anyone, no matter how jaded, not gasp in respect as your taxi twirls in bright, colorful, noon traffic around the Colosseum?

I met Michael at lunch time near Campo de' Fiori and we walked to an outside table to sit with an associate named Salvatore for an aperitivo. Prosecco arrived. I would learn that these two, one trim, intense and narrow and one round and extroverted with a pale, moon face, were known as The Odd Couple. Stiletto-sharp, witty, savvy. I liked them instantly. Talk was of my book, *KISS THE RISK*, of international call girls and power, money, control. It was half an hour of hilarity sitting under an umbrella. I was assessing them and they me. Michael had advised not to pay the men for water and wanted to know the status of my Palermo situation. They offered to help. There was no news about my visa.

I told them I was starting school in a few days, determined to speak Italian well. "When will you be in Rome again?"

I said, "I don't know but I will come back to get a pedicure and have my teeth cleaned." They liked that.

Later, that evening, Michael called and said, "I think you should know who you are dealing with." I was walking on via Monserrato, paying attention to paving stones in high-heeled sandals, as he told me they were apostolic appeal lawyers. I would discover that not only could they practice law in Italy but they were of the Roman Rota where all proceedings are conducted in Latin.

A few days later, on a grey Sunday morning on my way to Termini, I was not sad. I was leaving Rome but could come back any time. I was in the same country. I was one train away.

My Vatican lawyers had become allies. And I was going home to

La Tana, where I belong.

REVELATIONS FROM THE HAWK

Hawk and I met at the same little caffè at our regular table on a sunny September day. We were the only customers sitting inside where it was a bit dark. As she filled me in on the church situation, I felt a visceral sense of rage. "Just when I thought the Sparrows could not be more awful!"

Hawk was tight-lipped, angry. "The previous vicar was here nearly two months and that news was kept from Father Thomas. He was making the rounds when you would think that he would call on his replacement to say 'hello' and to wish him well but—"

"Well, that's one thing but you say they actually had cocktail parties and a special dinner for him?"

Hawk nodded. "Oh, yes, in a restaurant near the church and a woman, very elderly, I used to respect actually gave a party for him at her apartment. We discussed her before and I said she was not a Sparrow."

"I know who you're talking about. So Thomas was not only not invited but all this was done behind his back, kept a secret from him. It's horrible. Thomas is a good person and he has been so generous to these people . . ." I stopped and then realized. "That was why the church was so empty that Sunday."

Hawk nodded. "Yes. They were holding alternate services."

"Where?

"In people's gardens? In their houses? I don't know." She sighed and sipped her prosecco. She'd stopped with the tea. "I did take a stand on this and did not go to any of these gatherings and made it clear why not. I couldn't. I simply couldn't."

"Well, good for you!"

We chatted about my going to school and then asked for the check. Leaving coins on the table, we stood and nodded in farewell. Neither one of us could shake our sense of outrage. I left the caffè and went out into the blinding sun and the noise of via Roma thinking of Thomas.

THE SCHOOL FOR IMMIGRANTS

Defne and I had gone together to register at the school for immigrants which was a short bike ride across via Roma to via Maqueda towards the big Ballarò market. I received an email telling me to report for an evaluation test that following week. Defne called and said her test was Friday; mine was Wednesday. I went up a rather dark and narrow flight of stairs to a classroom with about six other people and was given a sheet of questions. Some were the same as the University of Palermo test I had taken earlier; I finished and turned it in.

My cell rang as I was unlocking my front door. Defne wanted to know how the test was. I said it was fine. She said, "How many questions? Were they multiple choice? Did you have to write complete sentences?" I laughed at this detailed inquisition and told her it was multiple choice. "Tell me the questions," she demanded. I said, "I can't remember the questions!" She was irritated and said, "I have to do well on this! I want to be in an advanced class!" I said, "Well, I'm the opposite. I'd rather be in a beginner class than in a class where I can't keep up."

"You're not like me," she said. "This is important to me!"

Defne was insistent that I tell her about the test. I told her there was a little story and you had to read it and answer questions about it.

"What was the story about?"

I was putting down my keys and kicking off my sandals. "Two people go to the movies and the girl doesn't like the movie . . ." my voice trailed off. She asked more questions and I tried to remember phrases. "Defne, this is just a placement test and it's not a big deal."

This made her angry and she said I didn't understand. I said, "You'll be fine. Your Italian is pretty good." We said goodbye but she was very annoyed that I didn't remember more details.

First day of school. The courtyard was crowded with women in robes, men in tunics and pillboxes, women in saris and others in jeans and Western clothes. A young Sicilian woman at the front desk looked up my name and told me I was to have class on Monday, Wednesday and Friday from ten to noon. She directed me to go around the side of the building to a certain door and up the stairs. About a dozen desks were in the room and balcony doors were open to the courtyard below. I sat alone until about 10:15 when the teacher arrived. A pretty brunette in her thirties. A Tunisian woman arrived, a Nigerian male. The teacher was introducing herself when the door opened and in walked Defne. She did a double-take when she saw me. "What are YOU doing here?" she demanded in a loud voice, obviously angry.

I was astonished as was everyone. The teacher asked her name and marked it on a list. Defne sat down and glared at me for two hours. It was her ugly sense of competition. When I was called upon, she often followed up with an explanation or a correction to my pronunciation. On Wednesday more students came. I started going Tuesday, Thursday and Saturday, too, so I was at school six days a week. Two hours without a break is long but class moved quickly and the open doors allowed a breeze to waft in. I stayed after class on that first Friday, approached the teacher and, in English, said, "We were friends ..." The young woman touched my arm and said, "I understand everything. Just ignore her." I did.

Defne dropped out of class a few weeks later and I would never see her again.

* * *

It took time but good people came into my life: Enzo, the carpenter/sculptor/marionette-maker, a few foreigners (Australian, German, Dutch, Irish, Byelorussian) who spent time in Palermo every year, two classmates who were from Ukraine and Kenya. I saw Giusi, the artist, every week. She was my conversation partner and became a trusted friend.

Giorgia, a nine-year-old who lived in the alley, and I became very close. I doubt she'd ever met an American before. It began when she admired my mandarini and did that little index finger twist in the cheek. We often chatted at my front door and she invited me to her first communion. I was the only woman not wearing an evening gown in what was said to be the oldest church in Palermo. I sat in back in a simple linen dress feeling very East Coast and Episcopalian.

Giorgia would come to my door after school and call, "Cici! Cici! April!" and I'd open the iron door. She'd often shout down from her balcony when she saw me turn into the alley on my bike. Sometimes she drew at my living room table as I had paper, stickers, colored pens. Often, we'd go to Lidl's or to a Bangladeshi store; this little girl was highly intelligent, clever, self-confident and I watched her 'read' people and bargain a price down. Of the two of us, she was the alpha female and, with my limited Italian, she assumed the role of adult. Giorgia often suggested we have an aperitivo and we'd sit in the cortile with our respective refreshments, light the candles and talk until it was time for her to go home to dinner. Because of our friendship, her parents decided I was okay and, in the future, I would be invited for Christmas and Easter and to celebrate family birthdays. Giorgia would change my life in the alley.

THE SWEETNESS OF STRANGERS

Two Sicilian men stood in a doorway and watched me arrive at school and tie up my bike every morning. It was always a smiling "Buongiorno" and sometimes a few questions. Was I a professor? Was I French? The pair seemed pleased that I was American. Those good feelings must be a holdover from World War II or maybe Obama because everyone expresses a strong dislike of Trump. After class, they were there as I unchained my bike and wished me "buona giornata." Nice men, grey hair, one stout, one thin. One morning I was having trouble with my padlock and when I came out at noon, the thin one had oiled it for me. Dolce/sweet.

I loved my school. The teachers were young, enthusiastic, patient and all Sicilian, of course. We students were Kenyan, Nigerian, Ghanaian, Tunisian, Moroccan, Bangladeshi, Ukrainian, Russian, from everywhere, all of us stumbling over verbs together. No one from the Western Hemisphere except me. No one from Europe or the British Isles. At about half past eleven, the scent of cooking wafted in from the piazza below to torture us. The Egyptian's phone chimed every day at one minute of twelve and then launched into the call for prayer. This signaled our pushing back chairs, the gathering of books and with a flutter of robes and a flash of blue jeans, we all clambered down the dark stairs and out into the sun.

* * *

One day in school, the eight of us crowded around a map of the world and the professoressa asked us each to point to our country of origin. First, it was Cote d'Ivoire then Madagascar. My turn came. I carefully said, in Italian, that I was born in Mississippi and pointed to it. Then I said that I had lived in New York. A Tunisian teenager beside me, demanded in English, "New York! What are you doing here when we all want to be there?"

A SMALL TRIUMPH

Finally. After months of asking for the plumbing and the electric certificates, they arrived. Gianni had told me at least a dozen times they had been sent, were not signed yet, were being signed, were in the mail, on and on. One more thing to check off my list.

DIRTY TRICKS AND OLIVE TREES

S<small>EPTEMBER</small> 30, 2022

I was going to buy lemon trees. The plan was for Melanie, a friend from the expats group, to come here at half past three and then we'd meet Angelo who is always on time and will be standing, smiling, beside his grey Mercedes.

My phone rang at eight o'clock this morning; it was a tecnico from AMAP.

He told me he was coming at 10 o'clock to turn off my water. No! I mentally screamed. I thanked him so much for calling and told him I was very sorry and would not be home at ten o'clock. We were the essence of cordial and he told me I should call him for another appointment when it was convenient for him to come and turn off my water. Certo! I said enthusiastically. Certainly! I thanked him, wished him buona giornata.

After my second call from AMAP I emailed the Roman legal beagles.

> *Two calls from AMAP today. I told Signor Bianco (phone 091 — — —), I would not be home at 1530 for him to come and turn off my water. He said that was fine as Signor Di Lauro would be there, that Signor Di Lauro had written a letter. I had told the previous AMAP person who called at 8 a.m. that I would not be home at 10 for his appointment to turn off my water.*

One Roman lawyer sprang into action immediately writing a letter to the commune of Palermo and to AMAP saying that if my water were turned off both entities would be taken to court. This document stated all his impressive lawyerly titles. It went via email and also in a registered letter. I was very grateful.

At 12:30, I rode my bike to the polizia and hoped Ispettore San Felice would see me. An escort took me up to the exalted 5th floor right away. San Felice had appeared to care what happened to me. However, he speaks in quick and complete paragraphs and I understand nothing. Today I stared into his eyes and tried to imagine what he might be saying. He called Dottoressa Spera/Claudia Cardinale. No answer. He called AMAP and nobody answered. San Felice shot a few more paragraphs at me. Finally, I said, in Italian, okay, here is the piano:

I will not be home at 15:30 and I will not have a confrontazione with Di Lauro (Trump of the Alley) or his tough son, The Enforcer. I will let them turn off the water. Tomorrow I will go to Claudia Cardinale and get it turned on again.

I confirmed with San Felice that yes, Di Lauro was breaking the law to turn off my water but since it is AMAP who is doing it there is nothing San Felice could do. He was very sorry.

I went home. Took a bath just because I could then texted Melanie to meet me at quarter after three at a palm tree in front of Lidl's instead of here at La Tana at half past three.

I left the house early to avoid Di Lauro and AMAP but the gang was already there in the alley at my front door.

The AMAP men in their blue polo shirts holding clipboards politely introduced themselves. Trump of the Alley and The Enforcer stood behind them looking smug. One AMAP man then told me they were turning off the water because I did not own the property and where were my documents? He then said the address was not vicolo della Gardenia, 1, at all and that it did not exist. Then, inexplicably, he said Signor Di Lauro owned it. I said I'd bought the property and it belonged to me and that this was, in fact, number one, vicolo della Gardenia. He wanted the deed but I said I was in a hurry as I had an appointment. I was told I could dig a line under the street which made no sense. Why would I do that if I didn't own the property? The AMAP men did not want me to leave. One extended a ballpoint pen and urged me to sign a page on his clipboard. I refused and walked away.

Melanie arrived since I hadn't shown up at the palm tree at Lidl's and was never late. Then an Italian I'd met at the expats group materialized on a bicycle. I told him to go away, to not get involved as the AMAP men began pleading their case. Melanie and I walked to Angelo's car parked near the train station in silence. In the front seat, shaken, I blurted out what had happened. Angelo was upset and insisted in emotional Italian, Move! Sell it! Get out! Those men are dangerous! They will hurt you! There are plenty of other places to live! You must leave!

I shouted back at poor Angelo in angry Italian. No! It is my house and I am staying! I have dealt with the Mafia in New York and in New Jersey sitting across a table wearing a wire, lying about my name, my past, everything. So how difficult is all this in Palermo? These people are ordinary thugs, thieves, crooks. They are not running me out like a scared little girl. No!

Add to this resolve a new kind of fury I have recently discovered. It is a rage summoned by being treated as stupid, weak, foreign and female. I feel like a goddammed lioness.

We reached the nursery and Melanie and I picked out two olive trees instead of lemon trees. They would be delivered. Afterwards we drove to Matteo's for two enormous terracotta pots I'd long coveted. Matteo told me his daughter is named Clarissa. Angelo and Matteo grew up together. I realize, yet again, that talk of a misdeed would travel a neighborhood with the speed of summer lightning.

Back at La Tana and I raced inside to check for water. Yes! Am I the only person in the industrialized world who prays before flushing the toilet?

Later I would discover that someone at AMAP read the legal beagle's email and called the tecnicos just in time. My lawyer said they were very embarrassed that Di Lauro had persuaded someone high up at AMAP that I had no right to have water. They acted illegally and I fought back legally.

• • •

I talked to one of the legal beagles the next day and told him that one anxiety haunted me. Gianni and his father, Luca Iwanttomarryhim, were in with the Di Lauros on the extortion. Gianni had brought in the notaio. What if the notaio were crooked and I did not own La

Tana? But, of course, I owned it because if Trump did then why would his son want to buy it from me?

I sent the deed off to the lawyers in Rome and all was in order and I do own this property.

How lucky was I to have the Vatican lawyers in my corner! Who could *invent* Vatican lawyers who will fight for me? Vatican Warriors. Who knew Vatican lawyers existed? Or that I would ever meet one?

The next day as I was tying my bike to a tree in front of the police station, I heard my name called. "Clarissa! Clarissa!" It was Ispettore San Felice, the man I'd hoped to see. White, neatly-trimmed beard, bright eyes, dressed in pale blue denim and running shoes. We stood on the sidewalk as he asked me about the water situation. I told him I had a lawyer in Rome and all about the letters and that things were okay for now. Dottoressa Spera/Claudia Cardinale wrote me that I will not have anyone cut off my water and that Di Lauro must legally prove that he has the right to my water. AMAP wrote the lawyers and sent six photographs of the water meter with my name in bold black marker on the valve. Di Lauro must have been foaming at the mouth upset because he may have had to unlock the padlock on the door for them to take the pictures.

San Felice was pleased. I know that he felt so bad not being able to help me when AMAP was going to turn off the water.

I asked him about the Registro della Notizie di Reato and San Felice said the magistrate had not signed it yet. It is a case number for a crime. No number yet means my interview, all the documents of what has happened are still unread. The magistrate has to read them and then tell the police to investigate.

It was not the police but the fierce letter from the Roman lawyers that won The Water War.

* * *

Angelo and I went to the nursery again for a pair of mandarin trees. The four trees now guard the front door of La Tana. The olive trees are named after my lawyers, Michael and Salvatore; the mandarini are called Oscar Wilde and Casanova.

Angelo told me how to make olive oil and that my olive trees were very young and would live to be a thousand years old. A thousand years! I always thought it wouldn't be fair to get a parrot. I planned to make olive oil but never did. One afternoon I saw that the branches were bent low, festooned with hundreds of olives; the next morning every single one was gone.

A DEBRIEFING WITH THOMAS

Thomas's travails at the Anglican church continued. His refrigerator died and his insistence on having another one was discussed and delayed. Money was the issue. He lived without a refrigerator for two months.

"But at least it's only the Sparrows and not the Mafia harassing me," he laughed as he poured the prosecco.

"They want you out of the church and they want me out of La Tana," I said. "But La Tana means I won't end up on a park bench surrounded by H&M shopping bags."

"You'd be homeless with a lot of panache," he joked as he took a sip of prosecco. "Yesterday I bumped into Jacob. You know who I'm talking about. He is a small man from Bangladesh and he comes every single Sunday."

I nodded. "I like that he wears a white shirt and a tie."

"Well, he is homeless and he washes that white shirt in the park and has strung up a clothesline there."

"Really? He looks immaculate!"

"He lives in that little park across from the Joli, the square you could see from your window."

I was amazed.

"Well, we chatted. I was on my way to my usual bar for my usual cappuccino. He handed me an envelope and I could tell there was money inside. He said, 'take this.' I was confused. Was it for the church? For me?"

I sipped prosecco and waited.

"As he walked away, he called over his shoulder, 'orange juice, a cornetto and coffee.' I went to my bar and they know me, of course. I was confused and told them what had happened. The barman took the envelope, someone prepared the order and a waiter put it on a tray to take to the park."

I laughed. "They do this for him?"

Thomas grinned. "Every morning! This man has his life under control!"

• • •

I would celebrate Oscar Wilde's birthday as I always did and have invited masses of people from New York, Paris, Rome, dappertutto/ everywhere. Some were friends of friends like the Russian writer and his concert pianist wife. He said, "Of course, we will come! There has never been a party for Oscar Wilde in Palermo so one must jump on it!" Most won't be coming but it's a way to let them know where I am these days and to remind them to toast Oscar on October 16th.

Oscar's party was coming together. I'd been stockpiling prosecco for weeks and I'd ordered miniature arancine, finger food and cupcakes from several places; all were to be picked up the Friday before Saturday the 15th. The party was the day before Oscar's true birthday but I didn't think he'd mind. Food would be served at room temperature. Person after person had never been able to light my oven and when anyone suggested I call the man who installed it, I rolled my eyes. Luca Iwanttomarryhim? Never.

A parade of electricians had tried to discover why La Tana was plunged into darkness at times. The last pair of these professionals announced there was water in the microwave and I said, yes, I know. They emptied it with a big splash and acted as if this were not normal as I shrugged and said it was my first microwave. So, my blackouts were not the Mafia but the microwave. I put it in the alley one night and in the morning it was gone.

Oscar would not mind room temperature though he'd probably make some pithy remark. At least I have a frigorifero. Time for a popsicle.

ALTHEA

It was after church as a dozen of us stood in the little courtyard with refreshments that I met Althea. At six foot four with a tiny dog named Flower, she was impossible to miss. Confident, chic, outspoken, a straight-shooter—I liked her instantly. South African, she'd worked on cruise ships and was about to marry Domenico, a Sicilian, a ship's engineer she'd met on board. I looked around for him and when she called, "Husband!" I saw him. Grinning loopily, he was a good-looking man in his forties, obviously in love and delighted to be summoned. Althea's Italian was limited as was Domenico's English.

Althea and Thomas and I would become a trio of confidantes. Thomas' and my debriefings seamlessly expanded for three. Well, actually four, as Flower, half pug with a chihuahua face, always had her own chair and cushion and was often dressed to rival Iris Apfel. Other than one sharp, happy bark when a prosecco cork popped, she listened quietly.

Althea and I would struggle with learning Italian, I would struggle with the Mafia, Thomas would struggle with the Sparrows and together we complained, commiserated, advised and celebrated. We spoke English, we connected, we trusted each other. All of us new to life in Palermo.

• • •

Lovely, soft rain pattering down. I always preferred penthouses so I could hear rain on the roof but now I can hear it falling out in the alley and in the cortile and it's just as peaceful. It was nearly nine o'clock at night and I locked the wrought iron door, pulled the Thai screen across so that no one could see in then sat down at my desk. The rain stopped and the noise of traffic on via Roma was so faint that I may as well be near the ocean. I sipped a goblet of my favorite rosé which comes in a box and costs about a dollar and five cents. Looking up at the Venetian chandelier and then at all my paintings that had survived the crossing, I thought: I am so terribly happy.

* * *

The Thursday before Oscar's party I felt unwell. I never get sick; my last cold was more than a decade ago. It was raining but I rode my bike to a rather faraway farmacia/pharmacy that offered COVID testing. After the swab, a dead-ringer for Marcus Welby in a white coat told me the test was positive. I'd had my fourth vaccine in London so it couldn't be true! I was anguished. "No!" I cried out. I explained that my party was in two days with guests coming from all over; he smiled and said not to tell them!

I was open-mouthed and stammered that I had to. Then we discussed the situation. I had no sore throat, no cough, just a headache and fever. I had outside space and maybe I'd feel okay on Saturday. I rode home in the pouring rain, stripped off my sopping-wet clothes and alerted my guests. All but three out-of-towners sent their regrets. Maybe for these diehards it had less to do with me and Oscar than with non-refundable tickets. Neither of my best friends in Palermo could come: James had COVID and Althea was getting married.

On Friday, I cancelled the cupcakes but nothing else as I could live on hors d'oeuvres for a long time. I stayed home, lounged on Moby Dick, popsicles lowered my fever and I felt like myself on Saturday.

I put on my dress, spritzed on perfume, lit candles and greeted my friends. Barbara, a photographer from Rome, and Sarah, a writer from Munich, and David from Paris who heads World Radio Paris and I all sat in the cortile, yanked off our masks and celebrated. We drank a river of prosecco and talked and laughed past midnight. Oscar was toasted and fondly remembered on his 168th birthday.

· · ·

The party was over and my friends had flown away. Last year I'd celebrated with Gema drinking tequila on the laundromat steps. I still had not been here a full year; the night before Halloween I'd arrived at the Joli and begun my life in the capital of the largest island in the Mediterranean. Closer to Africa than to Rome.

As I sat at my desk, I thought of my adversaries: Trump of the Alley, The Enforcer, Luca Iwanttomarryhim and his son, Gianni, whom I'd trusted. Then I thought of the men who'd helped me fight them: Marlon Brando, San Felice, the Vatican Warriors.

After seven trips to the appropriate office, I would learn that the Mafia investigation had been concluded and that there was a hearing date nearly three years from that first demand of money and the shouts of "Devi pagare!"

Bringing a case against the Mafia allowed me to stay in Italy.

Little Giorgia would give me news of The Enforcer. She extended chubby arms with crossed wrists and nodded knowingly. In the slammer in Milano. For eight years. We had no idea what he'd done.

Father Thomas would leave Palermo to become the vicar of an Anglican church in a northern Italian city. Althea and I would visit him as soon as Flower could get the passport she needed.

But on this October night in 2022, there was no court date, I faced The Enforcer every day and Thomas was still enduring the despicable Sparrows.

Rain suddenly swept the alley, pounding the stones. So much was flying through my mind. The Water War, The Padlock War, the Mafia. The Sparrows. My school. Faces. Every single character was new to me as was Palermo. Exotic, colorful, mysterious, quirky and confusing. I thought of the debriefings. No matter what the question, prosecco is the answer.

THE END

The Author

CLARISSA McNAIR was born in Mississippi and graduated from Briarcliff College in New York. In Toronto, she worked as a researcher for CBC-TV's award-winning documentary on organized crime, *Connections*. In Rome, she was a news writer, newscaster and producer of documentaries for Vatican Radio. In Los Angeles, McNair worked in film. She is now a foreign correspondent with World Radio Paris.

McNair is a private detective who worked undercover in NYC with the Joint Terrorist Task Force, the Organized Crime Intelligence Division of the NYPD and with the FBI. Her international and U.S. cases range from stolen art recovery and money-laundering to rape and murder.

Clarissa McNair lives in Palermo, Sicily.

www.ingramcontent.com/pod-product-compliance
Lightning Source LLC
Chambersburg PA
CBHW020444090526
44586CB00045B/846